Gush

Gush

Refreshment
for Thirsty Christians

Pastor Douglas W. Merkey

Gush: Refreshment for Thirsty Christians ISBN: 978-0-692-30212-5

© 2014 by Rev. Douglas W. Merkey. All rights reserved. No part of this book may be reproduced, stored in a retrieval system, or transmitted in any form or by any means — electronic, mechanical, photocopy, recording, or any other — except for quotations of less than 500 words (e.g., sermon, article, blog, review) that make up less than ten percent of a work's total word count. Proper attribution is required for such quotations. Permission for all other citations must be received in writing and in advance of use from info@getintolife.org.

Some of the illustrations in this book are true to life and are included with the permission of the persons involved. All other illustrations are either fictitious or are composites of real situations, and any resemblance to people living or dead is coincidental.

Unless otherwise indicated, all Scripture quotations are from *The Holy Bible, English Standard Version* (ESV), copyright © 2001 by Crossway Bibles, a division of Good News Publishers. Used by permission. All rights reserved.

Other versions of the Bible used and identified in this book are listed below. Out of respect, and for clarity, the author has capitalized pronouns and other words that refer to God.

The Message, copyright © 1993, 1994, 1995, 1996, 2000, 2001, 2002. Used by permission of NavPress Publishing Group.

The *New American Standard Bible*® (NASB), copyright © 1960, 1962, 1963, 1968, 1971, 1972, 1973, 1975, 1977, 1995 by The Lockman Foundation. Used by permission.

The *Holy Bible: New International Version*® (NIV®). copyright © 1973, 1978, 1984, 2011 by Biblica, Inc.® Used by permission of Zondervan. All rights reserved worldwide.

The New Jerusalem Bible (NJB), copyright © 1985 by Darton, Longman & Todd, Ltd. and Doubleday, a division of Random House, Inc. Reprinted by permission.

The *Holy Bible, New Living Translation* (NLT), copyright ©1996, 2004, 2007, 2013 by Tyndale House Foundation. Used by permission of Tyndale House Publishers, Inc., Carol Stream, Illinois 60188. All rights reserved.

Come, everyone who thirsts,
  Come to the waters.

    Isaiah 55:1a

Contents

About the Word "Gush"	9
Giving Thanks	11
Introduction: Our Voyage	13
Buoy I: Our Thirst	**21**
1 Life in the Desert	22
2 The Devil, Our Dehydrator	29
3 An Appetite for Desiccants	36
4 Our Supreme Thirst	45
Buoy II: God's Invitation	**53**
5 A Hearty Invitation	54
6 The Guest List	61
7 Party Particulars	68
8 Saying "Yes" to God	76
Buoy III: Water-Pictures	**83**
9 God, the Fountain	84
10 Like the Dew	91
11 Like the Rain	98
12 Like a Flood	104
13 Like a River	111
Buoy IV: The God of Gush	**119**
14 The God Who Gushes	120
15 Our Superlative God	129

	16	God, the Gushing Rock	137
	17	Being God's Beloved, Part I	145
	18	Being God's Beloved, Part II	152

Buoy V: Life in the Gush — 161

	19	Relationship and Radiance	162
	20	Going with the Flow	169
	21	The Law of the Gush	178
	22	Gush-Out Trifecta, Part I: To God and Self	186
	23	Gush-Out Trifecta, Part II: To Others	194
	24	Mutiny, Drought, and Kisses	201
	25	The Reality Sandwich	211

Buoy VI: Gush Everlasting — 221

	26	The Wrathful Gush of Hell	222
	27	The Sweet Gush of Heaven	230
	28	Our Voyage Continues	239

Appendices

	A	Am I a Christian?	249
	B	Gushcabulary	252
	C	The Attributes of God	256
	D	Postscript: Life in the Desert	259

Notes — 261

About the Author — 269

About the Word "Gush"

When people hear the title of this book, *Gush: Refreshment for Thirsty Christians*, they often wonder how the word *gush* can be associated with God. You may be wondering the same thing.

Maybe you associate *gush* with violent, destructive forces that threaten human happiness and safety, such as a deadly wall of water suddenly bearing down on a sleeping hamlet. Or maybe *gush* brings to mind an endless stream of superficiality, a tirade of criticism, or the unbridled and patronizing compliments of someone desperate for a sale.

But *gush* also has its positive side. It can refer to the spontaneous flood of joyful tears upon hearing "your cancer is in remission," or the waves of wonder elicited by a panoramic sky-igniting sunset, or the eruption of celebration in a dehydrated village as people watch water rushing from a newly tapped well. *Gush* may refer to the enraptured embrace of two lovers suddenly reunited after a long absence — or the sincere, lavish, and unstoppable demonstration of love, goodness, power, and commitment from the eternal God toward sinful humans in Christ.

As we explore God's Word in the following pages, I think we'll discover — pretty easily, in fact — not only that *gush* and *God* belong together in the same sentence, but also that God is the epitome of everything positive about the word *gush* in relation to His people in Jesus Christ. We'll be amazed to see how He gushes His love *to* us and *through* us. As we live in relationship with the God who gushes, we have the opportunity to be deeply hydrated.

Drink deeply, and may you be abundantly refreshed.

Giving Thanks

Thank You, Lord, for the many wonderful people you provided to help me write this book. Thanks for those who read various drafts of my manuscript and offered helpful comments: Bob, Carol, Doug, Jake, John, Kari, Katie, Madeleine, Rodney, Ruth, Sandi, Sheri, Terry, Veronica, and Robert. Thanks for Fran, my editor throughout the process, and for gifting her with the kindness, patience, and skill to help me. Thanks for John, Bob, and Deena, who provided beautiful places for me to think, pray, study, and write. Thanks for Paul, who helped me with the cover and other graphic designs related to the book. And thanks for the board and staff of Churches for Life, who recognized the value of this project and gave me opportunities to pursue it.

Above all, thanks for giving me the gift of Yourself. I love You, Lord. You've been amazing in how You've sweetly cared for me all my life. It's been wonderful to dream, plan, write, and publish *Gush* with You. Thanks especially for providing such a wonderful Navigator in Your Holy Spirit, and such a reliable map in Your Word. I pray that this book is faithful to that map, even as Robert Lewis Stevenson first drew from an actual island map upon writing his classic novel (and my favorite work of fiction) *Treasure Island*.

> But it is my contention ... that he who is faithful to his map, and consults it, and draws from it his inspiration, daily and hourly, gains positive support, and not mere negative immunity from accident. The tale has a root there; it grows in that soil; it has a spine of its own behind the words. Better if the country be real, and he has walked every foot of it and

knows every milestone. But, even with imaginary places, he will do well in the beginning to provide a map. As he studies it, relations will appear that he had not thought upon. He will discover obvious though unsuspected shortcuts and footpaths for his messengers; and even when a map is not all the plot, as it was in *Treasure Island*, it will be found to be a mine of suggestion.[1]

Introduction

Our Voyage

> *Then the eyes of the blind shall be opened,*
> *and the ears of the deaf unstopped;*
> *then shall the lame man leap like a deer,*
> *and the tongue of the mute sing for joy.*
> *For waters break forth in the wilderness,*
> *and streams in the desert;*
> *the burning sand shall become a pool,*
> *and the thirsty ground springs of water;*
> *in the haunt of jackals, where they lie down,*
> *the grass shall become reeds and rushes.*
> Isaiah 35:5–7

Rains from Up North

The location of the friend's house where I wrote the first draft of this book could be described as idyllic, exotic, striking, and intriguing. It's a gorgeous panorama of arid, scrubby ranchland, overlooking the azure waters of the Pacific Ocean. Maui rests on the horizon, looking like something that gurgled up from the sea in a *Godzilla* episode.

About ten feet from the living-room patio lies a naturally rock-walled stream and waterfall. When I first arrived, I noticed that the dry streambed was accented with dirt, dried mud, and sun-roasted animal droppings. The few remaining puddles shrank daily in the sun's merciless onslaught, showing only scant signs of life. Tiny minnows darted about in their ever-shrinking, stagnant water-worlds, probably unaware of their peril. Scrubby plants clung thirstily to rocky crevices and other depressions, which had at one time promised water. Like the river itself, these creatures depend entirely on rains to the north, in Waimea. And no rain up there means no water — and very little life — in the stream by the house.

Waimea lies about two miles uphill and about 500 feet higher in elevation than the house, waterfall, and stretch of riverbed just described. Waimea is a relatively cool place, both climate-wise and style-wise, and it often gets rain. Up north in Waimea, it's mostly green, and the grass grows thick year-round. Up there, creeks almost always trickle, and often gurgle richly, with fresh rainwater.

A bit later in my writing retreat, I discovered that when it rains heavily in Waimea, within less than an hour the dry waterfall and riverbed outside the house's patio are transformed into a torrential gush. Apparently, the downpour up north (rain in Waimea) causes a deluge down south (river water at the house). I was astonished to watch the dry streambed change from a silent, parched wasteland to a noisy, torrential flood in just ten minutes! The sound of the water itself was nearly deafening. But that was only the background to a chorus of gleeful birds who rejoiced at the revived stream. Later on, I'd hear the excited whoops and hollers of thrill-seeking kayakers who'd launched out into the stream that just a few hours earlier had been almost too shallow for minnows. What a transformation!

Before and After

The amazing change I just described reflects the Bible's many stories and lessons that speak of spiritual thirst and satisfaction. The passage quoted from Isaiah 35 at the beginning of this chapter is just one example of that theme. In those verses, God's people are pictured as the soul-dry blind, deaf, lame, and mute, whose hearts feel like burning sand and thirsty ground. In this "before" stage, we Christians experience spiritual and relational dehydration and pain. We're like the withering plants in the arid streambed.

In our "before" state, we're characterized by a spiritual dryness that comes with living in a spiritual desert and in seeking deep soul-hydration apart from relationship with God. By trying to experience lasting forgiveness, peace, meaning, and personal security and significance outside of God, we become spiritually and relationally weak and vulnerable. We can't cope. We feel spiritually lethargic. We become uninterested in all sorts of things that once gave us joy — including God. In fact, we may begin to feel that God has become distant, indifferent, or weak. What's really happening is that we're (re)discovering that we live in a sun-baked spiritual riverbed, and that God is the only person or thing that can satisfy our deepest longings.

It's against this stark reality that we see rain clouds form and then gush. God Himself — the "Great Up North" — causes waters and streams to break forth, scorched lands to become pools, and thirsty ground to be converted into springs. All these rich physical images point to God's lavish restorative power working in the hearts of His beloved people. Through Isaiah, we learn that God's hydrating gush causes wholesale celebration: Blind eyes are opened, deaf ears are unstopped, the lame leap like deer, and the mute sing for joy. This is a poetic way of saying that God revives our hearts and minds so we can know and experience Him more deeply, that He renews our wills to once again enjoy and serve Him, and that He hydrates our inner being so that we happily praise Him and sing for joy at all the amazing gifts He's given us. We become like kayakers whooping it up in the torrential gush of God's rehydrating grace and goodness.

This before-and-after, dehydrated-and-hydrated cycle appears throughout Scripture. It's the ongoing battle between our soul's deepest thirsts and the satisfaction to be found only in relationship with God. Here's another example, from Psalm 107. This is only one of several vignettes in this psalm in which people become so desperate in their thirst that they cry out to the God who alone can satisfy.

> Some wandered in desert wastes,
>   finding no way to a city to dwell in;
> hungry and thirsty,
>   their soul fainted within them.
> Then they cried to the LORD in their trouble,
>   and He delivered them from their distress....
> He turns rivers into a desert,
>   springs of water into thirsty ground....

> He turns a desert into pools of water,
> > a parched land into springs of water.
> > > Psalm 107:4–6, 33, 35

Thirsty?

So, as a Christian, how are you doing right now? Are you in the "before" or the "after"? Maybe you're somewhere in between. Maybe you aren't sure what this all means, so you're having a hard time figuring out where you are. Maybe you're not even sure you're a Christian (if you're in doubt, turn to Appendix A for help). Wherever you are at the moment, my desire in *Gush* is that we explore these ideas in the pages that follow. This includes traveling through the thirsty places of our hearts so we can rejoice in the spiritual water that God offers in order to satisfy us. Both the "before" and the "after" are important in this journey.

Ultimately, however, our goal should not be to simply understand the concepts, but to increasingly *experience* the "after" part of this process, which is marked by deep soul-satisfaction stemming from intimacy with God. This is exactly what He invites us, the thirsty, to enjoy in many places in Scripture:

> Come, everyone who thirsts,
> > come to the waters;
> and he who has no money,
> > come, buy and eat!
> Come, buy wine and milk
> > without money and without price. Isaiah 55:1

> On the last day of the feast, the great day, Jesus stood up and cried out, "If anyone thirsts, let him come to Me and drink. Whoever believes in Me, as the Scripture has said, 'Out of his heart will flow rivers of living water."
> > > John 7:37–38

To the thirsty ones who embrace His invitation, God adds many wonderful promises of holistic hydration:

> He [who trusts in the LORD] is like a tree
> > planted by streams of water
> that yields its fruit in its season,
> > and its leaf does not wither.
> In all that he does, he prospers. Psalm 1:3

> With joy you will draw water from the wells of salvation.
> > > > > > > > Isaiah 12:3

> For I will pour water on the thirsty land,
> > and streams on the dry ground;
> I will pour my Spirit upon your offspring,
> > and my blessing on your descendants.
> They shall spring up among the grass
> > like willows by flowing streams. Isaiah 44:3–4

> Blessed are those who hunger and thirst for righteousness,
> for they shall be satisfied. Matthew 5:6

Our Voyage

We'll call our quest for God a voyage, because it's an exploratory trip and because *voyage* goes well with the water metaphors of the Bible. In *Gush*, buoys are collections of chapters centered on one main theme. They mark significant milestones in our voyage and will help us track our progress. They won't guide us to a particular destination; in other words, they aren't a formula for "arriving" at the perfectly hydrated Christian life. Instead, they'll help us learn how to continually navigate the often-stormy sea of our ongoing relationship with our eternal God and Savior. As we'll see, we must constantly revisit these buoys for ever-deepening intimacy with God.

We'll set sail toward Buoy I by taking a closer look at why and how we thirst for God. At this stage, our aim is to honestly identify our need for God *as Christians*, and to feel the weight of that need. In the pangs of our renewed craving, we'll welcome the sight of Buoy II, where we'll hear the drenching sound of God's invitation to parched, weary people just like us. Then we'll be challenged and instructed to (re)embrace God's offer freely and joyfully.

At Buoys III and IV we'll reach the middle of our voyage and sail slowly around the God who calls Himself our "Fountain" (Psalm 68:26, Jeremiah 2:13). We'll take plenty of time to enjoy God and to let Him revive our dehydrated spirits. Appendix C complements the encouragement around these two buoys as a Bible-derived list of some of God's attributes that are super-hydrating. These two buoys and Appendix C should renew our hope and motivate us to explore how we can increasingly enjoy God.

At Buoy V, we'll explore our ongoing lives in relationship with the amazing God we've rediscovered at Buoys III and IV. We'll (re)learn the basics of a life lived in glad dependence upon God and how that life naturally yields praise to Him, love for others, and healthy love for ourselves. As we put Buoy V to our stern, we'll start looking toward the horizon as a future Day when we'll be free of the thirst and seasickness so common to our lives on this side of heaven.

Our voyage ends at Buoy VI with a glimpse of the eternal, saturating fulfillment in God that awaits Christians in heaven. As thirsty sailors' longing for rain is heightened by a baking sun, our desire for the hydrating delights of heaven will be heightened by looking into the blazing inferno of hell. This last leg of our voyage will also provide perspective for our entire trip. The final pages will confirm the main themes presented in *Gush* as an encouragement to revisit Buoys I through VI continually as we grow in relationship with God.

Our Navigational Chart

As we travel together, we'll discover that our navigational chart, the Bible, is brimming with water metaphors that point to spiritual realities. We already drank in this chapter from wet texts from Psalms, Isaiah, Matthew, and John. But there are many, many more! God uses these Scriptures to help us understand both our thirst and the satisfaction He offers those who trust in Him through Jesus Christ.

We'll learn more about our spiritual poverty, which is pictured as life in a desert, where people are parched and withered. We'll rejoice in the God who calls Himself our Fountain (Psalms 36:9, 68:26; Jeremiah 2:13,

17:13). We'll walk barefoot in the God who calls Himself our Dew (Hosea 14:5). We'll open our mouths wide to receive His cleansing, forgiving, righteous rains (Hosea 6:3, 10:12). We'll drink from His freely offered living water (John 4:6–26, Revelation 21:6). And we'll marvel at His wondrous river of eternal delights (Revelation 22:1–3).

As we prepare to embark, here are a few quick suggestions to help us gain our sea legs. First, expect to occasionally see new words and phrases that pick up on the positive meaning of the word *gush*. The meaning of most words in "gushspeak" is pretty obvious. But if you ever get confused, or just want to have some fun thinking about the hydrating truths presented in this book, turn to Appendix B for a helpful glossary.

Second, understand that this isn't a lazy pleasure cruise where we simply lounge by the deck pool during the day and catch a show in the evening. We're all sailors here — able-bodied men and women before the mast! That means you'll need to *exert* yourself by doing more than just reading. This exertion isn't so much about your doing something for yourself, however, as it is about letting God do something to you and for you. Your work will involve doing the things that (re)open you to thirst-quenching relationship with God.

In the grandest sense, this means taking a trusting, prayerful heart-posture that says, "Yes, God, I want you to work in my life." It also means confirming the credibility and applicability of God's Word to your life by saying at appropriate times, "Yes, God, I believe what you've just said, and I will respond accordingly."

From a place of trusting receptivity — ponder, wrestle, and at times sit still with the biblical ideas and challenges *Gush* presents. Use the "gushaholic's prayer" at the end of each chapter to pause, dive in, and swim around in the clear, refreshing, safe sea called God. Completing the "gushercises" — exercises designed to help us absorb the concepts of each chapter — will also help you get the most out of this book.

We're ready to go. So throw off all lines, weigh anchor, unfurl canvas, and let's set sail!

Gushaholic's Prayer

Lord, I'm excited about our voyage! Please use this book to reveal and rehydrate my heart in You as we journey together. Amen.

Gushercises

1. What do you hope to receive from God by reading this book?
2. Describe where you are at this moment in the before-and-after, thirst-and-satisfaction cycle.

Buoy I

Our Thirst

As we leave port, the light atop the first buoy we encounter beckons us to experience our thirst. That's necessary because only thirsty people seek satisfaction. This is true in every sphere of life. In fact, the thirstier we are, the more energetic we'll be about seeking satisfaction. Knowing this, God persistently uses the imagery associated with our physical thirst to point us to our spiritual thirst and our need for Him.

But what is spiritual thirst? What contributes to it? How can we feel it in a way that compels us to pursue God for hydration?

In the next four chapters we'll take a closer look at why and how we long for God. We'll become aware of our condition and the factors that contribute to it. We'll do this as an essential spiritual exercise designed to drive us to God and to a deeper experience of His amazing promise in Isaiah 58:11.

> And the LORD will guide you continually
>   and satisfy your desire in scorched places
>   and make your bones strong;
> and you shall be like a watered garden,
>   like a spring of water,
>   whose waters do not fail.

1

Life in the Desert

A PSALM OF DAVID, WHEN HE WAS IN THE WILDERNESS OF JUDAH.
O God, You are my God; earnestly I seek You;
   my soul thirsts for You;
my flesh faints for You,
   as in a dry and weary land where there is no water.

Psalm 63:1

The Ironman competition held on the Big Island of Hawaii every October is one of the most grueling tests of athletic endurance in the world. After a 2.4 mile swim in the open ocean, the triathletes must bike 112 miles on the Queen Ka'ahumanu Highway and then run 26.2 miles on that same road in and around the city of Kona. The whole race is punishing, but the bike segment is especially so because it occurs along a sun-baked, lava-surrounded, heat-radiating asphalt road. Scorching winds almost always whip down from the mountains to the sea, heating up as they traverse the aged black lava fields. These parching winds hit riders from the side and suck precious fluids from their bodies.

You could say that the bike portion of the Hawaiian Ironman is *aggressively* dehydrating. Not only is it waterless; it actively attacks the athletes, draining them of the water inside them. This is a very good picture of the world in which we live and of our journey through it, spiritually speaking. Not only is there no water for our souls, but whatever spiritual life we have within us is actively sought and sucked from us by the world.

Israel's King David was well acquainted with this dehydrating phenomenon. As a spiritual triathlete, he fully experienced living in a godless, parching world. In Psalm 63, he admits that this is a major contributing factor in his spiritual thirst and in his subsequent longing for God.

Waterless Means "Lifeless"

At this point you may be asking, "OK, but what exactly do you mean by 'the world'?" Good question! In Psalm 63:1, God helps us answer that question by using physical realities to clarify spiritual realities. When David bluntly says, "There is no water" in his surroundings, he means it in both aspects of human experience. In the physical sense, David's "world" refers to his desert surroundings that are materially dehydrating. In the spiritual sense, David's "world" is the collection of relationships, alliances, achievements, and so on that cannot satisfy his deepest longings for meaning, value, forgiveness from God, and soul-peace in relationship with Him. This fits with the New Testament meaning of "the world," which is most often translated from the Greek word "kosmos." Thayer's Greek Lexicon (i.e., dictionary) defines the spiritual sense of the word this way:

> [The world] refers to worldly affairs; the aggregate of things earthly, the whole circle of earthly goods, endowments, riches, advantages, pleasures, etc., which, although hollow and frail and fleeting, stir desire, seduce from God and are obstacles to the cause of Christ. [This includes] the incentives to sin proceeding from the world.[1]

Elsewhere in the New Testament, God says "the world" has the appearance of glory (i.e., value, magnificence, weight), but is ultimately vain and empty (Matthew 4:8, 13:22, 16:26; Galatians 4:3ff). God says that the world is dark, which means that it's fundamentally opposed to Him (Matthew 5:14) and does not know Him (1 Corinthians 1:21). He warns that the world tempts us to sin (Matthew 18:7, James 1:27), that it can even spiritually enslave us (Galatians 4:3), and that it is therefore condemned as foolish (1 Corinthians 3:19, 7:31). Perhaps the most blunt statement God makes about the world is a warning in James 4:4 — "You adulterous people! Do you not know that friendship with the world is enmity with God? Therefore whoever wishes to be a friend of the world makes himself an enemy of God."

For our purposes, we can understand the world as a network of values and invitations that ultimately lead us away from finding our soul's hydration in God.

The word for *no* in David's declaration in Psalm 63:1 is the Hebrew "particle for negation," *lo*. *Lo* is the strongest form of negation in the Hebrew language; it leaves no room for exceptions. The use of *lo* in Psalm 63:1 means that in the world where David lives there's *nothing at all* that can truly satisfy a thirsty soul or parched body. *Nothing.*

To add to this already blistered picture, David refers to his environment as "the wilderness of Judah." This is a real geographic area that ranges from extremely dry to mostly dry. Like the Queen Ka'ahumanu Highway, it's unfit for permanent human habitation. David goes on to describe the land as "dry" and "weary." The Hebrew word used for "dry" is *tsiyyah*, which means "a land of drought." The Hebrew word for "weary" (or as some translate it, "parched") is *ayeph*, which means "intensely thirsty, as if from exertion."

David's metaphors and similes lead us to one strong conclusion: His world is one long, parching Queen Ka'ahumanu Highway. His world is parched in a physical sense, but it's parched in a spiritual sense as well. And so is our world. Embracing and relying upon the world's values and invitations for lasting soul-hydration only enflames our thirst and leads us away from God to our own spiritual peril (and sometimes to physical, financial, or other kinds of peril, too).

Stay Thirsty, My Friends

One of the most ridiculous yet revealing examples of the dehydrating aggressiveness of the world is a popular promotional campaign for Dos Equis beer. These ads feature the so-called Most Interesting Man in the World hawking their beer in a variety of comical sketches in which he makes pithy statements about life. Nearly everything about this fictitious character illustrates the dehydrating farce and sawdust promises that the world offers in order to satisfy our souls: image, accomplishments, virility, swooning attention from members of the opposite sex, money, health, influence, prestige, and boastful intrigue.

In one clever ad, The Most Interesting Man is lounging at a lively bar. Surrounded by a bevy of alluring and adoring women half his age, he's laughing and enjoying himself as he glances toward a bowl of salty nuts on the bar. Next, we hear his charming yet leathery voice: "See those nuts? They're there to make us thirsty. While I don't like being coerced, in this case I'll make an exception." Then, looking straight into the camera, he smoothly concludes, "Stay thirsty, my friends."

It's hard to decide on the most scorching aspect of this cute little charade. Maybe it's the wry admission that the world actually puts out all kinds of salty nuts (i.e., anything enticing that offers soul-satisfaction but that, in fact, makes us even thirstier). Maybe it's the idea that the world's temptations to false satisfaction run perilously close to coercion. Maybe it's the twinkle-eyed suggestion that it's okay to give in to these temptations. Maybe it's the bold-faced insanity of the concluding shot that it's actually good to *stay* thirsty. Or maybe it's the deluded thought that siren singers who embody such emptiness and vanity are our friends.

You decide. But whatever you conclude, remember this: Nothing that the world has to offer will ever satisfy our soul's deepest thirst. *Nothing.*

Like The Most Interesting Man, the world — the network of values and invitations that ultimately leads us away from finding our soul's hydration in God — is *lost* in its thirst. The world constantly sets out "salty barroom nuts" that seem to promise satisfaction but only inflame our deep longings. In a strangely horrid way, the world actually perpetuates its own thirst and somehow enjoys it in a constantly changing, ever-present, complex web of similar invitations. These invitations are accompanied by false promises of satisfaction apart from relationship with God. Accepting these invitations (i.e., trusting them for the satisfaction only God can provide) always makes us thirstier in the long run.

What of The Most Interesting Man in the World? Worldly messengers like him are described in several places in Scripture. Notice the water/thirst imagery in these verses:

> For the fool speaks folly,
>   and his heart is busy with iniquity,
> to practice ungodliness,

> to utter error concerning the LORD,
> to leave the craving of the hungry unsatisfied,
> and to deprive the thirsty of drink. Isaiah 32:6

> These are waterless springs and mists driven by a storm. For them the gloom of utter darkness has been reserved.
>
> 2 Peter 2:17

Do We Believe It?

Do we really believe this is an accurate spiritual picture of the world we live in — not only that there is *no* soul-satisfying water in the world, but also that the world actually *inflames* our thirst and *sucks* the spiritual life out of us? Do we realize that the basic value system around us, along with its ever-changing invitations, is opposed to God and actively hostile to a healthy spiritual lifestyle?

Maybe you live in an actual physical desert, maybe not. But I know that we all live in a *spiritual* desert as David did. Maybe you're like Sharon, a sixteen-year-old Christian who's been allured by a version of The Most Interesting Man who vainly promised her that the right clothes, the right friends, and the right boyfriend would bring a lasting feeling of personal value. Or perhaps you're like Dave, who loves Jesus but has embraced the world's belief that a successful career is what really holds the key to his heart's delight. Maybe you're like Tasha, a single thirty-something who's getting more and more anxious to realize the world's promise of satisfaction in the form of a husband and children.

It could be that you're like Sam, a ministry leader who's swallowed the world's deadly value attractively cloaked in religious garb that whispers, "What you need is more baptisms … more members … more young people … a bigger building … an expanding radio ministry." Or maybe you're like Susan, the faltering Christian who's bought the lie that increased religiosity — Bible study, prayer, church involvement, taking the Lord's Supper, and the like — will merit God's smile and love.

Who or what is *your* Most Interesting Man? What does his voice sound like? Which of his alluring promises grab your attention? How are you chafing in service to his deception? What is he telling you that's ultimately leading you away from God as your ultimate satisfaction?

Realizing the dehydrating deceptiveness of the world can be a real bummer, to say the least. But it's absolutely essential. Unmasking its slick cruelties for the first time can be like revisiting Disney World as an adult. When I went there as a child, I was totally captivated by the magic of it all. I thought that Goofy and Mickey Mouse were actually giant, happy cartoons come to life. I thought Cinderella's castle was real. In my innocent little heart I really believed that "it's a small world after all" and that people everywhere lived with perpetual smiles. It was amazing.

But then I visited Disney World as an adult. I still had fun, mind you, but my mature eyes saw through much of the make-believe. I ached at the price of admission and parking. I knew that there was probably a sweaty person inside that Mickey suit. I saw the hook beneath the glitzy surface and recognized how much the operation was geared toward selling Disney paraphernalia and junk food. I even realized that buildings were built with shrunken second and third floors to make kids feel bigger. As an adult, my experience was tempered with reality; it was disillusioning and sad.

Looking at the reality and ploys behind the show at Disney World may seem superficial to you, or just plain mean-hearted. What we're aiming at here is unvarnished frankness about things of much greater importance. We must see that in this world there are all kinds of schemes that are just that — schemes. When we identify their work in our hearts, we're to point them out and say, "I see you for what you are! You're a lie that's designed to lead me away from finding my ultimate satisfaction in God." Recognizing these deceptive schemes is absolutely essential to life in the gush of God. If we fail to unmask them, we'll blindly chase the sad illusion of The Most Interesting Man in the World: *Stay thirsty, my friends*. And our longings for God will be stunted.

Gushaholic's Prayer

Lord, thank You for showing me that the basic value system of the world I live in is spiritually dehydrating. I'm glad You've helped me realize that nothing the world offers me can satisfy the deepest longings of my soul. Please reveal the ways that I've bought into the world's parching lies. Amen.

Gushercises

1. Explain what it means that the world you live in is a "dry and weary land where there is no water."
2. What's the difference between *staying* thirsty in a worldly sense (which is bad) and re-experiencing spiritual thirst that drives you to find satisfaction in God (which is good)?
3. Describe The Most Interesting Man/Men and their messages that tend to attract your attention and devotion. As you do, be honest about whether or not your pursuit of them is bringing you the deep and lasting satisfaction you desire.
4. After reading this chapter, you may wonder if there's any legitimate pleasure to be found in this world — even in eating a fistful of nuts, for instance! To help you think this through, turn to Appendix D, a postscript to this chapter.

2

The Devil, Our Dehydrator

The thief [the devil] comes only to steal and kill and destroy. I [Jesus] came that they may have life and have it abundantly. John 10:10

Be sober-minded; be watchful. Your adversary the devil prowls around like a roaring lion, seeking someone to devour. 1 Peter 5:8

How do you feel about vampires? That's right — I'm asking what you think about a creature that the dictionary defines as a "bloodsucking evil spirit," and that, according to European folklore, is a dead person believed to rise each night from the grave and suck blood from the living for sustenance. So — what do you think?

Maybe pinpointing your feelings about vampires is too abstract or corny. In that case, let me ask you a related question: How do you feel about mosquitoes, ticks, leeches, and horseflies? "What?!" you're secretly thinking. "Our author's cheese has finally slid off his cracker!" I don't think so. All these questions — while potentially revolting — are meant to shock us into thinking soberly about the nature of the devil and about his role in our lives.

That's because the devil is a lot like all the creatures we've just considered. He *is* a creature, and like the other creatures he's a bloodsucker. The devil, however, lives off our *spiritual* vitality instead of our *physical* vitality. He's spiritually aggressive and violent, but not necessarily obvious in what he does. In fact, his "bites" often go undetected — at least until they get infected and pose a serious threat. The devil, like a vampire, can be alluring. He and his demons love to craftily lead us away from the safety and satisfaction of intimacy with God — and then, when we're most vulnerable, they pierce our souls with woes that will drain us of our spiritual vitality.

It's time for us to wake up to the reality of this voracious enemy of our souls. It's time for us to be appropriately disgusted with this wily dehydrator and his host, and to feel the burden of their presence. As we do so, our thirst should increase, making us even more inclined to seek God alone for our safety and satisfaction.

Steal, Kill, Destroy, Devour

The two verses quoted at the beginning of this chapter are among the Bible's most vivid descriptions of the devil. They point out his spiritual agenda by using words we normally associate with the physical world. Let's examine the list below to get a better sense of the Bible's description of the devil. As you read, consider whether or not your lifestyle reflects a posture that recognizes the existence of such a creature. The Bible says the devil is a being who ...

1. Steals. The word for *steal* is *klepto* (yes, from which we derive *kleptomaniac*), and it means "to take away something secretly, without the owner's permission."[1] The Bible actually calls the devil a *kleptes* who *kleptos*, "a stealer who steals."
2. Kills. The word for *kill* is *thuo*, which means "to sacrifice, offer, slaughter in sacrifice, slay, or kill for food."[2]
3. Destroys. The word for *destroy* is *apollumi*, which means "to ruin, destroy, kill, or cause something to come to nothing, perish, pass away, or cease to exist."[3]
4. Devours. The word for *devour* is *katapino*, which means, literally, "to drink or gulp down, swallow; used as part of a metaphor to denote the devil's activity against someone, completely overpower, bring under control"; or figuratively, to "overcome, destroy; of waves of water, overflowing someone; drown."[4]

Steal, kill, destroy, and devour: This is the devil's job description. Pretty intense, huh? You bet! And we, fellow voyagers-in-God's-gush, are the object of all that viciousness. Let's not be fooled about this. The devil isn't some comic-book character in a red suit who prances around giving us bad hair days and making our coffee cold just for laughs. Rather he and his allies (demons) work to destroy, or at least pollute, our intimacy with God and our satisfaction in Him. In the terminology of gushspeak, we'd say that he wants to *dehydrate* our souls.

How does the devil steal, kill, destroy, and devour? The texts above say he "roars" and "prowls around." Both words carry a strong sense of action. In a sense, he *assaults* us and whatever is godly in our lives. It can be a full-frontal assault, or a sly, back-door attack. To borrow a phrase used in twelve-step recovery programs, we could say that he's "cunning, baffling, and powerful."[5] He's sneaky. He's real. And he's all business. We who acknowledge these facts should learn as much as we can about our enemy so we can be on our guard.

Enemy Tactics

Mainly, what the devil and his demons do is *tempt* us. To *tempt* (*nasah* in Hebrew and *peirasmos* in Greek, along with their derivations) basically means "to conduct an experiment, a trial, or a test to learn our character."[6] When evil spirits tempt us, they do so to get us to sin, to forsake God, and to ruin our character.[7] Theirs is a test with an *evil* motive for an *evil* end. In doing this, the devil is a creative opportunist (Ephesians 4:27) and a schemer (Ephesians 6:11) who lays snares (1 Timothy 3:7, 2 Timothy 2:26) and shoots flaming darts (Ephesians 6:16) to get us to sin. These tactics are personified by the seductress of Proverbs 7:

> And behold, the woman meets him,
>   dressed as a prostitute, wily of heart....
> She seizes him and kisses him,
>   and with bold face she says to him,...
> "Come, let us take our fill of love till morning;
>   let us delight ourselves with love...."
> With much seductive speech she persuades him;
>   with her smooth talk she compels him.
>   Proverbs 7:10, 13, 18, 21

The saddest part of the situation just quoted isn't the siren's temptation, but the young man's ignorance, shown below in additional verses from Proverbs 7. This is a picture of us when we refuse to acknowledge the existence and craftiness of our enemy, the devil.

> I have perceived among the youths,
>   a young man lacking sense....
> All at once he follows her [the adulteress just described],
>   as an ox goes to the slaughter,
> or as a stag is caught fast
>   till an arrow pierces its liver;
> as a bird rushes into a snare;
>   he does not know that it will cost him his life.
>
> Proverbs 7:7, 22–23

Are you getting the picture? The devil, personified here as a seductress, is a dehydrator extraordinaire with a burning zeal for his job and many weapons in his arsenal. If you're a Christian, the devil and/or his demons hate you and do all they can to parch your soul. We must recognize these facts if we're to find our hydration in God.

The Terminator

Let's turn to the movies for help grasping the Bible's description of the devil. The Terminator, the bad guy from the classic movie and television series by that name, is an excellent example. The Terminator is a human-looking, nearly indestructible robot covered with human flesh. He's a creature from the future, built by machines that want to exterminate the human race. The Terminator is incredibly resilient, intensely mission-minded, and obsessively active. As you can guess from his name, a Terminator's sole job is to, well, *terminate* his human target.

In the 1984 film that started it all, the Terminator tirelessly seeks his mark, Sarah Connor. He wants to kill her. Explosions, machine-gun fire, being smashed by a truck, being hit with a crowbar — it seems that nothing can stop that Terminator. Toward the end of the movie, he gets torn in half, and you think it's all over. But you're wrong! With a jolt, he's clawing his way toward Sarah, his target, with his one remaining arm. He's a relentless killing machine.

So is the devil. He doesn't give up. Even if he had only one arm, he'd be clawing his way toward us to do us harm. He's active. He hates God and Christians. His greatest passion is to entice us so he can steal, kill, destroy, and/or devour us and our relationship with God. In short, he wants to dehydrate our souls. He's so crafty, baffling, and powerful that he makes the Terminator look like Bambi.

My Response

I experienced at least one devilishly dehydrating spiritual attack while writing *Gush*. After writing the first draft, I felt more connected to God than I had in a long time. I had a renewed sense of praise to Him, felt at peace with myself, and had a positive outlook toward those around me. I was sleeping better and was physically rested. My condition was clearly a gift from God and bore the marks of His goodness as described in places like Galatians 5:22–25.

It wasn't long after I returned from my writing retreat that difficulties began popping up all around me. Each bore demonic claw-prints — the problems came from outside me and threatened to steal, kill, destroy, and devour the sweet intimacy with God that I was experiencing. First, sudden betrayals and rumors sprang up around me and about me at work. Second, the utility company surprised me by unnecessarily mangling the beautiful dogwood tree in my backyard, despite my warnings not to do that very thing. Third, there was an increase in lustful images that "just so happened" to cross my path. Fourth, some projects at work designed to grow people in Christ ran into significant, unexpected roadblocks.

Unfortunately, I responded to the devil's enticing campaign by sinning in a variety of ways. I actually participated in his dehydrating activities, gulping down salty barroom nuts in a vain attempt to slake my increasing thirst. In other words, I fell for his temptations. I fell for his dehydrating campaign by forsaking God and turning to sin for temporary, superficial relief from my frustration and for satisfaction of my inflamed supreme thirst.

My prayer life tanked because I reverted to self-reliance. I ramped up planning and list making, trying to tighten control over my life instead of remaining open to God and acknowledging His power and interest in my plight. I let my problems and pains, not my belovedness in Christ, define me. This made me anxious and irritated. For relief I indulged in lustful thoughts instead of talking with and trusting in God and the community of people He's placed around me for support.

During this time, I became thirstier and thirstier. I found myself feeling further and further from God, which is exactly what the devil and his minions wanted. Maybe you can relate to the attack I've described and to the failure I've confessed.

It's unreasonable to attribute all my sin to the devil or demons. I'm sure that both the generally dehydrating nature of this desert-world (Chapter 1) and the parching work of my own flesh (Chapter 3) also contributed. However, the boldness of the temptations and their intense enticement to do evil at least hinted at the involvement of our dehydrating foe. They fit his job description perfectly.

Your Response?

Before you can identify the devil's dehydrating activities in your own life, you have to accept the fact that he's real. You must admit that we have an enemy who's violently passionate about stealing, killing, destroying, or devouring us and our relationship with God by enticing us to sin. By *sin*, I mean "trying to find peace with God — and the joys that come with it — outside of the forgiveness offered by Jesus Christ and an ongoing relationship with Him."

A good next step is to identify happenings in your own life that mirror mine as described above. Look for temptations coming from outside your own head that seem strangely direct or unexpected, and that are designed to lure you from God.

Remember that the devil's basic objective is to dehydrate us by attacking our relationship with God by enticing us into sin. How has he — or more likely, his demonic allies — been invading your life? A new opportunity for an illicit relationship? Surprise temptations to rob God of His tithe by splurging on some "need" you've just "got to have"? Sudden physical chaos, to which the easiest solution would be to sin? A seemingly harmless enticement to twist the truth just a little so you can get that promotion, grade, friend, control, compliment, or advantage you crave? Yet one more invitation to work late and miss another important family event you promised to attend?

If you're coming alive to the reality of the devil and his dastardly, dehydrating ways, that's great! You're making progress in our voyage according to God's warning in 1 Peter 5:8 — "Be sober-minded; be watchful. Your adversary the devil prowls around like a roaring lion, seeking someone to devour." Together, we're building on the admissions we made as we considered the last chapter, regarding which of the world's dehydrating messages we find most alluring. As we add our recognition of the devil and his demons' work in us, our thirst should increase. And, contrary to the world's enticement, we're not to *stay* thirsty (as if staying thirsty were a good thing); instead we're to let our new recognition of thirst drive us to God for satisfaction.

As we grow more aware of our need, don't despair! For one thing, God has the devil on His leash (see Job 1 and 2). Amplified recognition of thirst paves the way for amplified celebration of God and His opulent, gushing invitation of forgiveness, fellowship, love, and grace. It also opens up revitalized love toward ourselves and others. So hang on as we turn inward to examine our longings.

Gushaholic's Prayer

God, thank You for being honest with me about our enemy the devil. Please keep me from paranoia while helping me to recognize his attacks. Help me feel my thirst when he and/or his demons attack me so that I run to *You* for safety and satisfaction. Amen.

Gushercises

1. In general terms, describe the devil's purpose and work.
2. Where and how have you noticed the devil and/or his demons attacking you?

3

An Appetite for Desiccants

For I delight in the law of God, in my inner being, but I see in my members another law waging war against the law of my mind and making me captive to the law of sin that dwells in my members.
Romans 7:22–23

Have you ever bought a new pair of shoes, a purse, or a piece of electronic equipment? Upon opening the box, or looking inside the item itself, did you notice one or more strange little white packets printed with the following words: "Silica Gel — Do Not Eat — Throw Away"? Have you ever wondered what those little packets are for?

The answer is that they're desiccant packets. They contain materials, like silica beads, that absorb moisture. Manufacturers ship moisture-sensitive items like electronics with these packets to protect the items from the damage and decay caused by dampness. This is one use for desiccants that's *good*.

But we Christians aren't shoes, purses, or electronics. For one thing, we're *alive*! And because we're alive, we need to stay hydrated. We can't survive more than a few days without water. Spiritually, we need the hydration that comes from being in an intimate, ongoing relationship with God, who's our spiritual water. Things that rob us of this kind of moisture are our enemies. So for us, desiccants are *bad*. They deprive us of the precious spiritual humidity that's essential to our survival.

The problem is that we Christians retain an annoying *internal affection* for desiccants. We still occasionally desire to eat the very thing that would dehydrate us: sin! This is the third aspect of the parching trio we battle in this life. It's in addition to the *external* enemies (our desert home, and the devil and his demons) that work to ruin our connection with God.

In Romans 7:14–25, the apostle Paul gives a vivid and anguished description of his own battle with his remaining internal desiccant-loving nature. We'd be right, upon reading that entire passage, to get the feeling that a terrorist lives within Paul, driving him — against his redeemed will — to sin. Paul calls this conflict a war within him (v. 23), between his redeemed nature and his remaining sinful nature. It's a war that can be very fierce and maddening at times.

This desiccant-loving internal enemy tries relentlessly to get Paul to eat desiccants — to sin. Hating good and loving evil, just as the world and the devil do, the foe wants Paul to forsake God. Like the devil, this enemy works to get Paul to do things that will "make him captive" to sin. This "body of death" (v. 24) — this rebellious, unwanted internal terrorist — tries to induce Paul to turn his back on God and turn instead toward spiritually dehydrating things for soul-satisfaction. All this is true, despite the fact that Paul is a bona fide Christian who, in his redeemed nature, is indwelled by the Holy Spirit, embraces the Lordship of Christ, and seeks to love and serve Him. It's also true for every Christian before Paul and since Paul. That includes you and me.

Our Internal War on Terror

Consider the early stages of the international community's war on terrorism in Iraq. In 2003, U.S. Marines captured the murderous dictator Saddam Hussein. He was later put on trial, condemned, and executed. There's no doubt whatsoever (since he's *dead*) that Saddam will never again dominate Iraq. At the same time, America and several other nations remained in Iraq to install a peaceful, orderly humanitarian government that would work for the good of the nation. We could say that, at that time, Iraq's official government really and objectively shifted from a bloodthirsty dictatorship to a peaceable body of law and order.

Despite this official and very real shift in power, terrorists and terrorist cells remained within Iraq. At times they still flare up, doing what they've always done: bombing, killing, and causing chaos. From within the nation, they recruit disenchanted citizens to join them in their murderous acts. Their ultimate aim is to overthrow the new government from within. They aren't officially in power, but they "wage war" against the new government that *is* in power.

This is a good illustration of every Christian's internal world as described by the apostle Paul and exemplified by his own life with Christ in Romans 7:14–25. When we embrace the gospel, Christ overthrows our sinful nature and installs Himself as King of our lives. Our redeemed nature lives joyfully under His reign and cherishes the wholesome spiritual fruit that comes from intimacy with Him.

Unfortunately, a spiritual terrorist remains within us, just as physical terrorists remain in Iraq and other peaceable nations of the world. That's what Paul calls "sin that dwells within me" (v. 17). From time to time, this indwelling sin-terrorist flares up against Christ's power in our lives and tempts us from within to do things that would undermine Christ's reign and cause us to seek our satisfaction elsewhere. Our foe entices us to eat spiritual desiccants, to sin. If we're honest, we'll admit that we often grab what God forbids simply because we acquiesce to this otherwise unwelcome internal affection for sin, or we simply get tired of resisting its temptations. Our willful surrender to our flesh's desiccant-eating enticement, along with our desert home and the devil and his demons, leads to our spiritual dehydration.

Snatching Cortez's Treasure

It's time for us to admit that we're sometimes no different from Captain Barbosa and his cursed crew of pirates in the movie *Pirates of the Caribbean: The Curse of the Black Pearl*. Even though we're Christians, there remains a part of us that's just like him — driven to take the very things that would dehydrate our souls. In an impassioned speech to his captive, Elizabeth Turner, Captain Barbosa describes how the impulse to take all 882 gold pieces from Cortez's sacred treasure led him and his crew from bad to worse. Listen as he laments giving in to his own lust by snatching a treasure that he had been told beforehand would desiccate him and his greedy crew.

> Find it we did. There be the chest. Inside be the gold. And we took 'em all. We spent 'em and traded 'em and frittered

'em away on drink and food and pleasurable company. But the more we gave 'em away, the more we came to realize that drink would not satisfy. Food turned to ash in our mouths. And all the pleasurable company in the world could not slake out lust. We are cursed men, Ms. Turner. Compelled by greed we were. But now, we are consumed by it.[1]

I'm not saying Captain Barbosa was a Christian. I'm saying that in Romans 7 God reveals that every Christian, like the apostle Paul, has to regularly deal with a terrorizing inner desiccant-loving Barbosa that never feels godly remorse. Notice that the result of his treasure-grabbing is increased thirst: "But now, we are consumed by it [greed]." That's the end result of eating desiccants. They not only fail to satisfy; they also lead to increased pain, spiritual dehydration, and captivity to the desiccant itself (John 8:34).

When was the last time you felt your inner Barbosa flaring up? Forget the pirate hat, the swashbuckling accent, and the rotten teeth. Can you admit that you've felt the effects of your own internal terrorist waging war *within* you? Have you ever been compelled *from within* to do something you knew would hurt God, yourself, or someone else? Have you ever gone ahead and done that very thing while inside simultaneously screaming both "Yes!" and "No!" Have you wrestled with or been revolted by the darkness of your own thoughts? If so, then you've felt the dehydrating campaigns of your internal desiccant-loving terrorist.

Exposing Our Internal Terrorist

The most distinguishing mark of our internal desiccant-eater is that it's, well, *internal*. It elicits impulses *within* our own being — via our very own thoughts, feelings, and desires — that lead us away from finding forgiveness and ultimate contentment in God. This coercive insider has a variety of tactics. In Galatians 5:19–21, God helps us by providing a grand exposé of our internal foe's most popular strategies. The following list has been compiled from a study of the Greek meaning of the key words in this original text, and is expressed as a series of impulses we might feel inside ourselves. As we read, let's ask God to expose our desiccant-loving ways to us and to increase our thirst for Him.

1. Sexual immorality (*pornea*): persuasions that push us to engage in any kind of extramarital, biblically unlawful form of sexual intercourse, including physical or emotional unfaithfulness either inside or outside of marriage. It also includes thoughts or feelings that move us to forsake the Lord by being unfaithful to Him or His calling upon our lives (i.e., idolatry, spiritual adultery).
2. Impurity (*akatharsia*): enticements to immoral living in general, or wasteful, extremely extravagant living in particular
3. Sensuality (*aselgeia*): desires to throw off moral restraint as particularly evidenced by a drive toward licentious behavior (unchecked, selfish sexual immorality)
4. Idolatry (*eidololatria*): urges to give ultimate adoration, love, or honor to any created thing, including material things (person, house, car, body, prized possession, etc.) and immaterial things (relationship, idea, cause, etc.)
5. Sorcery (*pharmakeia*): inclinations to rely upon magic or spells, or to ascribe mystical/magical powers to drugs, people, ideas, or campaigns
6. Enmity (*echthra*): compulsions that move us toward hostility or hatred as an inner disposition or an outward opposition
7. Strife (*eris*): cravings that move us to wrangle or quarrel in a contentious manner and in a way that leads to discord and rivalry
8. Jealousy (*zelos*): rising internal bitterness or discomfort over another's situation in life, along with a sinking attitude about one's own situation
9. Fits of anger (*thumos*): intense or sudden impulses toward violent, uncontrolled anger, rage, or wrath
10. Rivalries (*eritheia*): resentment based upon someone else's advantage, and/or the impulse to want to be better than someone else

11. Dissensions (*dichostasia*): desires to tear a group that should be one into two, usually including the basic desire to make people hate (or at least dislike) each other
12. Divisions (*hairesis*): wishes to separate from the true exposition of the Christian faith and follow one's own tenets (heresies), which are false or unbiblical teachings
13. Envy (*phthonos*): feelings or actions of ill will toward another because of a real or perceived advantage that that person possesses. This is often accompanied by a growing desire to have whatever the other person has.
14. Drunkenness (*methē*): impulses to bring oneself under the controlling influence of an intoxicating substance in general, or alcohol in particular
15. Orgies (*komos*): cravings to indulge in alcohol or other inebriating substances, often accompanied by other immoral behavior, such as sexual impropriety
16. And things like these: This means that Paul's list isn't complete. It shows us that our flesh has even more strategies to try to satisfy our thirst, and that they'll generally bear these kinds of traits.

Whenever we hear an *internal* prompting toward any of these listed thoughts, feelings, or actions, it's very likely that we're experiencing a dehydrating temptation away from God and toward sin. Our indwelling desiccant-lover assaults us on two fronts: It elicits doubts about God, and it entices us to look elsewhere for satisfaction. In our times of thirst, the still-immoral part of us wants us to leave God as our Fountain *and* reach for any number of parching alternatives.

For example, we envy (*phthonos*) when we heed our inner voice's suggestions that God isn't giving us the advantages we need in life. The voice also fixates us on others who have the advantages we think we need. We sit and stew over this, listening to our fleshly, parching voice that whispers, "You know, if God really cared about you, He'd give you what that other person has. You really need that thing, after all, to be valuable and to get Him to forgive you and like you. It wouldn't hurt for you to take matters into your own hands, at least a little bit. Why don't you send an email to your [boss, teacher, sibling, classmate, parent] — expressing your discontent? Don't be too direct about it. Be subtle. Do what you must to get what that other person has so you can get ahead and *be* somebody."

Or consider what happens when we indulge in sensuality (*aselgeia*) by going along with the internal prompting that tells us that God is really not the most satisfying thing in town *and* that there are better ways to get the pleasure, intimacy, and strength we crave. Again, this two-front war is waged quite subtly at times by our inner desiccant-lover who tempts, "What's up with God? Doesn't He know you have legitimate sexual and relational needs? How can He expect you to confine those to marriage? In fact, just look at this person over here that seems ready, willing, and able to give you the satisfaction you deserve. Why don't you indulge a little?"

Or reflect on the temptation to engage in strife (*eris*). The backdrop for this desiccant-loving Barbosa is often a dispute over anything from doctrine to the proper way to change a diaper. Our flesh seizes its chance and whispers, "What?! How can that person hold that view? You've got to show them the error of their ways, no matter what the cost. If they escalate, you must escalate. You must meet fire with fire. You can't afford to lose this debate, even if it means losing the friendship or causing public scandal."

Maniacal! Twisted! Parching! What all these terrorizing inner promptings have in common is that they move us away from relishing meaning, joy, and satisfaction in God. No wonder Paul exclaimed with exasperation in Romans 7:24, "Wretched man that I am! Who will deliver me from this body of death?"

Feeling Thirsty?

It's important that we, *as Christians,* regularly echo Paul's vexed cry. Remember — Paul was a mature Christian when he penned that cry in his letter to the Roman Christians. Who among us hasn't experienced their inner Barbosa trying to yank them away from God to seek soul-fulfillment elsewhere? Who among us hasn't felt the parching reality of Paul's heartfelt plea in Galatians 5:17? I've personalized the pronouns so we can read this as a confession:

> For the desires of my flesh are against the Spirit, and the desires of the Spirit are against my flesh, for these are opposed to each other, to keep me from doing the things I want to do.

Experiencing our thirst at the hands of our own internal desiccant-eater is a burden. But it's a burden that leads to life when our thirst drives us to God for satisfaction (instead of *staying* thirsty, as the world advises). In fact, the thirstier we are, the more vigorously we'll seek God, and the more exuberant we'll be when we receive His gush of mercy, grace, forgiveness, and love. As we feel this great burden of our thirst, we may even lose some sleep, just as the late singer-songwriter Rich Mullins did on an occasion when he was wrestling mightily with his own internal desiccant-lover.

Rich describes this struggle in his 1995 hit song "Hold Me, Jesus." He wrote the song while on tour in Amsterdam. Rich had been lying awake all night in his hotel room, "waiting for his roommate to start snoring" (i.e., fall asleep) so he could "take a walk and be tempted" among the intensely immoral streets of the city. He lay there all that night, fighting with his internal sin-terrorist's campaign to lead him into finding joy outside of God and His perfect moral will. At 5:00 AM, Rich got out of bed and wrote these words:

> And I wake up in the night and feel the dark
> It's so hot inside my soul
> I swear there must be blisters on my heart
>
> So hold me, Jesus, 'cause I'm shaking like a leaf
> You have been King of my glory
> Won't You be my Prince of Peace[2]

Rich's song is a song of a man who recognizes his thirst but doesn't want to *stay* thirsty. It beautifully expresses the longing of a Christian who's aware that there are forces around *and inside* of him that want him to leave God and seek satisfaction elsewhere. At this point in our voyage, we need to accept that part of our story matches Rich's, or if you prefer, the apostle Paul's as recorded in Romans 7:14–25. We must acknowledge that there remains inside of us a dark internal terrorist who, while no longer in official power, still flares up from time to time to tempt us away from God. Recognizing our internal terrorist will heighten our thirst, which is a good thing, for I can hear thunder up north, which signals rain clouds a-comin'.

Gushaholic's Prayer

Use Rich's prayer, or any one of Paul's confessions in this chapter, as your prayer.

Gushercises

1. Read Romans 7:14–25. In your own words, describe what Paul's going through.
2. Slowly and prayerfully reread this chapter's sixteen-item list of internal sin-impulses. How have you experienced the work of your own internal sin-terrorist?
3. How do you resist your indwelling sin-terrorist? (If you don't have a plan, don't worry — read the next chapter for help!)

4

Our Supreme Thirst

As a deer pants for flowing streams,
so pants my soul for You, O God. Psalm 42:1

Hydrophytes are plants that grow only when wholly or partially submerged in water, or in saturated soil. Some of them even use water as their support structure (for example, lily pads — the leaves of water lilies, the most famous hydrophytes — float on the water's surface). Even more than hydrophytes, we're hydro*philes*. *Hydrophile* is the fusion of two Greek words: *hydros* (water) and *philos* (loving friendship). Literally, hydrophiles are "water lovers"!

We're hydrophiles in the most comprehensive sense. We depend on water both literally and figuratively. When we don't get the water we need in any area of our lives, we thirst. Unfortunately, the world in which we live isn't very friendly to comprehensive hydrophiles like us. In fact, it's often downright hostile. Our fragile bodies lose physical water in the withering summer sun and in the dry winter air. We suffer emotional dehydration through common and extraordinary stresses of all kinds. We get relationally dried out by conflict with our family, coworkers, neighbors, and friends.

In the three preceding chapters, we've seen that we're also spiritual hydrophiles that can get spiritually dehydrated. In fact, we've seen that there are three entities that relentlessly try to rip us from God, our water home. To the degree that these entities succeed, our souls thirst for God. At times, this thirst is practically unbearable, even when we can't label it or pinpoint it. Whenever our souls cry out for satisfaction of soul-needs (e.g., love, respect, value, meaning, forgiveness of sin, and peace of heart), they're ultimately crying out for God.

We've seen that the world brazenly wants us to "stay thirsty, my friends" and campaigns to that end. We've seen that the devil and his fellows work to lure us away from water (i.e., God) with temptations galore. And we've seen that our own remaining internal desiccant tries to convince us that the hot sands of sin will actually refresh our souls. No, this world isn't friendly to hydrophiles like us.

Our voyage so far has been charted to raise our awareness of these facts and to help us admit our need for God. In order to go deeper with these admissions, we still need to ask a very important, if not ridiculously obvious, question: What, exactly, is spiritual thirst? Answering that question will help us sail deeper into the heart of our God, whose gush gives us lasting and true soul-satisfaction.

What Is Thirst?

The English word *thirst* indicates a strong craving, desire, or yearning. In Psalms 31:9–10, 42:1 (noted at the beginning of this chapter), and 143:6, King David and the sons of Korah (Old Testament worship leaders, song writers, and gushaholics) use the word *thirst* and several synonyms to help us understand what they're experiencing. Their description is what we also experience — at least to some degree — when we thirst.

"Pants" (*ayyal*) means that they long for or crave as an intense throbbing of the soul. "Distressed" (*tsarar*) means that they feel bound or tied up, restricted, narrow, scant, and cramped. This word depicts a person in the fetal position, curled up in an attempt to preserve himself from suffering or weakness. "Wasted" and "wasted away" (*ashesh*) mean that they feel weak, thin, ravaged, destroyed, exploited, or killed. This is a picture of a person wasting away from disease — with hollow, sunken eyes, protruding bones, and stringy hair. Like "pants," "wasted" is used twice, amplifying its intensity. "Spent" (*kalah*) means that they're exhausted or finished — like an athlete who collapses just after crossing the finish line. That their strength "fails" (*kashal*) means that they're stumbling, staggering, or tottering. This word portrays an athlete who's crawling toward the finish line.

David and Korah's sons are obviously thirsty. God inspired each of them to use vivid, robust words to describe his experience. But remember that you don't have to be crawling across a physical or spiritual Death Valley, about to expire, in order to feel some semblance of yearning or craving. You need only to understand the fundamental landscape of thirst and to basically confess, "God, I *am* thirsty. I *do* have a craving for something deeper, something more."

The big question, then, is what (or who) is that *something*? What are we really thirsty for? Asking these questions — and receiving their answers — sets the stage for gigantic leaps forward in our life in the gush of God!

Our Supreme Thirst

Identifying the *something* can be tough, because the word *thirst* can be applied to almost anything. We can thirst physically for water, food, pain relief, safety, quiet surroundings, or bodily warmth. We can thirst relationally for respect, companionship, or love. We can thirst intellectually for knowledge, answers, or academic growth. We can even thirst sociopolitically for world, national, state, or local harmony and peace. Are any of these the true *something* we thirst for? Or are we really and more deeply thirsting for something (or Someone) else?

King David felt thirst in every area of his life, just as we do. In Psalm 38, he describes nearly every kind of thirst a person can experience. In verses 3, 7, and 10 he laments his physical thirst. In verses 4, 6, 8, and 10 he is grieved by his psychological thirst, which causes him heaviness, sadness, weakness, mental anguish, and a throbbing heart. In verses 11, 12, 19, and 20 he bewails his social thirst — how his friends, companions, and kin have left him, and how his foes assail him.

As important and parching as all these thirsts are, they aren't the deepest part of David's lament. They don't represent his *supreme* thirst. They aren't the ultimate *something* for which he's thirsting. That spot is reserved for God alone. David puts it this way in Psalm 143:6 — "I stretch out my hands to You; / my soul thirsts for You like a parched land." Here are several verses from Psalm 38 in which David admits his supreme thirst *for God*.

> O Lord, all my longing is before You;
> > My sighing is not hidden from You....
> But for You, O LORD, do I wait;
> > it is You, O Lord my God, who will answer....
> Do not forsake me, O LORD!
> > O my God, be not far from me!
> Make haste to help me,
> > O Lord, my Salvation! Psalm 38:9, 15, 21–22

In the New Testament, the Greek word for *thirst* (*dipsao*) brings the idea of spiritual craving into even sharper focus. It's used to describe those "who painfully feel their want of, and eagerly long for, those things by which the soul is refreshed, supported, [and] strengthened."[1] John 4:13–14 is one place where *dipsao* is used figuratively to highlight our supreme thirst — our spiritual yearning for peaceful relationship with God. In this scene, Jesus is talking with a woman who's had five husbands and who is presently living with a man who is not her husband. It's sadly obvious that this woman is trying to satisfy her soul's thirst with the *something* of male companionship, commitment and/or sex. Jesus helps her by pointing out the vanity of her chosen *something* ("this water") and points to Himself ("the water that I will give him") as that for which she truly thirsts.

> Jesus said to her, "Everyone who drinks of this water will be thirsty [*dipsao*] again, but whoever drinks of the water that I will give him will never be thirsty [*dipsao*] forever. The water that I will give him will become in him a spring of water welling up to eternal life."
> > John 4:13–14 (see also 6:35 and 7:37)

All this leads us to one strong conclusion: *Our supreme thirst is for intimacy with God.* This is the thirst that goes deeper than all our other thirsts. It's the *something* and *Someone* for which we most deeply thirst. It's the thirst that underlies many of our other thirsts. It's our most basic and significant craving. Anything that sidetracks our yearning for God, or tempts us to try to satisfy that yearning outside of relationship with

Him, only inflames it. When we give in to those diversions or temptations, we sin and stoke the parching fires already started by the world, the devil, and our flesh. Here are a few examples to unpack this extremely important part of the Bible's gushology.

Consider the Christian twenty-something who's embraced the illusion that personal value and soul-peace can be found in physical beauty and the attention it brings. In service to this lie, she turns her back on the God who offers her indelible value, and she tries to earn life and peace on her own. She does this by spending endless hours at the gym, at the cosmetic counter, in fashion magazines, and before a mirror. She's not denying her supreme thirst; she's trying to satisfy it without God. That's sin. And sin will only inflame her supreme thirst, which is for intimacy with God.

Or consider the youth group teen who's swallowed the dehydrating myth that personal worth is determined by athletic performance. In slavery to this sinful lie, he rejects the God who continually declares Him beloved (and therefore, immeasurably valuable) in Christ. In rejecting God, he practices relentlessly, and sacrifices friends, family, and other pursuits in order to get to tournaments, special practices, and coaching camps. He isn't denying his supreme thirst; he's just trying to slake it without God. He's swapped the powerful, satisfying intimacy with God for the slavery of athletic performance. That's sin. And that sin will only magnify his thirst until he wakes up and turns back to the God who's his Hydrator.

Or consider the middle-aged churchgoer who foolishly believes that he'll satisfy his longing to feel strong and loved if he can have the naked vixen on his computer screen. In sinful lust, he rejects the God who alone can satisfy his heart's desire for a sense of personal strength and belovedness, instead pursuing a mirage that leaves only guilt and shame. He's fallen for a lie — that his need for sensual pleasure is his supreme thirst — and he's trying to satisfy that lie in wicked ways. He needs to realize that the sense of strength and love he craves are gifts that God gives opulently through relationship with Him.

Or consider the believer who's committed to living out a strange fusion of Christian and cultural virtue: raising well-behaved children, loving his wife, going to church, keeping a tidy lawn, avoiding "big" sins, and paying his taxes. Day by day he tries to satisfy his thirst for a meaningful life by way of his own moral performance. But then he suddenly and violently loses his temper with his son, clicks a strange link that plunges him into a night of sensual indulgence, or heartlessly degrades his wife over the temperature of the dinner she's prepared. Suddenly the something that he thought would satisfy his thirst (moral performance) fails him. In his confusion and despair, he wonders if he's been looking in all the wrong places for the lasting joy and peace he so strongly desires.

Finally, consider the once-thriving youth group member who went off to college and fell away from fellowship with God. She's desperate for release from the shame, guilt, and misery of recent years poorly lived: promiscuity, abortion, alcohol or drug addiction, failing grades, and general rebellion against parents, teachers, society, and God. In her deep darkness she cuts herself, lets others treat her like a sexual toy, and parties to try to satisfy or numb her screaming thirst. In her vain attempts, she's only making things worse. She'll continue to do so until she (re)realizes that every thirst of her withered heart — for forgiveness, dignity, relational security, soul-peace, and love — are met in the God who sweetly and enthusiastically invites repentance and soul-hydrating relationship with Him.

Now consider the unique circumstances, habits, and yearnings of your own life. What do they say about you and your thirst? Why do you do the things you do? Why do you crave the things you crave? Is there a deeper thirst, a supreme thirst — yet unrecognized — that you're futilely trying to satisfy outside of intimacy with God? Or when you admit your desires, does your yearning for God appear at the top of the list? Do you recognize that *this* is your supreme thirst?

Admitting the Obvious

Seeing our craving for God's forgiveness and for intimacy with Him as our supreme thirst is simple, profound, and essential. This superlative need reminds me of the identifying emblem chosen by a church in downtown St. Louis named "Crave." The image they've attached to themselves is a straightforward drawing of a hand reaching upward, fingers straining for the sky (i.e., God). With this basic icon, Crave has done a wonderful job of identifying itself as a community that acknowledges that its supreme longing is for God.

To confirm its identity, Crave has emblazoned its thirsty-hand logo on a wall in their church, on mugs, on apparel, and on other objects. If King David and the sons of Korah could have bought a garment to express the parts of Psalms 31, 38, 42, and 143 we've discussed, it's likely they would have bought a Crave T-shirt! The question before us today is whether or not we'll adopt Crave's thirsty-hand logo as the logo of our own lives. Doing so is to admit that our supreme thirst is for relationship with God.

Once we recognize that our supreme thirst is for intimacy with God, the only remaining question is whether or not we'll continually *reach* for Him. We aren't called to *stay* thirsty, after all! We're invited by God to experience satisfaction in Him. Of course, by definition, Christians are people who *have reached* for Him at some time in their past in order to be saved (see Appendix A for help with this). But we Christians also need to remember that we must constantly reach for Him as He reaches for us. We do this not to be re-saved, but rather to find ongoing hydration in a parching world.

As Buoy I fades from view, my hope is that we'll embrace Crave's thirsty-hand logo as the emblem of our own hearts. I also hope we'll deeply acknowledge that it's God — and God alone — who can satisfy our thirsty souls. As we do this, and as Buoy II enters our view, we'll find that God's hand is actually reaching out for us — not to smack us or berate us, but to give us the very thing we crave the most: Him.

Gushaholic's Prayer

Lord, I'm thirsty. All of the things I've done to try to get deep satisfaction have left me wanting more. I'm tired of that, Lord! I want true satisfaction of my supreme thirst. I know that that's found only in relationship with You. So please show me, thirsty as I am, what it means to be truly hydrated in You. Amen.

Gushercises

1. Describe the concept of supreme thirst as explained in this chapter.

2. When you feel your thirst — perhaps now for the first time — how do you express it?
3. What keeps you from expressing your thirst to God?
4. Try to express your thirst for God to Him in writing. Be as specific as you can. Try to get underneath your "surface thirsts" as we did in the examples in this chapter. For example, if you're obsessed with athletic achievement, describe it. Then write about why, deep down, you're so driven to perform in sports and hear the "well done" of fans, friends, and family.

Buoy II

God's Invitation

Buoy II is a welcome sight for parched people like us! That's because as we sail around it, we get to take in His hydrating voice that says, "Gushing God Seeks Parched People!" In the next four chapters, we'll dive into God's invitation and ultimately see how and why Christians need to say "Yes" to Him on a daily basis.

5

A Hearty Invitation

Ho! Every one who thirsts, come to the waters.
Isaiah 55:1a (NASB)

Sally Mae Pew. There she stands, glued by sticky insecurity and personal neediness to the greasy cinder-block walls of the high school gymnasium. She's quite a sight in her rumpled plaid skirt, knee-high wool socks, her dad's mauve sweater, and tilted Coke-bottle eyeglasses. She's come alone to the annual Harvest Fair dance at the urging (threatening, actually) of her parents. As she stands motionless, like a barnacle fixed to the wall, she's more aware of her privation than ever.

Nobody really likes Sally Mae. She's just too "unique." She's a social black hole with a gravitational pull that threatens the public persona of anyone who comes near. To be considered her friend is the equivalent of a social death knell. Her popularity-draining pull is so strong that being seen talking with her, or just inadvertently lingering in her vicinity, is enough to suck popularity points from even the most savvy high school socialite. This ability, though quite innocent and unintentional, is repulsive to everyone, and Sally Mae knows it. She feels it. So it isn't strange that the next hour passes with nobody talking to her or even acknowledging her presence.

But then something amazing happens: Blake Remington enters the gym. *Pierces* might be an even better word. That one seemingly insignificant act is more than enough to supply fodder for the front page of the high school newspaper, countless social media posts, and billions of megapixels of cell-phone photography. That's because Blake is a star. To say he's well liked might be the understatement of the century. He's captain of the football team. He gets good grades, has classy parents, a shiny sports car, lots of shiny trophies, and even shiny teeth. He's class president, in the honor society, and is liked equally by band geeks, jocks, and potheads. Incredibly, he's even *nice*. He tutors kids in the city, encourages teammates when they're flagging, takes out the trash at home, writes letters to his grandma, and goes to his church's youth group *gladly*.

Blake is the antithesis of need. He's a walking, talking, living, breathing picture of relational provision. In all of this, he remains sincerely humble. If Blake had a soundtrack, it'd be the sound of a spring-fed mountain stream with birds chirping and pines rustling and beavers beavering. All this opulence and genuine warmth seem to gush out of him from a mysterious place of eternal abundance.

What happens next is *beyond* amazing. Blake Remington fixes his steel-blue eyes on Sally Mae Pew. He politely, yet urgently, shakes off the squeals of a gaggle of starstruck cheerleaders and begins to stride across the gym toward her. He walks confidently, ignoring adoring classmates and leaving palm-up offers of multiple high-fives unrequited. With jaw-dropped disbelief, the entire student body parts like the Red Sea to let him through. Then, the unspeakable: Blake Remington asks Sally Mae Pew for the next dance.

Bowing low, he pleads earnestly, "Sally, may I have the pleasure of your company?" The crowd lets out a gasp. Adult chaperones frantically text their friends to start the PTA gossip chain. Cheerleaders weep. The DJ's digital music begins to skip repeatedly. A baby cries, and a dog howls in the distance. But none of this fazes Blake Remington. Still bowed, he gently extends his hand. And Sally Mae Pew whispers, "Yes."

You're Invited

Who do you relate to most in this story — Sally Mae or Blake? We're supposed to relate to Sally Mae. Like her, we ooze spiritual and relational need, or to use a word we've become pretty familiar with, we *thirst*. Our entire voyage has been driving us to this basic admission — one that might make us feel at least a bit embarrassed or offended. It's even natural that we'd fear — at least a little — that we too will be left ignored, like a crusty barnacle fearfully gripping the wall with no one asking for our company.

"Who'd ask me to dance," we might ask, "being that I've just admitted I'm so thirsty and needy? Who'd be crazy enough to invite me, the relational vacuum that I am, to find my deepest needs met in relationship with him?" For Christians, who have already accepted this invitation at least once, the problem might be to believe that anyone (especially God) would *re*-invite us to intimacy after we've freshly revealed our neediness. For this reason, it's normal for Christians to ask, "Who'd re-invite me?"

God, that's who. He's pictured as Blake in the parable. He's the antithesis of need. He's focused on us with sincere and passionate warmth. In the gospel, He strides toward us Christians and constantly invites us to re-experience His forgiveness and love. Whether our thirst is mild or whether we feel we're about to expire from spiritual need, God comes to us and asks, "May I have the pleasure of your company?" It's up to us to say, "Yes."

This parable is just a different way of presenting the core idea found in Scriptures like Isaiah 55:1, quoted at the beginning of this chapter. In that verse, God is striding across the universe to invite His parched and thirsty people to find in Him everything their souls need. In this chapter, we'll reflect on how *zealous* God is about making this invitation. In the next two chapters, we'll look at even more details of God's invitation that should move us to say or re-say "Yes" to God.

A Hearty Invitation

If our parable of Sally Mae and Blake were to accurately reflect God's zest in seeking out thirsty Christians, having Blake simply *stride* across the gymnasium would be inadequate. Instead, we'd have to pick a verb gushing with passion and urgency, like *bolt*, *dash*, *race*, or *sprint*. Blake would need to *blaze a trail* to Sally Mae, leaving a flaming slash in his wake. He wouldn't even wait for the student body to part. He'd rip across that hardwood floor for the sole object of his affection, overcome with his yearning to see her deepest needs sated. That's closer to the picture we get of God's invitation to Christians who admit their thirst.

If this kind of passion seems too melodramatic, consider the first word in Isaiah 55:1. It's the word that kicks off God's invitation to the thirsty in the verses that follow. (Unfortunately, the ESV and the NIV don't include this word in their rendering of the Hebrew text as the NASB does). The best translation of this word is actually not a word at all, but the sound of a man whistling urgently to get someone's attention. The best words we can offer in our English translations are words like *Come!*, *Hey!*, or *Ho!*

In Hebrew the word is *hoy*, which is a "particle of interjection." It reveals God's *heart* in what He's about to say, exposing His joyfully excited longing and anticipation. God is exuberant about inviting the thirsty (that's us) to Himself! He's passionate, energetic, and enthusiastic! He puts this small, but powerful, signal word at the beginning of His speech so that we pay attention and know that He's speaking to us joyfully and urgently.

God's *Ho!* is followed by four *come*'s — three in verse 1 and one in verse 3 (the NASB translates this passage accurately). The repetition of the word *come* amplifies its intensity. God really, really, really, *really* (four times over) wants His thirsty people to draw close to Him. What's more, all four of these *come*'s are imperatives, which means that God is forcefully saying, "It's absolutely necessary and crucial that you come to Me." God knows He's our only hope of hydration, and He unabashedly meets our need head-on with an invitation so energetic and passionate that it is off the Richter scale.

This same energy is reflected in Jesus' invitation to the thirsty in John 7:37.

> On the last day of the feast, the great day, Jesus stood up and cried out, "If anyone thirsts, let him come to Me and drink."

It's easy to see the similarities between God's invitation here and the one He makes in Isaiah 55. God's exuberance is unchanged. In John 7, Jesus "stood up and cried out" to invite the thirsty. The form of the verb translated "stood up" (pluperfect active of *histemi*) indicates that Jesus was holding His ground, or as we sometimes say, "making His stand." This is no slouching, tired rising to one's feet. It's the firm, authoritative posture of someone about to say something crucial and urgent.

Once on His feet, Jesus "cried out." There are several words the Holy Spirit could have used here to tell us that Jesus was about to say something. Interestingly, He chose just about the most intense word for speaking — *krazo*, which means "to scream, shriek, shout, or clamor in an almost annoying manner." The point is obvious: God is *rambunctiously* trying to get our attention. He's robustly inviting us, the thirsty, to come to Him for satisfaction.

Let's also notice that Jesus waits until "the last day of the feast, the great day" to stand up and cry out. This detail refers to the final day of the seven-day Passover feast celebrated by the Jews to commemorate God's rescuing them from bondage in Egypt. This "last day" is different from the other days in that it was a day of solemn assembly (Leviticus 23:36, Numbers 29:35), upon which no one could do any work. The last day was the punctuation mark at the end of a celebration that memorialized a time when God had heard the cries of His thirsty, enslaved people and had come down to deliver them from slavery in Egypt (Exodus 3).

By saving His loud declaration for the last and greatest day of this feast, Jesus magnifies His invitation exponentially. "God's deliverance from temporal slavery and thirst in Egypt was just a foretaste of what I'm offering," Jesus seems to say. He continues, "So come to Me right now and receive satisfaction so much deeper that it's beyond comparison!" What Jesus is clamoring about, of course, is the spiritual hydration He's vigorously and gladly extending to soul-thirsty people of every kind, including Christians.

Believe

What if in our opening story Blake Remington had *slowly sauntered* over to Sally Mae? What if he had danced with ten other girls first, paused for some yearbook photos, schmoozed with the faculty chaperones, gotten a snack, eaten the snack, and *then* casually approached Sally Mae? What if he had been timid in his actual request for a dance? What if he had added, "But you know, Sally Mae, if you don't want to dance with me, I've already got Susie and Jane lined up, so no big deal."

Thank God that we don't have to muse over any of these what-ifs when it comes to His invitation to us, the thirsty. God isn't distracted or nonchalant about any of it. He's completely, unreservedly focused and passionate about inviting us to find satisfaction in Him. Perhaps our biggest challenge at this point isn't simply to believe that He's inviting us, but to believe that He's inviting us *robustly*. A muffled "Well, um, I guess, maybe, that God is sort of inviting me" denies the emphatic oomph that we've just discovered in God's heart.

As Christians, it's our privilege to daily embrace God's invitation and His exuberance in extending it to us. We do this by first believing that the invitation is genuine — that God can and will do what He says He'll do, and that He sincerely wants us to accept His invitation. We've already seen God's passion in extending His invitation to us. If we believe and accept His invitation, we'll be able to stand with godly joy and confidence in the gymnasium of life, surrounded by those who avoid, bully, tease, dismiss, and disgrace us. "My Father is happy in my company," we'll affirm, "so my soul is hydrated, no matter who harms or ignores me." When we accept God's invitation daily, we're not re-saved — we're set free to thrive in our salvation. God's enthusiastic and recurring invitation is a constant summons to live a hydrated life in relationship with Him.

As we, the Christian Sally Mae Pews of the world, re-say "Yes" to God's invitation, it's likely we'll become aware of how strong our dehydrating enemies are. The desert world, the devil, and our desiccating flesh will all assault the idea that God is inviting us. They're likely to invest even more energy in attacking the idea that God is *exuberant* about His invitation. They'll play on our wounds and frailties, tempting us to disbelieve. They might say things like "What?! I really doubt that God would invite *you* to be with *Him*! I mean, look at you! You're Sally Mae Pew — needy, and thirsty. Sure, I know you're a Christian already, but you keep failing to love and obey God. Don't you think God can find better company? Even if He *is* inviting you, you can be sure He's not all that thrilled about it. Chances are, you're His last resort. You're only daydreaming if you think God's happily excited about *you*."

It's these sorts of lies about the nature of God that are like treacherous rocks that threaten our voyage in the Christian life. So beware and steer clear by believing the truth about God's invitation to the thirsty: "Hey! Everyone who thirsts, come to the waters. It doesn't matter if you aren't attractive. It doesn't matter if you've spent whatever attractiveness you think you have on meaningless adventures. I'm offering you the lavish gush of relationship with Me, totally free of charge. That's right! I'm taking My stand and imploring you! If you're thirsty, come to Me and drink! Let nothing hold you back. It's *you* that I want, thirst and all. You're invited!"

All that's left now is to believe. Take God at His word, even if it's your umpteenth time doing so. Believe, and say "Yes" to Him.

Gushaholic's Prayer

Lord, thank You for robustly inviting me to Yourself, even though I'm a spiritual Sally Mae Pew. Help me believe and say "Yes" to your exuberant invitation.

Gushercises

1. What might keep you from embracing the *robustness* of God's invitation?
2. How do you feel, knowing that God is inviting you to Himself *exuberantly*?
3. Write out your "Yes" to God. If this is your very first "Yes," please turn to Appendix A for a little help. If you're already a Christian, you must re-say "Yes" to God — not to be re-saved, but to be re-hydrated in your salvation. This exercise is for brand new Christians and for long-time Christians as well!

6

The Guest List

Come, everyone who thirsts,
come to the waters;
and he who has no money,
come, buy and eat!
Come, buy wine and milk
without money and without price.

Isaiah 55:1

I was once invited by a world-class photographer to model in Hawaii. Now don't get the wrong impression. I'd never modeled before in my life. I'm *not* that good-looking, and this was definitely *not* a swimsuit photo-shoot! I was playing the part of a middle-aged dad with a photo-wife, photo-daughter, and photo-in-laws having fun at a resort. We were photographed playing croquet, riding horses, shooting skeet, playing tennis, hitting golf balls, shopping, going for strolls, and bowling on the lawn.

When I got that invitation, I was absolutely dumbfounded. Me? He wants *me* to be in a photo-shoot? In Hawaii? All expenses paid? Plus a stipend? At a five-star resort? For a week? You've *got* to be kidding!

The invitation was so good that I lived in mild fear that the inviter would realize he had made a mistake inviting *me*. I felt so unqualified and insecure. So I anxiously waited for the phone call in which he'd say, "I'm sorry, Doug. We got someone better-looking with more experience. I don't know what I was thinking when I asked you." Of course, this photographer wouldn't have done that at all. I was just creating a scenario in my mind based on my own fear, brokenness, and disbelief.

In the same way, it can be hard to believe that God is specifically inviting *us when we're thirsty* (i.e., unqualified and insecure) to enjoy such a lavish experience with Him. Even if we believe He's enthusiastic, we may still harbor a nagging doubt that it's actually *us* that He's inviting. Most Christians I know doubt this, at least sometimes. I do. This chapter will reveal some wonderful, biblical reasons how we can know that God is inviting us*, specifically when we're thirsty*. Our only remaining decision will be whether we'll receive and rest in God's delightfully specific offer, or suffer in disbelief as I first did when my photographer friend invited me to be part of an exotic Hawaiian photo-shoot.

Everyone Who Thirsts

One reason we know that God specifically invites those who thirst is that our thirst and His invitation are unmistakably and directly paired in the Bible. Recognizing this fact is like putting on an outfit that's been perfectly tailored to fit your exact figure. "This outfit was made just for me!" you exclaim as you happily move toward the checkout counter to make it your own. In the same way, God tailors His invitation specifically to the nuances of our thirsty hearts. The precise fit of His summons with our exact condition as thirsty people is designed to make us exclaim, "This invitation was made just for me!" In this case, too, we rush to make His invitation our own, not with cash, but with repentance, faith, and trust in His Word.

We've already seen that in New Testament Greek the word for *thirst* (and its derivatives, like *thirsty*) is *dipsao*. In Chapter 4 we looked at John 4, where a woman, talking with Jesus near a well, uses *dipsao* to reveal her thirst. Jesus then uses the very same word, *dipsao*, to invite her to find her satisfaction in Him: "Jesus said to her,… 'Whoever drinks the water that I will give him will never be thirsty [*dipsao*] forever'" (verses 13–14). The words used for the woman's thirst and for God's invitation are a perfect match. God, the ultimate Tailor, has fashioned His invitation so precisely that it's impossible to deny and delightful to embrace.

We see this tailored fit appearing in the Old Testament, too, where the word for "thirst" is *tsame*. God inspired both King David and the sons of Korah to use this word to affirm their supreme thirst in Psalms 42:2 and 63:1, saying, "My soul thirsts [*tsame*] for God." In Psalm 107:5,

God describes His people as "hungry and thirsty [*tsame*]; their soul fainted within them" while they wandered in the desert after being delivered from Egypt. In Isaiah 5:13, He describes His people, being chastised by Him for their sin, as being "parched with thirst [*tsame*]."

Notice that, in a tailored match, God uses the very same word for thirst, *tsame*, in His invitation in Isaiah 55:1 — "Ho! Every one who thirsts [*tsame*], come to the waters" (NASB). In Nehemiah 9:15, God clarifies that He gave Israel water from the rock in order to satisfy their *tsame*. In Isaiah 41:17 He clarifies yet again that He's the God who specifically invites the *tsame*:

> When the poor and needy seek water,
>   and there is none,
>   and their tongue is parched with thirst [*tsame*],
> I the LORD will answer them;
>   I the God of Israel will not forsake them.

Still, you may ask, "Yeah, but what if I'm thirsty because I've really blown it and gone off on a desiccant binge? In fact, what if I don't have anything to offer God *but* my thirst? What if I had no 'money' in the first place to buy this tailored invitation God makes to the thirsty?" Not a problem, according to God. If we read Isaiah 55:1–2 carefully, we see that God addresses His invitation specifically to these sorts of people. In those verses, "money" stands for whatever we think we possess that might buy us peaceful relationship with God. He goes on to say that the people who have no money, or those who have wasted their money on desiccants, are exactly the people He's inviting!

Christians Too

It should be obvious by now that God's invitation is to every single thirsty person on the face of the earth. If you're a human being, if you live on the face of the earth, and if you're thirsty, then you're invited. Let me remind us that this includes Christians. We need to remember this, because we Christians are sometimes the last people to believe that God is re-inviting us to Himself. There are many reasons why we might feel this way. A main one can be the unspoken, silly delusion that Christians aren't supposed to get thirsty. "We have Jesus already," this nonsense goes, "so how could we ever feel want?" A variety of desert winds can contribute to this parching lie.

I remember going through a church membership class in which we were encouraged to adopt a cheerful attitude whenever we were in the church building. While it's certainly true that joyful celebration and worship at church are appropriate, that exhortation smacked of naïveté at best and spiritual bondage at worst. It reinforced the illusion that Christians shouldn't thirst — or at least shouldn't *show* their thirst. It could even imply that God likes only happy, hydrated Christians. All of these misconceptions deny the specificity of God's invitation to the thirsty, including thirsty Christians, in both public and private contexts of communion with Him.

Photos of buttery-skinned, silky-haired, perfect-toothed, glowing Christians adorning covers of Christian-themed books, albums, and conference programs don't help the situation. Misleading book titles that promise endless glee this side of heaven are a slap in the face to believers who live in the real world, grappling with the desert, the devil, and their own flesh. Snappily dressed, constantly smiling worship leaders and choruses can perpetuate the idea that the Christian life is all gladness, and never includes sadness or thirst. Worship services that seldom or never pause to truly lament — ignoring more than half of the psalms — can make it very hard for Christians to believe that thirst is a legitimate part of the Christian life or that God has any genuine, caring interest in thirsty people.

Falling into the comparison trap might be another reason we doubt God's invitation to us. In the comparison trap we look at other believers, based on their status alongside some arbitrary standard of value we devise, and judge them to be more worthy of God's invitation than we are.

Yet another reason might be besetting sin, which is a sin we tend to struggle with regularly. After such a failing, a fleshly mind game can ensue in which our internal desiccant whispers, "Not again! Well, now you've done it. God's probably had it with you now. Regular thirst is one thing, but parching yourself with the same old desiccant is another! Why would He waste Himself on a repeat offender like you?"

To these dizzying, dehydrating deceptions, the devil might even add Psalm 23:1 as a prooftext for this lie, taking the following verse out of context: "The LORD is my Shepherd; I shall not want." Though God did indeed employ King David to write Psalm 23 — taken in context, verse 1 is David's admission that he *is* wanting. It's part of an entire psalm in which David admits his need and speaks to his own soul, reminding Himself of God's sufficiency to satisfy his thirst. He *isn't* saying, "I never feel any cravings, yearnings, or needs." That's preposterous, not only in light of this psalm as a whole, but also in light of David's many confessions in the texts we've explored so far in this book.

We must recognize that anything that tempts us to believe that God isn't inviting us to get (re)hydrated in Him might be nothing more than The Most Interesting Man in the World wearing clerical robes to hide his typical farce behind a religious disguise. It's just like him to say with a wink, "Christians should never be thirsty, my friends." Or "You might have enjoyed God's kindness once, but there are limits, my friends." Or his favorite advice, designed to steer us completely off course, "*Stay thirsty, my friends.*" Ugh! Believing these deceptions will leave our souls dry and downtrodden.

Let's not fall into these traps, fellow voyagers! In fact, let's remind ourselves that texts like Isaiah 55 — one of God's clearest invitations to the thirsty — was written specifically to God's people. This proves that there are thirsty people among us. Let's remember and believe that we're included in the "anyone" of John 7:37 — "If anyone thirsts, let him come to Me and drink." And just in case you're not sure you're one of God's people (i.e., a Christian), turn to Appendix A for help figuring that out. God's invitation to the thirsty is for you, too!

It's for Real

Let's return for a minute to the amazing invitation I received to do some modeling in Hawaii. Despite all my doubts that it was real, and despite my fears that the photographer was going to change his mind, the call retracting the invitation never came. It was for real! The inviter meant it! He did want me to receive this fantastic adventure, even though I had no modeling experience and was not the best-looking man on earth! So I went on the trip and had one of the best times of my life.

We realize that on a human level, people do sometimes rescind their invitations. On that level, we may have felt the pain of being uninvited. Unhealed brokenness in this area may be a chief reason why some of us fear that God will renege on His exuberant summons. But God will never inflict that pain on us. He'll never withhold or withdraw His invitation. When He says, "I'm inviting anyone who's thirsty," He invites *everyone*, and He won't change His mind. To abate this fear, just take a swig from Numbers 23:19.

> God is not man, that He should lie,
> or a son of man, that He should change His mind.
> Has He said, and will He not do it?
> Or has He spoken, and will He not fulfill it?

Let's apply this same Scripture to the concepts of this chapter, customizing it for our spiritual hydration.

> God isn't lying or deceiving us when He invites us to satisfy our supreme thirst in Him. He isn't someone who sends out invitations and then changes His mind. Has He said, "Hey! Come, everyone who thirsts, and I will satisfy your soul!" and then not followed through? Has He made these invitations to the thirsty time and time again in Scripture only to turn His back and fail to fulfill?

What do we say to these questions, fellow Christians? The answer of faith and trust has to be, "No! God isn't a deceiver! Yes! He's invited me, and He means it! No! He'll never take His invitation back!" Soak in that confession as we move on to marvel at the God who's inviting us to find our satisfaction in Him.

Gushaholic's Prayer

God, thank You for tailoring Your invitation specifically to the nuances of my thirsty heart. Your invitation is impossible to deny and delightful to embrace! Please help me to trust You completely and to accept Your invitation again and again. Amen.

Gushercises

1. What makes it hard for you to believe that God invites you to come to Him precisely *when you are thirsty*? Be as personal and specific in your answer as possible. Perhaps reflect on a time when you were thirsty and someone you trusted gave you sand to swallow.
2. Summarize some biblical truths in this chapter that God has provided in order to allay your doubts about His enthusiastic desire to call you to Himself when you are thirsty.
3. Pray that God will stir up His Spirit within your heart to displace the difficulties you described in response to question 1 with the truths you cited in response to question 2. It may be helpful to write out this prayer as an aid to future hydration.

7

Party Particulars

Incline your ear, and come to Me. Isaiah 55:3a

What would you do if you were invited to an exclusive dinner with the reigning monarch of the United Kingdom? And what if you were also invited to a similar evening hosted by the president of the United States of America? What if these two events were rolled into one, and you received an invitation to a dinner with these two heads of state and their spouses? Well, that's exactly what happened to 130 A-list guests who received invitations to a lavish white-tie dinner at the White House in May 2007.

Really. Imagine it. Imagine you were one of those invitees. Imagine slogging to your mailbox, with your typical lack of interest, to retrieve your mail. Imagine sorting through the regular junk and a few bills to find a strange envelope wedged between the latest *Reader's Digest* and a coupon for Bed Bath & Beyond. Mildly surprised and curious, you pull out the interesting item and carelessly toss your other correspondence aside.

As you handle the unusual envelope, it feels rich to your touch. It's hand-addressed in exotic navy blue calligraphy, and to your shock, you find the presidential seal on the back. In wonder, you run your fingers over the embossed emblem before carefully opening the envelope. As the flap comes up, a translucent sheet of delicate paper flutters in the breeze. From beneath this protective inner paper blanket, you slowly remove a heavy gilt-edged card.

"This is definitely not something from a discount quick-print service," you think to yourself. As the card rests in your clammy palms, you spy another presidential seal, this one printed neatly on the front of the card. You go on to read your full name, exquisitely hand-printed at the top. As your eyes widen and dart onward, you read that the President and First Lady of the United States request the honor of your presence at an elaborate state dinner at the White House. Upon further exploration, you learn you'll be sharing the evening with Her Majesty the Queen and His Royal Highness.

A wave of shock sweeps through your mind. Your breathing becomes shallow. Your pulse quickens. Your clammy palms have melted into *sweaty* palms. "Me? The queen? Dinner? The White House? The president? I ... I ... I ... Why *me*?"

I'm pretty sure that the White House sends out lots of invitations each year. Some come from ranking officials, and some don't. Some are inviting people to exclusive personal engagements with those officials, and some aren't. I'd guess that there are purchasing agents who invite food suppliers to deliver sacks of flour to the kitchen, facility managers who invite carpet cleaners to clean carpets in obscure hallways, and maybe even mid-level staffers who invite the press to a special briefing in a pressroom.

But it's noteworthy when the president of the United States invites 130 people to an elite white-tie dinner honoring Her Majesty the Queen and His Royal Highness. The difference is in *who's* doing the inviting and in *what* the guests are being invited to. In fact, the *who* and the *what* make all the difference.

The Who: God

In the biblical gospel, the *who* isn't a purchasing agent, a facility manager, or a mid-level staffer. It isn't even a queen, a prince, or a president of any earthly nation. It's none other than the King of Kings and the Lord of Lords. It's the triune God: Father, Son, and Holy Spirit. It's the Creator of the Universe, who commands heavenly armies, gives breath to every living thing, and balances galaxies like tops. The Savior who lived, died, and rose again is the One who makes this invitation. This astounding fact makes all the difference.

Let's remember that God is always the One who personally calls us back to Himself for satisfaction. Even if He employs prophets, preachers, or Sunday school teachers to speak the actual words, He's ultimately the One doing the inviting. In Isaiah 55, it's very clearly God who says, "Come to the waters." In John 7:37, the text plainly says that it's Jesus who takes His stand and cries out, "If anyone is thirsty, let him come to Me and drink." In Revelation 22:17, it's the Spirit of God who says, "Come," to anyone who's thirsty and desires to gulp the water of life without price.

It may be hard for us to be moved by the fact that it's God who's inviting us. After all, we can't audibly hear God's voice. And when we hear His invitations read aloud from Scripture, it's only a human voice — our own or someone else's — that we literally hear. Maybe if we experienced what Israel experienced at Mount Sinai, we'd be a bit more awed by the fact that God is the One doing the inviting.

> Then Moses brought the people out of the camp to meet God, and they took their stand at the foot of the mountain. Now Mount Sinai was wrapped in smoke because the LORD had descended on it in fire. The smoke of it went up like the smoke of a kiln, and the whole mountain trembled greatly. And as the sound of the trumpet grew louder and louder, Moses spoke, and God answered him in thunder.... Now when all the people saw the thunder and the flashes of lightning and the sound of the trumpet and the mountain smoking, the people were afraid and trembled, and they stood far off and said to Moses, "You speak to us, and we will listen; but do not let God speak to us, lest we die."
>
> Exodus 19:17–19, 20:18–19

Imagine that you were in that crowd of Israelites to meet the LORD — who descended in fire! Imagine the trumpets, the thunder, the lightning. Now *that's* a *Who*! Fearsome, yes. But magnificent, awesome, and inspiring as well. This reminder of the *Who* of our invitation should gush into our hearts and change us. It should fill us with awe, joy, urgency, humility, astonishment, and gladness. It should take our breath away. "*God?* You mean *God* is personally inviting *me* to come to *Him?*" we might ask. "Wow! I mean, *WOW!*" is a fitting reply, as we comprehend the staggering privilege of being invited by such an indescribably magnificent Host.

When was the last time you pondered the *Who* of this invitation we've been exploring? This blessed honor is an exercise in and of itself. I recommend that either now or later — or both! — you spend some time camping in Appendix C, which was written specifically to help us marvel at our great Inviter.

The What: God

Have you ever been invited to be a "special guest" at an event a friend was hosting, only to find, upon attending, that your friend wasn't able to spend any time with you at the event itself? Maybe you enjoyed the hors d'oeuvres, some casual conversation with other guests, and assorted party festivities in a beautiful setting. But sadly, all your friend/host was able to give you was a quick "Hey, good to see you!" That seems to be my standard experience at most weddings to which I'm invited. I'm able to enjoy all the typical wedding merriment, but I usually get only twenty-three seconds to hug the bride, shake the groom's hand, and say, "Congratulations!"

It's certainly great to know that it's God who's inviting us, isn't it? But *what*, exactly, is God inviting us to? Is it an experience where He's a distracted, unavailable host surrounded by so many swarming admirers that we never get to meaningfully interact with Him? If we show up, are we going to get just ten seconds of eye contact with Him before we're shuffled off to the dessert buffet? Or is He inviting us to an exciting evening that He won't attend at all? The answers to these questions get at the *what* of God's invitation. The *what*, along with the *who*, makes all the difference.

The *what* of God's invitation stands in stark contrast to the sad picture of attending a friend's party, only to find that friend unavailable. That's because the *what* of God's invitation is God Himself. God always invites us to intimate, joyful (re)connection with Him.

In Isaiah 55:1–3, a text with which we're becoming very familiar, God specifically points out that He's the One to whom we're being invited: "come to the waters [*mayim*]" (v. 1), "listen diligently to Me" (v. 2), and "come to Me" (v.3). The latter two instances obviously point to

God, but what of the first? "The waters" also points to God, since He's so often referred to in the Bible as the "Fountain of Living Water" (Chapter 9). It makes no sense that He'd invite us to a literal brook or cistern to satisfy the soul-thirst He's identified in this passage.

It's only when we receive *God* that we're truly satisfied, as is undeniably evident in places like Psalm 1:3 and Jeremiah 17:8. God is the Water for which the sons of Korah thirsted in Psalm 42:1. Just as physical waters are cleansing and refreshing to our bodies, so will our time with God be cleansing and refreshing to our souls. It's important that we understand exactly what God will be giving us. We shouldn't picture Him giving us a cup of water unless we realize that *He's the water in the cup*. God is the refreshment we're looking for. He's the *What* of His own invitation.

God moves on to say that enjoying Him as the *What* will be like enjoying milk and wine. "Milk" (*chalab*) highlights the abundance of the experience. This is substantiated by God's use of this word to describe the opulence to be found in the Promised Land — "a land flowing with *milk* and honey" (Exodus 3:8, Deuteronomy 6:3; emphasis added). "Wine" (*yayin*) signifies that our time with God will be gladdening and renewing.

God then describes the waters, milk, and wine as "good" and as "the richest of fare," in which our souls will "delight." These words don't describe just the *experience* we're going to have; they also describe the *What* of that experience: God Himself. It's to *Him* that we're invited. He Himself embodies all goodness, richness, and delight! He is, after all, the object of our supreme thirst. He's the living water, milk, and wine for which our souls thirst. Altogether, these pictures tell us that our experience with God is going to be deeply enjoyable and comprehensively satisfying to our souls.

Still, there's an even more astonishing *what*-phrase that soars above the rich imagery of waters, milk, and wine. It comes at the end of Isaiah 55:3 — "I will make with you an everlasting covenant, / My steadfast, sure love for David." In this one phrase, God gushes a delightfully explicit and plain description of the *what*. Let's look at this important verse as we usher the excited quivering of our hearts up into our minds and out through our lips in the form of a happy "Yes, God!"

The Grand What-Phrase

First, God's relationship with us in Christ is a covenant (*berith*) relationship, a bond of intimate attachment, affection, and personal self-disclosure. *Berith* is a technical term that signifies a binding, blood-sealed association. God makes, or "cuts," this covenant, which means that it's a completely irreversible commitment on His part. Elsewhere in the Bible, God likens His covenant (*berith*) with His people to a perfected form of marriage between husband and wife (see Isaiah 62:1–5). It's quite fitting to say that God is asking for our hand in marriage — our *parched* hand, I might add — without any possibility of His ever filing for divorce.

Second, God's relationship with us in Christ is a loving (*chesed*) relationship. This word sparkles like the ocean at sunset as it reflects the dazzling fullness of God's emotional and willful affection for us. Most broadly, *chesed* means that the association God desires with us is marked by kindness and goodness on His part. The relationship also glitters with grace, which means that God freely, faithfully, and affectionately extends Himself to us, despite our thirsty, wandering, and occasionally desiccant-eating ways.

Third, God's relationship with us in Christ is an eternal relationship. The infinite duration and durability of what God is offering is signaled by two modifiers: "everlasting" (*olam*) and "steadfast" (*aman*). The meanings of these two words coalesce like two golden streams to form one immeasurably beautiful river of relationship that is true, authentic, accurate, loyal, trustworthy, dedicated, committed, constant, and staunch. Considering our remaining thirst and our occasional desiccant binges, this is stupefying news! It means that God will *never* completely withdraw Himself from us, but will *always* gush toward us with His love.

Best of all, this relationship we've been talking about is a relationship with *God*. It's "an everlasting covenant, *My* steadfast, sure love for David" (emphasis added). This carries us right back to where we started — to God — the glorious *What* of His own invitation. The invitation is about being with a *Person*, fellow voyagers! This amazing fact should compel us to join the apostle Paul in his declaration in Philippians 3:8 — "Indeed, I count everything as loss because of the surpassing worth of knowing [experiencing, being in relationship with] Christ Jesus my Lord."

This idea that God is the *What* of His own invitation might hit us sideways, at least for a moment. One big reason for this is that we're often consumed with our requests for lesser *whats*: better hair, grades, human relationships, athletic performance, social standing, career opportunities, sex, neighbors, pastors, moral performance, political leaders, financial returns, health, and/or possessions. As good as some of these *whats* may be, they all fall pitifully short of the only *What* that can satisfy our supreme thirst. To focus on them as our *what* is like getting to the party but never going in! It's like staying in the parking lot and splashing around in its greasy puddles instead of entering the building to enjoy the host and the delights that surround him. When we stop short of accepting God as the *What* of His own invitation, we fail to receive what He really wants to give us (Himself) and we miss out on lasting soul-hydration.

But God isn't calling us to a free shopping spree in His "warehouse of circumstantial remedies." He isn't inviting us primarily to a financial windfall, a clear diagnosis, an acceptance letter from the college of our dreams, a job promotion, or any other legitimate earthly pleasure. As good as all those things may be, He isn't inviting us to get hydrated by letting Him give us good stuff or remove bad stuff. He wants to give us *Himself*. And that's better by far.

When was the last time you heard God inviting you to Himself? When was the last time you said to God in your thirst, "Yes, God, I know that You're *What/Who* I really need! Thank You for inviting me to come to You. Even if You choose to change nothing about my desiccating situation, I know that in close relationship with You, I can live as a hydrated person, no matter what."

A Divine Invitation

Think of an Evite or another invitation you've received. My guess is that your initial reaction, like mine, takes place even before you open the invitation itself. It probably happens when you see who sent you the invitation. Is it a person you know? If so, how well? Is it from someone you'd like to spend time with? If so, how much and what kind of time? All these are questions about the *who* — questions in which we ask, "Who's inviting me?"

If the *who* checks out, you'll probably move on to consider the *what*. That is, you'll see just what kind of event this is. Does it sound fun? Will you fit in? Is it expensive? Is it far? Do you have anything suitable to wear? And, of course, will you get to spend any time with the friend who's invited you?

God's invitation to come to Him for the satisfaction of our souls is the best invitation we'll *ever* receive. It's *from* Him and it's *to* Him, and He gushes it to us constantly. So what's your response? Will you respond (with a mouse-click or otherwise) "Yes," "No," or "Maybe"? To be a Christian means that we've already said "Yes" once in order to enter into relationship with God (Appendix A). But it also means that we *daily* have the opportunity to say "Yes" to God's invitation — not in order to be re-saved, but to experience true joy through deeper intimacy with Him. In the next chapter, we'll look at the glories of saying "Yes."

Gushaholic's Prayer

God, thank You for inviting me to continually come to You to spend time with You! Please captivate me with the astonishing fact that You're inviting *me*, and that You're inviting me to be with *You*. Please wash away anything that might keep me from saying "Yes." Amen.

Gushercises

1. Read John 7:37 and Matthew 11:25–30. Describe the *who* and the *what* of God's invitation to the thirsty in those passages.
2. Describe a time when you wanted a blessing from God other than God Himself to satisfy your supreme thirst. How would you change your request to reflect the idea that God is the *who* and the *what* that you need most?
3. Read Appendix C and pick a few attributes of God that you've never thought much about. Read all the prooftexts for those attributes and marvel at the God who's inviting you to come to Him.

8

Saying "Yes" to God

Repent therefore, and turn again, that your sins may be blotted out, that times of refreshing may come from the presence of the Lord.
Acts 3:19–20a

On November 16, 2010, the airwaves buzzed with the news that England's Prince William had proposed to Kate Middleton — and that she'd said "yes." Kate's "yes" sparked a media frenzy as people all over the world watched her "yes" unfold. On a practical level, there would be guest lists to build, invitations to send, gowns to select, menus to plan, media to manage, hairdos to create, and an actual wedding ceremony to rehearse. Over the ensuing months, countless words would be written about all those things. To many onlookers, Kate's "yes" was embodied by these external trappings.

Sadly, thirsty Christians sometimes make the same mistake when it comes to re-embracing God's invitation. We go astray when we focus on the *results* of our "Yes" rather than on its foundations. This happens when we think saying "Yes" simply means amplified religious activity or emotional excitement. We assume that a Christian, someone who's said "Yes" to God, has left the world of religious mediocrity and ho-hum worship for a life of intense service, theological study, and effervescent worship. But as healthy as those things can be, they aren't at the heart of saying "Yes" to God.

The core of our "Yes" is the internal shift we make from trusting false fountains to trusting *the* Fountain — God — for our soul-hydration. This trust is a Spirit-empowered act of our will that includes our whole being: heart, spirit, mind, emotions, and oftentimes our body.

It means forsaking our commitment to a bevy of dehydrating suitors and allying ourselves with the only Suitor who can satisfy our souls. This is what the Bible calls "repenting" or "turning," and it must be the essence of our "Yes."

"Yes" and "No"

Whether she knew it or not, Kate was actually turning, or repenting, when she said "yes" to Prince William. In fact, saying "yes" to any option requires a person to turn away from other competing options. In Kate's case, saying "yes" to William meant that she had to turn her primary allegiance away from a single life, her parents, and all other suitors in order to turn toward Prince William as her priority. The same is true of us when our Royal King, Jesus Christ, invites us to come to Him to find satisfaction for our supreme thirst.

When we say "Yes" to God, we must repent, or turn, by also saying "No" to other suitors. In keeping with the Bible's water imagery, "other suitors" are all the other fountains from which we've been trying to satisfy our supreme thirst for things like peace with God, a sense of personal value, and meaning in life. When we turn from our other suitors, we identify and renounce them, recognizing that they weren't satisfying fountains at all. We must simultaneously turn toward God, affirming His personal integrity and embracing Him as our Source of Hydration. The essence of our "Yes" is a shift we make in our inner being: By God's grace, we turn our allegiances away from other fountains toward God, *the* Fountain.

The idea of turning from desiccants toward God is clearly seen in Acts 3:19, quoted at the beginning of this chapter. In this one verse, God uses two Greek words that embody turning: *metanoeo* and *epistrepho*. Both are commands, and both involve a change in one's inner being and its allegiances. In this verse God assures those hearing or reading His words that if they turn to Him, they'll receive two of the most amazing promises possible: He promises that He'll forgive their sins, and that they'll experience "times of refreshing [that will] come from the presence of the Lord."

Friends, this is a critical point in our voyage. All we've explored so far in *Gush* has led us to this pivotal issue. We've seen how hard our maniacal enemies (the world, the devil, and our desiccating flesh) work to dehydrate us. We've considered their presence in our own lives, and we've begun to more deeply feel their parching sting. We've sorted through our various forms of thirst in order to isolate our one supreme thirst: intimacy with God. Then we heard God's drenching voice inviting thirsty people like us to get our supreme thirst met in relationship with Him.

So now is the time to repent. As Christians (i.e., those already saved), now is the time to turn *once more* from our other suitors to God. Taking our cue from Isaiah 55, now's the time to tell God, "God, I hear you calling me to 'Come!' As You do, I realize that You're right. I *am* thirsty. I've been dehydrating my soul spending money I don't have on things that can't satisfy. Let me list the so-called fountains I'm now turning away from so I can come to you.... I'm saying 'No' to them and 'Yes' to You as the only One who can slake my supreme thirst. Thank You for inviting me to come to You!"

As Christians, we remake this turn not in order to be re-saved, but to come in from the various spiritual deserts to which we often wander. Like God's people in Isaiah's day, we're to do this as often as necessary — maybe even several times a day! There's no such thing as (re)turning to God too often. The important thing is that we do it whenever we realize that we're seeking to satisfy our supreme thirst in something or someone other than Him.

And just in case you're not sure you're a Christian in the first place, now is the time to settle that question once and for all. Turn to Appendix A for a simple, biblical explanation of what it means to come out of the desert to say "Yes" to God for the first time. Whether it's your first time or your thousandth time saying (or re-saying) "Yes" to God, you still may need some help making this turn. You'll find the help you need in Isaiah 55. But first, an illustration.

Driver's Ed

Do you remember taking driver's education? Maybe you took an actual class, or maybe a parent or other adult gave you the informal version in a parking lot. I had both. If you've never taken it, the basic idea is that someone is teaching you how to drive a car. One thing I remember about driver's education is learning how complex it was to make a proper turn: signal so many feet in advance, slow down, check the mirrors, watch for traffic, and confirm that there were no turning restrictions. I was grateful to have an instructor with me for my first several turn attempts.

If you're a Christian, you already have some understanding of what it means to turn to God. But for our own refreshment, let's revisit some basics that will help us in this extremely important maneuver. As One who's supremely interested in our successfully navigating our (re)turn to Him, God is our driver's ed Instructor. He offers plenty of wonderful help to make sure we joyfully execute our "No" and "Yes."

In Isaiah 55:1–3, God gives us specific ways by which we can admit our thirst, turn from false fountains, and reenter His gush. He instructs us to come, buy, eat, listen diligently, delight ourselves, incline our ear, and hear. In the original Hebrew, all but one of these instructions are imperatives (i.e., commands), which means that God is requiring action from us. To increase the likelihood of our safety and success, He breaks our turn into a step-by-step procedure. Following God's instructions makes our turn smooth and secure, ensuring that we'll get where we want to go. As Christians making frequent turns, we can be thankful that God gives us such excellent assistance in leaving the desert and returning to Him.

Notice that all these instructions implore us to enjoy God Himself as the substance and destination of our turn. By explicitly or implicitly attaching Himself as the object of these commands, God vigorously reminds us that our turn is all about relationship with Him: Come to Me, buy from Me, eat what I'm offering, listen diligently to Me, delight yourself in Me, incline your ear toward Me, and hear Me. This turn isn't about successfully completing some cold religious exercise! It's about re-experiencing personal connection with the God of the Universe for our hydration and His glory.

As we look more specifically at God's instructions in Isaiah 55:1–3, we see that they involve quite a lot of action. Turning by saying "No" and "Yes" is a sweaty exercise of faith. First and foremost, it means confirming that the affections of our redeemed inner being are for God and His gush. It means granting priority to the pure desires of our redeemed hearts as "new creatures" in Christ, who long for fellowship with God (Ezekiel 11:19–20, 18:31; Romans 6–8; 2 Corinthians 5, especially verse 17). This saying "Yes" to God includes saying "No" to our own rebel desires, relegating them to their "conquered" status in Christ. Oftentimes, we must accomplish this inner shift by moving our physical bodies, changing our circumstances, or reprioritizing our relationships. Like physically turning a car, making a spiritual turn involves synchronizing several actions.

To "come" means that we move our entire being from a dehydrating set of affections — to God. As with turning a car, it means saying goodbye to the road we're already on in order to travel a new road. To "eat" means that we need to partake of God's presence and promises as our soul's sustenance. This usually includes spitting out the desiccants we've been chewing. To "listen diligently" means that we must concentrate on what God is saying, and show that we take it seriously by responding to His words. This often involves blocking (i.e., tuning out) the parching messages of the world, the devil, and our desiccant-loving flesh. In fact, the Hebrew form of *listen diligently* in Isaiah 55:2 is emphatic.[1] The NIV does a good job reflecting this emphasis by rendering the phrase "Listen, listen."

God speaks to our hearts by His Holy Spirit through His Word, the Bible. In many ways, He's inviting us to gulp Him as He's revealed in the Bible. We can do this by participating in individual or group Bible studies, reading Bible-based books, enjoying biblically true music and art, and listening to live or broadcast biblical teaching and preaching. As we say "Yes" to these blessed privileges, we also need to turn away from the countless false "bibles" all around us. These include rancid messages from The Most Interesting Man in the World, dehydrating temptations from the devil and his demons, and the skewed ideas coming from our remaining internal desiccant.

The Many Turns of a "Performance Junkie"

Up to this point in my life I've been a full-time student, a corporate executive, a professional sculptor, and the CEO of a Christian ministry. For almost my entire life, the world, the devil, and my own internal desiccant have been singing a dehydrating song across all these vocations that goes something like this, "Doug, you are what you do. Your value as a person, and God's attitude toward you, depend upon how you perform at your work. That's your real fountain: your vocational performance. Don't you want to be satisfied deep down inside? Then perform! Get results!"

I can't begin to tell you the number of times I've confessed to God that I, at least momentarily, believed those lies. Each time God brings me back to my spiritual senses, I'm compelled to repent by turning away from the false fountain of my own performance back to the one true Fountain — God. Here's a succinct conglomeration of the kinds of confessions I've made over the years: "Lord, I've tried to satisfy my need for meaning, for personal value, and for peace with You based on my performance as a [student, executive, artist, minister]. I've done that by forsaking friends in dire need in order to get a better grade, by working ridiculously long hours to post big results, by fretting over a client's reaction to my art proposal, and by losing sleep worrying about what people will think of this book. Please help me to stop relying upon my performance for soul-satisfaction and to (re)start looking to You instead."

Along with that confession, I've needed to do things like apologize to my friends, cap the number of hours I work, and take a healthy disinterest in the feedback of art clients and book readers! At the same time, I've needed to re-hear God's invitation as we explored it earlier in our voyage around Buoy II. I've needed to be reminded that God doesn't despise me for my thirst, my sin, or my confession. I've needed to be reminded that it's people just like me that He enthusiastically invites and re-invites to Himself for satisfaction. Then I've needed to take Him at His word and act on my belief by resting my heart, mind, emotions, schedule, money, and everything else on Him. I have completed my turning back to Him when I'm able to say, "God, I am so happy that You still love me when I'm thirsty. Thank You for wanting to be with me so that You can satisfy me — and so I can know and experience the satisfaction that you still abundantly gush toward me."

I hope that sharing my own struggle to say "No" to false fountains and "Yes" to *the* Fountain has encouraged you to begin thinking about what that looks like in your life. The gushercises at the end of this chapter will help you work through this. They'll also prepare you for Buoy III and an extended time marveling at God as the Satisfier of our thirst.

Gushaholic's Prayer

Thank You, Lord, for showing me what it really means to say "Yes" to You. Please help me to identify the false fountains where I've been seeking to satisfy my thirst. Help me to turn away from them and turn to You with my whole being. Amen.

Gushercises

1. Describe the actions involved in saying "No" to false fountains.
2. Describe the actions involved in saying "Yes" to God, the one true Fountain.
3. Where do you need to say "No" and "Yes" as described in your answers to questions 1 and 2, above? How can you act on this need (i.e., repent) right now?

Buoy III

Water-Pictures

In the 2010 film adaptation of C. S. Lewis's *The Voyage of the Dawntreader*, Eustace, Lucy, and Edmund find themselves arguing over the existence of a magical place called "Narnia." As the argument heats up, Lucy becomes captivated with a mysterious painting that's hanging in the room where they're all standing. It's a painting of a sailing ship on a rolling sea. All of a sudden, the painting begins to drip — then spritz — then *gush*. The deluge coming from the picture is so tremendous that it quickly fills the room. The children are soon overwhelmed and find themselves swimming amid the room's water-borne furniture. As they swim, they're transported to the wonderful blue waters of Narnia itself — a land full of adventure and truth, and home to Aslan, the great lion king who knows and loves them.

At this buoy, we'll explore five soul-hydrating water-pictures of God. Having been painted and hung by God for our hydration, these pictures will sweep us away to a land of deep soul-delight in relationship with Him. We should hope that our hearts will become drenched, as Eustace, Lucy, and Edmund did, with the lavishness of God that gushes from these biblical water-images.

9

God, the Fountain

> *Bless God in the great congregation,*
> *the* LORD, *O You who are of Israel's Fountain.*
> Psalm 68:26

I am known to take long walks year-round in St. Louis's famous Forest Park. The perimeter of the park is about 6.2 miles, and on a hot summer day, I can get quite thirsty. Thankfully, I know the location of every single water fountain in the park. I even know the nature of the different fountains: Some trickle, some gush, some take a while to flow, some don't work at all, some are in buildings, some have a side bowl for dogs, and some include a faucet under which I can plunge my sweaty head. On really hot days, I'll arrange my walk to make sure I get to the next fountain soon enough so that I stay hydrated.

Occasionally I walk in the park with friends who are less familiar with the area. If it's hot, they'll often load up with bottled water until I tell them, "Don't worry — I know where all the fountains are." With that important information, we're free to enjoy the park without carrying water or worrying about dehydration. This is a good picture of what God desires for our voyage through the Christian life. He wants us to know Him as our Fountain so we can live with substantial soul-freedom and joy in a hot, waterless world.

Knowing the truth about God is absolutely essential — because, spiritually speaking, our entire life is like one long walk through Forest Park. Actually, we're walking through a searing spiritual desert, there's an enemy who wants to dehydrate us, and we have a nagging disposition to eat desiccants. Oh, and there is only one water fountain that can satisfy our supreme thirst — God, our Fountain. When we forget this marvelous truth about God, we'll dig anywhere in search of the value, peace, love, meaning, and forgiveness we crave. By reminding us that He is our Fountain, God intends for us to survive — even *thrive* — on our journey through this fountainless land. He beckons us to learn to soak in Him as our internal and relational Source of Life. Let's do just that as we explore the details of this beautiful water-picture.

Source of Life

In Psalm 68:26, God calls Himself "Israel's Fountain," highlighting the idea that He's the internal and relational Source of Life for His people. A similar idea is expressed in Psalm 36:9 — "For with You is the fountain of life; / in Your light do we see light." To receive maximum hydration from these saturated biblical truths, let's first think about the idea that our Fountain is a *Source* of *Life*.

The word *fountain* (Hebrew: *maqor*) in these texts specifically indicates a source where water originates, such as a spring — as compared with a storage vessel for water, such as a cistern. A *maqor* is the source for water that flows, streams, or gushes.

God perfects this physical representation of a fountain, since He originates with absolute independence. This means that as a Source, God depends upon no one but Himself to gush Himself and all His benefits to us. He's self-sustaining. He's the Source that's sourced only in His infinite, immutable (unchangeable) Self! For this reason, God surpasses any physical picture of a fountain/source, including every spring whose flow can ultimately be traced back to some other source (e.g., glacial melt from a distant mountain range).

This is incredibly good news for those of us who sometimes worry that we, the devil, or the desert might plug or dry up God. Impossible! Ridiculous! By definition, God can't be dried up, because He doesn't depend upon anyone but Himself to be "wet." God's propensity or ability to gush can never be diminished, because He's the Source. He's like the bubbling spring that's *always* full — no matter how hot and dry it gets outside, no matter how many siphons or pipes we build to tap into Him, and no matter how many fires we ignite to dehydrate Him.

Recognizing God as our self-sustaining Fountain should bring us tremendous internal peace. We can be completely assured that God will always supply what we crave most deeply: forgiveness, value, peace, meaning, love, and hope. He will provide *everything* He promises[1] *every time* we come to Him. Unlike our parents or our spouse or our friends, God will never disappoint us by breaking His promises because He's tired, sick, or busy. We'll never find Him with a sign around His neck that says "Out to Lunch" or "Out of Stock" or "Out of Order." Never! As the Source sourced in Himself, His constant mode is "Open for Business — Running at Full Strength — Ready, Able, and Willing to Fulfill All My Promises."

But just *what* does God, the Source, always gush toward us? The answer is easy, yet incredibly profound: Life! God is the origin of our vitality — an all-encompassing *joie de vivre* — that animates everything about us as human beings (except our sin, for which we alone must accept authorship). As our Redeemer, God especially sends forth eternal life through Jesus Christ. But He's also the ultimate Cause behind all that "moves" our bodies, emotions, thoughts, and affections in godly ways and directions.

This, again, is great news! That's because the "Forest Park" in which we live (a desert), and unseen enemies (the devil) suck vitality from us in every way. Even our remaining flesh deals death on a regular basis (Romans 7:24). This makes us ask, "Where can we go to get life?!" In answering this question, The Most Interesting Man in the World, the devil, and our own flesh sing in perfect harmony, "Oh, let us show you the possibilities!" They then roll out temptation upon temptation to try to lure us to build our lives around non-fountains that can deliver only dust and ashes for every part of our lives, including our hearts.

In weaker moments, we often give in to those temptations. We do so by seeking life from any person, place, or thing that seems to be a fountain, but isn't God. We then build our lives around dry springs, such as our children, career, pleasure, academic achievement, physical vitality, popularity, financial security, or athletic accomplishment. We can even treat religious activity as a fountain, thinking that our rigor in serving God will give us the life we crave.

But none of those things is a *source*. Each one depends upon something else for its flow. Usually, that "something else" is us! And none of those things delivers life. They all ultimately deliver misery as we slave away to keep them going. Therefore, to build our lives around any of those false fountains, or to look to them for the vitality we crave, is a monumental error that will have terrible consequences for our hearts.

Thankfully, all our momentary lapses of spiritual reason do not dehydrate God. He's sourced in Himself, remember? He alone is the Fountain of Life, remember? As His fountainlike Spirit brings us back to our spiritual senses, we find Him as we left Him: gushing away. As we come back to Him again and again (by repenting/turning, remember?), He gushes life into our hearts in the form of forgiveness, mercy, and love — all to satisfy our supreme thirst.

An Internal Fountain

God as our Source of Life is only the beginning of this beautiful waterpicture. It gets even more hydrating when we consider that God is a Fountain that bubbles up *inside of us*. God as our *internal* Spring is proven in a passage we've looked at before, which involves Jesus' conversation with a woman standing beside a physical well (John 4:13–14). In this passage, Jesus points out the severe limitations of "this water" compared with the overflowing opulence and internal sourcing of "the water I will give him." The former refers to the physical well, which represents the dry fountain of male companionship, in which this woman has sought satisfaction (see verse 18). The latter refers to Jesus Himself.

> Jesus said to her, "Everyone who drinks of this water will be thirsty again, but whoever drinks of the water that I will give him will never be thirsty forever. The water that I will give him will become *in him a spring of water welling up to eternal life*." [emphasis added] John 4:13–14

In this text, Jesus, the Fountain Incarnate, explains that to receive Him is to receive a life-giving Source that takes up residence inside us. This teaching would have been a radical idea in Jesus' day. Everyone knew that springs were stationary and that people, like this woman, had to travel to get to them. But Jesus says, "When you welcome Me, I will plant Myself within you so that you will always have the Source of Life giving you life, no matter where you are. With Me inside you gushing life, you need never run spiritually dry." This aspect of God as our Fountain is astounding!

The picture of God as our internal Source of Life reminds me of the defibrillator my grandfather had implanted in his chest. This amazing little unit regularly sent electronic pulses to his heart at the optimal interval and strength to make sure his heart would beat properly. A main beauty of that technology is that it went with him everywhere, because it was *inside* him! For my grandfather, that internal device was an always-available internal spring of health and vitality. For him, it meant the difference between physical life and death.

That's what God, the Fountain, is for His people: an *internal* Source of spiritual life. When we trust in Jesus Christ, God plants Himself within us as an infinite, living "Device" who mysteriously becomes "in [us] a spring of water welling up to eternal life." He's constantly sending spiritual pulses from within us at the optimal interval and strength to make sure we stay at peak spiritual health. We feel these pulses (or "welling up") when we sense God bringing to our hearts and minds life-giving words, convictions, and impulses that match Scripture. In those very moments, we're receiving the life-giving gush of God! Embracing that life often means the difference between spiritual life and death.

It's a great privilege to have the Fountain of God implanted within our hearts. As we walk through the Forest Park of this life, we don't even need to know where the fountains are, because the Fountain lives inside us! He's always there, gushing life to us in the most intimate and accessible way possible — directly from His heart to ours, internally. The magnitude of this honor compels us to gush gladness and gratefulness to God, and to remain sensitive to His gush of life. Let's celebrate the fact that God always sends forth life from within our hearts to slake the flaring thirst of our oft-parched souls.

A Relational Fountain

The refreshment continues as we remember that God as a life-spring within us is *warmly intimate*. In His affection and love, God differs completely from a cold, impersonal defibrillator implanted within. He cares about us deeply and personally as He gushes life from within us. We could say that His movements within us are *friendly* movements. They are peaceful actions tailored to our particular personalities and circumstances for our ultimate, god-ward well-being. This is true even when God is convicting us of our sin. As a relational Fountain, He perfectly adapts His gush of life to us all the time so that we can find life in Him — and enjoy Him and respond to Him.

Have you ever stood under a showerhead that barely trickled? Have you ever tried to get a drink from a water fountain that violently sprayed an eye-poking jet three feet into the air? Each of these situations is a case of need/fountain incompatibility. Frustrating, isn't it? It's frustrating to be dirty and need a shower with water pressure sufficient to get you clean — only to find barely enough spray to moisten a washcloth. It's frustrating (if not startling and hazardous) to be thirsty and go for a drink from a water fountain that's so over-powered that you might lose an eye in the process. But when it comes to God, the *relational* Fountain, we'll never face these frustrations. With Him, we'll always experience the joy of need/Fountain compatibility.

We may have trouble believing that God knows us perfectly and adapts His gush within us to our own unique needs and circumstances. Perhaps there have been times in our lives when people were weak when we needed strength, or were rough when we needed tenderness. Because we've been conditioned by our experiences with flawed human beings, we may expect God to behave the same way. This is where we're challenged to trust that God will perfectly tailor His gush to our needs.

Remember: God's strength and sensitivity as our Fountain do not depend on us! They depend on *Him*. And He's happy to invite and re-invite us to Himself — a self-sourced, infinite Source of Vitality. As we continue repenting, we'll discover that He alone is the place where we can find unending forgiveness, mercy, meaning, grace, joy, peace, love, and every other good thing that hydrates our souls. As that happens, we'll be able to join the chorus of God's people of old who have sung His praises in places like Psalm 36:9a — "For with You is the fountain of life" — and Jeremiah 2:13, where God is called "the Fountain of Living Waters."

We may also join some more recent choruses that reflect this same theme. For example, we might look to William Cowper's famous 1771 hymn, "There Is a Fountain Filled with Blood," and make his words our own. Let's do that right now, fellow voyagers, as we affirm our faith in God, our Fountain of life that's internal and relational. Let's plunge our hearts beneath His hydrating gush.

> There is a fountain filled with blood, drawn from Immanuel's veins;
> and sinners, plunged beneath that flood, lose all their guilty stains:
> lose all their guilty stains, lose all their guilty stains;
> and sinners, plunged beneath that flood, lose all their guilty stains.
>
> The dying thief rejoiced to see that fountain in his day;
> and there have I, as vile as he, washed all my sins away:
> washed all my sins away, washed all my sins away;
> and there have I, as vile as he, washed all my sins away.
>
> E'er since by faith I saw the stream Your flowing wounds supply,
> redeeming love has been my theme, and shall be till I die:
> and shall be till I die, and shall be till I die;
> redeeming love has been my theme, and shall be till I die.[2]

Gushaholic's Prayer

O God, my life-giving Fountain! Thank You for gushing within me with relational warmth. Help me to forsake every false fountain, and to drink only from You, my marvelous, never-ending Source of Life. Amen.

Gushercises

1. How do you have trouble believing — and living out your belief — that God is your only Fountain?
2. How do you struggle to embrace the fact that God is an internal and relational Source of Life as described in this chapter?
3. Describe a time when you experienced God the Fountain swishing around inside you, bringing words or other encouragements of life that matched Scripture.
4. Based on this chapter and any other Bible passages that come to mind, describe God as a Fountain.
5. How can you daily plunge into the God who's your Fountain?

10

Like the Dew

I will be like the dew to Israel;
   he shall blossom like the lily;
   he shall take root like the trees of Lebanon;
his shoots shall spread out;
   his beauty shall be like the olive,
   and his fragrance like Lebanon. Hosea 14:5–6

Have you ever seen a spiderweb laden with dew early in the morning? Even if spiders freak you out, you have to admit that it's a beautiful sight. The delicate droplets hang on slender threads of silk, sparkling on a magical tapestry of dancing sunlight. Like dewdrops on spider's silk, the water-picture of God as our Dew elicits ideas of tender hydration. It reminds us of God's gentle and quiet provision for our thirsty souls. This is true whether God is pictured as the *Giver* of dew, or as One who's *like* the dew.

Provision and Blessing

To Israel, dew meant much more than beautiful spiderwebs. Dew, or night-mist (*tal*), was seen as a gift from the sky that brought fertility, welcome and gentle refreshment, and nourishment. Dew was an important source of moisture for plants, and therefore was an important source of life. As the Giver of dew, God is described as the One who bestows blessing or favor. Details of God's blessing are beautifully expounded as sweet droplets in Hosea 14:5–6, quoted above. They're also noted in other places where dew (*tal*) is used in the Bible. Here are a few of those places.

> May God give you of the dew of heaven
> and of the fatness of the earth
> and plenty of grain and wine. Genesis 27:28

> So Israel lived in safety,
> Jacob lived alone,
> in a land of grain and wine,
> whose heavens drop down dew. Deuteronomy 33:28

> For there shall be a sowing of peace. The vine shall give its fruit, and the ground shall give its produce, and the heavens shall give their dew. And I will cause the remnant of this people to possess all these things. Zechariah 8:12

The idea of God giving dew goes well beyond the mere physical act of His providing water for His people. As with the other water-pictures we're exploring, the physical represents the spiritual. To say, then, that God gives dew is to say that He brings us spiritual blessing and nourishment. It means that He continually gives us what our souls crave most: Himself and His benefits — forgiveness, mercy, meaning, and even more. The idea of God giving dew overlaps the idea that God is our Fountain. God means for the poetic similarity of these two water-pictures to further convince us that He alone satisfies our supreme thirst.

Quiet and Gentle

A distinguishing characteristic of dew, compared with other water images like fountains, rains, and floods, is that dew is very quiet and gentle. To really grab hold of this idea, just camp out in the grass on a spring evening, and see if you can hear the dew forming in the early morning hours. You can't! It's silent. Yet when the sun rises, there it is, carpeting the field! So it is with our God in His likeness to the dew. His hydrating love is often undetectable until we've discovered that we're covered in it.

What a delight that is — to awake at various points in our life to experience the dewlike refreshment of God.

That God likens Himself to dew is particularly helpful for those who've been badly wounded or abused. It's welcome news for all of us, because we live in a generally harsh and thorny world. It's in those circumstances that we especially appreciate God's tender nourishment. To both Hosea's and Zechariah's hearers, this aspect of God's dewiness would have been important. Those prophets were writing to God's people who'd undergone painful chastisement by Him for their desiccant eating. God wanted them, and us, to know that He's as gentle and mild as dew with people when they're broken — even when their brokenness is a result of their own sin.

How might our hearts be affected when we gaze at this picture of the God who is sometimes like the dew in His love for us? For one thing, we may find that we feel safe to expose the tenderest places of our souls to Him. These are the places we may have closed to God's hydrating presence, because we knew Him *only* as the universe-creating, earth-shaking, thunder-cracking God. And while He *is* those things (like a flood, as we'll soon see), He's also like the dew.

As with all the other water-pictures we'll survey, a key to reaping the benefit of God as the dew is to exercise faith. We must believe and trust that God can really be tenderly hydrating. This often opens the door to a fresh experience of God's sweet healing presence and refreshment, as noted in this dewlike invitation — "Come to Me, all who labor and are heavy laden, and I will give you rest. Take My yoke upon you, and learn from Me, for I am gentle and lowly in heart, and you will find rest for your souls" (Matthew 11:28–29).

Someone with a wounded heart might express her faith by saying, "God, it can be hard for me to open certain sensitive areas of my parched and wounded heart to You — in part because I so often think of You as an earth-shaking God. But now I'm beginning to understand that You're also like the dew. So I'm going to trust in that fact and talk with You now about some very broken, dehydrated parts of my life. Thank You for giving me this water-picture that makes me feel safe to talk to You about these things. I'm so looking forward to Your gentle, quiet presence and hydration. Amen."

Quiet and Opulent

Just because God can be like the dew doesn't mean that He's a small, stingy Giver. "Individual dew droplets are small," we might say to ourselves, "so maybe God gives only sweet little blessings." We must avoid this mistake! The following true story serves as an example: About 1.2 million Israelites and their livestock were camped out in the desert, just after God had liberated them from Egypt. Notice how God watered those thirsty mouths daily with dew, then fed them with manna.

> In the morning dew lay around the camp. And when the dew had gone up, there was on the face of the wilderness a fine, flake-like thing, fine as frost on the ground [i.e., manna]. Exodus 16:13b–14

Some may read these verses and say, "Yeah, but the dew dried up to provide manna, so Israel didn't get watered with dew." Not so fast! It was normal for people in those days to take morning walks with cloths tied around their ankles in order to collect dew. Then they'd wring out those cloths and drink the precious, hydrating water. How else would they get water in a dry land with very few springs, rivers, and lakes, and almost no rain? Why else would God send dew, if only for a little while, before He evaporated it to reveal the manna? So we see that it's reasonable that Israel relied on God's dewy provision to water all 1.2 million people, plus their livestock, for forty years in the desert. *That's* opulence!

There are many dew images in the Bible that speak directly to God's lavish provision and blessing. The blessing of Genesis 27:28 is one example: "May God give you of the dew of heaven / and of the fatness of the earth / and plenty of grain and wine." Another is the rich description in Psalm 133, where dew is mentioned in a water-picture of generous goodness and pleasure (emphasis added).

> Behold, how good and pleasant it is
>   when brothers dwell in unity!
> It is like the precious oil on the head,
>   running down on the beard,
> on the beard of Aaron,

> running down on the collar of his robes!
> *It is like the dew of Hermon,*
> *which falls on the mountains of Zion!*
> For there the LORD has commanded the blessing,
> life forevermore.

If none of these biblical examples convinces you, just go outside some morning when dew covers the grass and roll around in it for a while. I guarantee you'll get soaking wet! Something like this happened to me when I was hired to take some pictures of a family farm. To get the best light for the shoot, a friend and I drove to the location very early in the morning. Once there, we put our equipment in a four-wheel ATV and set out around the property, trying to get pictures in the soft, early light. We hadn't counted on the amount of dew we'd find. After just a few stops, our ATV was drenched, and our shoes and the bottoms of our pant legs were completely soaked. Our soaking may have happened quietly, but it certainly was opulent!

So it is as we voyage through the Christian life with the God who often surprises us with quiet, yet lavish, dewlike hydration. It can happen when we read Scripture — often half-awake early in the morning or dead-tired late at night — and God's Spirit sweetly reveals to us a truth we weren't expecting but greatly need. It can happen when God plays a song on the radio with the exact lyrics and tune that encourage us to persevere amid trial. It can happen when we blankly stare at a painting and God suddenly causes its composition, colors, and theme to warm some cold place in our souls with the peace we crave. It can happen when we sit exhausted in the church pew and God softly hydrates our hearts through the singing and praying of His people, the reading and preaching of His Word, and the quiet celebration of His sacraments.

Knowing that God often works this way should encourage us to relax a bit in our relationship with Him. It should relieve us from frantic, water-grabbing hyper-vigilance, and release us from the slavish idea that we must always "do our part" in order to enjoy God and His blessings. Instead, we can take pleasure in commands that beckon us to "be still and know that I am God" (Psalm 46:10a). The "be still" of this verse literally means that we let ourselves go slack by resting from our frenzied attempts to grab hydration. As a field lies still and receives abundant dew, at times we too must lie still to receive God. We do this simply by trusting and waiting on Him as the dewlike God who loves to hydrate us quietly and opulently, without a lot of spiritual gyrations on our part.

Back to Spiderwebs

God's longing for us to know Him as the Dew is illustrated by a beautiful scene from the 2006 film *Amazing Grace*. The movie shows William Wilberforce at a pivotal point in his young career as the English legislator whom God would use to end the slave trade in the British Empire. The scene opens with a tender piano refrain and a very close shot of Wilberforce in his garden in the early morning. (Close camera angles often imply intimacy.) He gazes in sweet astonishment at a dew-covered spiderweb and gently touches it with his finger. Then he happily looks up to the sky, smiling, and plops down with his books on the dewy grass. He's so overcome that he can't even open the book he's chosen to read and instead lies back in the wet meadow, given over to the marvel of God. After a brief interruption by his chief butler, Richard, a dialogue ensues that reveals the heart of a man being hydrated by the God who's like the dew:

> WILBERFORCE: Richard?
> RICHARD: Sir?
> WILBERFORCE: I know that lying down on the wet grass is not a normal thing to do.
> RICHARD: None of my business, sir.
> WILBERFORCE: Truth is, I've been even more strange than usual lately, haven't I?
> RICHARD: [responds with a speechless look of mild affirmation]
> WILBERFORCE: It's God. I have 10,000 engagements of state today, but I would prefer to spend the day out here getting a wet ass, studying dandelions, and marveling at bloody spiders' webs!
> RICHARD: You found God, sir?
> WILBERFORCE: I think He found me.[1]

I'm not sure whether the actual William Wilberforce had a dew-experience and dialogue exactly like the one pictured in that movie. But it's historical fact that around age twenty-six he had a profound experience of God that resulted in his conversion to Christ and that positively altered the course of his life. It's interesting to me that the filmmakers chose to demonstrate this radical, life-changing experience with God in a scene that associated the experience with spiderwebs and dew!

The Bible is clear that God intends for us to associate dew with His quiet, gentle, and opulent way with those who seek Him. He especially wants those who are weak, broken, and fearful (all of us, at times) to realize as they consider this water-picture how inviting He is. When, by faith, we recognize this tender, abundantly generous, aspect of God, we may ask in astonished wonder as Job did, "Has the rain a father, or who has begotten the drops of dew?" (Job 38:28). Oh, that we might lie down in our God who gives the dew and is like the dew. Through faith, we shall indeed.

Gushaholic's Prayer

Lord, thank You for this refreshing water-picture that reveals you as giving the dew and being like the dew. Please help me to drink it in, believe it, and thereby experience your soul-hydration in all its quiet and tender opulence. Amen.

Gushercises

1. What's your reaction to the idea that God-like-the-dew is quiet, gentle, and opulent?
2. By trusting in the God of this water-picture, what tender places in your heart might you expose to God for healing and hydration?
3. How can you "be still" to receive God as a field quietly rests and receives abundant dew?
4. Create a work of art (e.g., a drawing or photographs) with dew as the theme.

11

Like the Rain

Let us know; let us press on to know the LORD;
His going out is sure as the dawn;
He will come to us as the showers,
as the spring rains that water the earth. Hosea 6:3

Forrest Gump (the 1994 movie and its title character) produced some pretty famous pop culture slogans in America, such as "Life is like a box of chocolates; you never know what you're gonna get." You might also recall the famous "I was run-ning!" Well, one of my favorite scenes in that movie is a very wet scene: Forrest is slogging with his platoon through a Vietnamese swamp when torrents of rain suddenly begin to fall. Here's how Forrest describes the change in the weather:

> One day, it started raining, and it didn't quit for four months. We been through every kind of rain there is. Little bitty stingin' rain ... and big ol' fat rain. Rain that flew in sideways. And sometimes rain even seemed to come straight up from underneath.[1]

It's fun to imagine a conversation between Forrest Gump and an Old Testament Israelite — because of their shared awareness of rain types. However, ancient Israelites derived a lot more meaning from rain than Forrest Gump ever did. To Forrest, rain was mainly an annoyance. But to Israel — and to us — rain is valuable and multifaceted. Its biblical water-pictures tell us much about the God of gush and the gush of God. Here's a sampling of words that God's people during Old Testament times used to describe rain. As you read this list, it'll be helpful to know that many of the Israelites' crops — including their main crops, barley and wheat — were planted in the autumn and harvested in April and May.

1. *geshem* or *matar*: rain or heavy showers
2. *yoreh* or *moreh*: early, autumn rains lasting from late October to early December
3. *malqosh*: later, spring rains lasting from March through April
4. *rebibiym*: abundant showers (literally, "abundance of droplets")
5. *zerem*: violent or flooding rain
6. *sagrir*: dripping, annoying rain

The Bible is actually a very rainy book! As we survey the rains (or lack of rains) in the Bible, we'll find that the Holy Spirit was very specific about which rain-words He used to make a point. To grasp the impact of this water-picture, we must remember that Israel was an agricultural society living in an arid climate. Because rain was essential for the Israelites' sustenance and survival, its type and timing was a subject of intense concern, carrying meaning well beyond the physical. We'll discover more truths about God as we examine the first three kinds of rain listed above and soak in this valuable water-picture.

Comprehensively Hydrating

Hosea 6:3, quoted at the beginning of this chapter, says that God and His actions toward His people are "as the showers [*geshem*], as the spring rains [*malqosh*] that water the earth." Notice that *geshem*, used early in the verse, is the general word for rain. The general becomes specific when, later in the verse, God likens Himself to *malqosh* — the later, spring rain lasting from March through April.

Malqosh rains were essential for bringing crops to maturity. They were seen as a sign of God's blessing, favor, and pleasure. As One who comes like *malqosh*, God wants us to know that He'll stick with us and nourish us so that we mature and bear fruit as Christians. We needn't worry that He'll give up on us in the middle of a challenge. He'll ensure that we'll get what we need in order to know, honor, enjoy, and serve Him *all the way through* each season or issue of life.

But God isn't only like *malqosh* rains. He nourishes us at the beginning of a season as well as at the end. He tells us this in these texts by likening His work to *moreh* and *yoreh* rains.

> Be glad, O children of Zion,
>   and rejoice in the LORD your God,
> for He has given the early rain [*moreh*] for your vindication;
>   He has poured down for you abundant rain [*geshem*],
>   the early [*moreh*] and the latter rain [*malqosh*], as before.
>   Joel 2:23

> They do not say in their hearts,
>   "Let us fear the LORD our God,
> who gives the rain [*geshem*] in its season,
>   the autumn rain [*yoreh*] and the spring rain [*malqosh*],
> and keeps for us
>   the weeks appointed for the harvest." Jeremiah 5:24

Unlike *malqosh* rains, *moreh* and *yoreh* rains come at the beginning of the growing season (late October through early December). These two words clarify the type of *geshem* (i.e., general rain showers) referred to in both texts just quoted. They were very important for preparing the dry, barren soil to receive the farmer's seed, and for ensuring seed germination and sprouting. As One who comes like *moreh*/*yoreh* rains, God wants us to know that He'll supply what we need at the beginning of various spiritual challenges, including the start of the grand challenge of living in relationship with Him in such a dry, barren world.

It's wonderful that God likens Himself to *geshem, malqosh, moreh,* <u>and</u> *yoreh* rains! The tight proximity of these words to each other in these and other Bible texts paints a lush and powerful image of God's comprehensively hydrating character. He's a lavish God who expansively and consistently provides soul-nourishment from beginning to end. He won't give up on us. According to His perfect timing, He'll come to us like early (*moreh/yoreh*) rains and like late (*malqosh*) rains, watering our hearts with His presence and goodness.

God's faithful provision to our souls from the beginning to the end of our earthly lives is described this way in Philippians 1:6 — "And I am sure of this, that He who began a good work in you will bring it to completion at the Day of Jesus Christ." It's also explained this way in Hebrews 13:5 — "I will never leave you nor forsake you." Interestingly, this verse is quoted from Deuteronomy 31:6 and 8, and Joshua 1:5, which find Israel on the brink of a tremendous challenge: to enter the land God had promised to them hundreds of years before. It's at times exactly like this that the Israelites — and we — need to hear that God comprehensively hydrates His people. This is true when we face challenges throughout life, including the event that can be the greatest challenge of our lives: our death.

As a pastor, I've witnessed many instances of God hydrating His people through their lives *and* their deaths. In one notable instance, I was caring for a young man who was dying of cancer. God had gotten him off to a good start in His Christian life with His abundant *moreh/yoreh* (early) rains. As the cancer increasingly ravaged his body, it became apparent that my friend would need abundant *malqosh* (later) rains from God.

Very near the end, during a solemn moment in the hospital room, I remember my dear Christian brother welling up with fearful tears as he asked me in a soft, broken tone, "Am I going to be all right?" It was the cry of a suffering Christian and dear friend with a parching heart in dire need of God's later rains. In response, I moved very close to his face and gently put my hands on his head. Then, looking tenderly into his eyes, I said firmly, "You will be just fine. God will carry you through this door and will be with you on the other side. He promises you this in the Christ you received by faith. You will be just fine."

Through the expression on his face in the moments that followed, I could see the effect of God's hydrating later rains on my friend's heart. Though much physical pain still remained, I could tell that God was hydrating his heart with the later-rain truths he needed most at the end of his life's journey: I love you; I forgive all your sins through your faith in My Son; I will not leave you; I am holding you securely; I will receive you upon your death with gladness and strength. A few days later, my friend died. I can't wait to see him again, perfectly hydrated and radiant!

Even if you aren't facing the trial of death at this present moment, we all long to experience God as the One who is comprehensively hydrating. We long to keep hearing His soul-reviving songs of forgiveness, grace, love, and strength in the water-pictures that liken God to *geshem, malqosh, moreh,* and *yoreh* rains. By faith, we can own these truths to our heart's delight in every trial of life.

Rain in the Forecast?

The summer of 2012 sparked a new interest in The Weather Channel for many Midwesterners, especially farmers. Having received hearty early rains, most crops got off to a good start. But as a hot, rainless June gave way to an even hotter, rainless July, concern was the only thing that was growing. Suddenly, the forecast for continued drought became big news across the nation. A headline on the front page of the August 17–19, 2012, edition of *USA Today* was typical: "Parched U.S. Overheated into Fall." The story lamented the perils of not receiving much-needed late-season rains: "But while rainfall may improve some, the drought seems likely to 'persist or intensify' from California to southeastern Illinois through November."[2]

Like Midwest farmers facing too many hot, rainless weeks in a row in the summer of 2012, we too remain fixed on the forecast during difficult seasons of our lives. However, our obsession isn't with the possibility of physical water droplets but with God's faithfulness. When the chips are down and the heat is on, we often panic and wonder whether God will stick with us.

We seldom give voice to our secret fears, of course. But inwardly, our desiccant-loving flesh whispers, "I wonder if God will hang around. It's getting pretty hot, you know. This trial's going on longer than normal, don't you think? I don't see any clouds of relief on the horizon, do you? Maybe God's not going to carry you through. Maybe He's just not that reliable. Maybe He's only interested in giving you a start and seeing how far you can get on your own."

The challenge of faith in moments like these is to remember that God has been and always will be like the *malqosh, yoreh,* and *moreh* rains to

His people. Whether He hydrates our souls temporarily on the earth, or whether He decides to bring us through death into a perfected experience of His soul-rains in heaven, God *will* hydrate us. One way or another, His rain-like hydration will come — guaranteed.

Gushaholic's Prayer

God, I thank You that You are comprehensively hydrating like the early and late rains. I need constant reminders from You that I am forgiven, valued, and loved. Please help me hear Your voice raining in my heart, especially at the beginning and end of trials. Amen.

Gushercises

1. Describe a time when you were thankful for rain.
2. How might you fear that God will fail to nourish your soul from the beginning to the end of your life and/or during a season in your life? Let your answer be a confession to the God who's truly like *malqosh*, *yoreh*, and *moreh* rains.
3. The next time it rains, stop and listen: Consider how God is like the rain and hydrates your soul.

12

Like a Flood

And he went up to Baal-perazim, and David struck them [the Philistines] down there. And David said, "God has broken through my enemies by my hand, like a bursting flood." Therefore the name of that place is called Baal-perazim. 1 Chronicles 14:11

I write this book as a resident of St. Louis, Missouri. Being situated near the confluence of the Mississippi, Missouri, and Illinois Rivers, St. Louis has had its share of floods. I recall a minor occurrence in 2008, which, among other things, totally washed away a two-lane asphalt road that I used to get to work. In 1993, before I moved here, the region was devastated by a more serious flood. Houses were swept away, crops were destroyed, businesses were ruined, and lives were lost because of the watery deluge. Many memorials around our city remind us of the Great Flood of 1993 and of the devastation that was caused by rising waters.

Floods are among the most powerful natural phenomena on earth. Basically, a flood happens when water overflows, or otherwise gushes, into an area that had previously been dry. While we may typically think of a flood as being sad and catastrophic, that isn't always the case. For example, floods can be agents of cleansing. It's very fitting, therefore, that God sometimes likens Himself and His work to a flood. In this water-picture, God identifies Himself with three main kinds of floods, each with a different purpose. Although these purposes often overlap when floods are associated with God in the Bible, in order to get the most from this fascinating water-picture, we'll look at each of the three purposes individually.

First, God likens Himself to "floods of deliverance" — as One who rescues His people by overwhelming and conquering sin and other enemies. Second, He sends "floods of conviction" to wake people to their sin and to induce heartfelt repentance for the purpose of their own good and His glory. Third, He authors "floods of judgment," by which He either literally or metaphorically judges and/or cleanses the world of sin and sinners and establishes His glorious righteousness on earth. Let's look at these three amazing aspects of the floodlike nature and work of God as we continue to soak in His gush.

Floods of Deliverance

1 Chronicles 14:11, quoted at the beginning of this chapter, paints a dramatic picture of God acting like a flood of deliverance. This verse recounts an event that happened just after David was anointed king over all of Israel. David's, Israel's, and God's enemies (the Philistines) heard of David's anointing and came to wage war against David in the Valley of Rephaim. As David and his army went out to meet this enemy, David witnessed God's delivering torrent ("like a bursting flood") through his own hand against his and God's foes.

This incident compels David to give God the name "Baal-Perazim," which literally means "the Master of Breakthroughs." David then honors God by giving this name to the site where God's conquering floodlike victory occurred. David thus praises God for delivering the Israelites by destroying their enemies and for cleansing his new kingdom from this great evil.

God used this aspect of Himself to hydrate me at a time in my own life when I was surrounded by enemies and trials. The floodlike deliverance pictured in David's experience inspired me to create a sculpture that I titled *Master of Breakthroughs*. I sculpted a massive fist violently smashing through a thick steel plate from underneath. The plate represented the evil I was battling within and around me; the hand represented David's and my flooding, delivering, conquering God. Together, these two components depicted God "like a bursting flood," smashing our enemies with the force of His conquering, delivering gush. It was my own personal testament, designed to encourage my heart in the truths we're presently discussing.

How does picturing God as a flood of deliverance encourage your heart? This question may be challenging, since we usually think of floods as unwanted or harmful events. But when we're surrounded by trials, the image of God as a delivering flood can be tremendously uplifting. What Philistine armies or thick steel plates are you up against? Do you believe that the God who can break through like a flood can deliver you?

This is the challenge of faith associated with the picture of the God who can work like a flood of deliverance. The question is whether or not we believe or trust that God is still the Master of Breakthroughs. We engage in battle as David did, believing in the God who often delivers through our actions. As usual, the world, the devil, and our desiccating flesh will try to convince us otherwise, thereby sending us into a desert of hopelessness. "God can't help you," we'll hear. "He's not strong enough to deliver you from your sin, addiction, fear, worry, hopelessness, grief, or [your own personal enemy]. He's no Master of Breakthroughs! At least not for you in this situation."

Lies! God was, is, and always will be our Flood of Deliverance. He may not do exactly what we'd like Him to do when we'd like Him to do it. But He can and will break through when and how it is best. Consider this water-picture of God as it overlaps with our next royal painting of the God who brings floods of conviction.

Floods of Conviction

In Scripture, God sometimes graciously threatens physical floods or associates Himself and His judgment with a flood in order to convince people of their sin. He mercifully intends those warnings to compel otherwise ignorant or hard-hearted Christians and non-Christians to repent (Chapter 8). Jesus taught His disciples using this water-picture.

> As were the days of Noah, so will be the coming of the Son of Man. For as in those days before the flood they were eating and drinking, marrying and giving in marriage, until the day when Noah entered the ark, and they were unaware until the flood came and swept them all away, so will be the coming of the Son of Man. Matthew 24:37–39

In this text, Jesus refers to the Flood, a God-caused calamity of epic proportions in time-space history that unequivocally demonstrated God's judgment toward unrepentant people (Genesis 7–9, to be discussed shortly). This warning was and is to be heeded by Jesus' disciples above all, since they/we are the ones to whom He specifically directed this message (Matthew 24:3). It's like a siren designed to wake us from complacency, sin, and ignorance so that we return to enjoy God as the King and Satisfier of our supreme thirst. David heeded a warning like this when He cried out in conviction in Psalm 69:15–17.

> Let not the flood sweep over me,
>   or the deep swallow me up,
>   or the pit close its mouth over me.
>
> Answer me, O LORD, for Your steadfast love is good;
>   according to Your abundant mercy, turn to me.
> Hide not Your face from Your servant;
>   for I am in distress; make haste to answer me.

Whether we consider God's flood warnings to be kind or annoying depends in part on how well we know Him, how much we value Him, and how much we value our own true (i.e., God-defined) well-being. If we know Him to be the God who does what He says; if we know Him as the God who's always concerned for our good and His glory; if we value our relationship with Him; and if we acknowledge that a life lived in His gush is the best life possible — then we'll be grateful for His gracious flood warnings. We will, in fact, thank Him for sometimes jolting us from our desiccant-eating ways to re-experience life in Him.

In addition to the occasional flood, we St. Louisans must sometimes deal with tornadoes. (Despite all these potential natural disasters, St. Louis is a great place to live! Really!) That's why authorities have installed tornado-warning sirens all over the region. They test these sirens at the beginning of every month. If they go off at any other time, everybody knows they're supposed drop everything and take cover, preferably in a basement. But do you think everybody is convicted to comply with this warning system? Hardly.

I confess that there was a time when I didn't comply with the warnings. If the sirens went off, I'd look out my window, and if I didn't see anything dramatic, I'd go about my business. That was until Good Friday, 2011, when some twisters touched down not far from my house. In the days that followed, I got news that some very good friends nearly lost their lives in that catastrophe. I even had family in town that weekend who could not return home because our airport was shut down due to storm damage. Suddenly the threat of tornadoes became very real, and my attitude toward the warning sirens changed from one of mild interest and occasional compliance to one of thankful attentiveness and absolute compliance.

Whether we're talking about St. Louis's tornado sirens or God's Scriptural flood sirens, we must take heed! We must consider the power of God, His majestic holiness, and His passion to see us honor, enjoy, and serve Him. It's healthy for us to *thank* God for His gracious flood warnings and the conviction they bring! Let's let King David's confession in Psalm 32:5–6 serve as a model for our prayers in this regard.

> I acknowledged my sin to You,
>> and I did not cover my iniquity;
> I said, "I will confess my transgressions to the LORD,"
>> and You forgave the iniquity of my sin.   Selah.
>
> Therefore let everyone who is godly
>> offer prayer to You at a time when You may be found;
> surely in the rush of great waters,
>> they shall not reach him.

Floods of Judgment

The final flood-picture we'll discuss is that of God as One who's like and who sends floods of judgment. This image comes into clear view after God's warnings have been ignored and He has righteously decided to judge unrepentant sinners. These floods present God's people with a picture of Him that is both fierce and comforting.

God's floods of judgment are pictured with great clarity in an event appropriately called "the Flood," as recorded in Genesis 7–9. Having had enough of mankind's rebellion against Him, God righteously decides to judge mankind and cleanse the earth of evil by causing "the fountains of the great deep" to "burst open" and the "floodgates of the sky" to open (Genesis 7:11, NASB), thus sending a literal "flood of waters." The Flood "blotted out every living thing that was upon the face of the land" (Genesis 7:23a, NASB). However, God mercifully provided for the rescue of Noah, his family, and pairs of animals that had boarded the ark.

The Flood is such an epic picture of God's judging and cleansing power that it's pointed to again and again throughout Scripture as a symbol of both warning and encouragement. We already saw how Jesus referred to the Flood in Matthew 24. It also occurs in 2 Peter 2:5 and 9, written well over two thousand years after the Flood:

> If He [God] did not spare the ancient world, but preserved Noah, a herald of righteousness, with seven others, when He brought a flood upon the world of the ungodly,... then the Lord knows how to rescue the godly from trials, and to keep the unrighteous under punishment until the Day of Judgment.

Christians should be tremendously comforted by the fact that, as He did during the Flood, God will one Day judge everyone and everything in the whole world. We needn't fear this; in fact, we can look forward to it because of God's mercy and forgiveness that we've freely received through faith in Jesus Christ (Appendix A). As pilgrims often harassed by evil in this world, we can be encouraged, knowing that God will one Day set all things right and put an end to all evil. Just as a flood tears condemned crack-houses and brothels from their foundations, so too will God one Day condemn everything corrupt, washing it away to leave only beauty, wholeness, and life.

This judging and cleansing theme is pictured beautifully in a scene from the film version of *The Lord of the Rings: The Two Towers*. At a pivotal point in that story, an army of Ents (walking, talking trees) battles the evil wizard Saruman and his hordes. At a crucial point in the battle, the Ents' leader shouts to his compatriots, "Let loose the river!"[1]

With that, a platoon of Ents breaks the dam upstream from Saruman's stronghold. The pent-up waters gush forth with violent force — down the mountainside and onto the battlefield. The flood douses Saruman's fires, destroys his war machines, and sweeps away his armies. Eventually, it disarms Saruman himself by confining him to his tower. As the floodwaters begin to subside, the Ent leader solemnly declares, "The filth of Saruman is washing away."[2]

As people who know that God will one Day bring a final flood of judgment,[3] we can echo the Ent leader's statement on many levels. We can rejoice that God will permanently wash away the filth *around us* by ridding this world of all who refuse to repent of their hatred of God. We can rejoice that He'll permanently wash away every last trace of affection for desiccants that remains *within us*. And we can rejoice that in all of this, we need not fear, because on the cross Jesus Christ has already absorbed the flood of God's judgment that we deserved for our sin.

Even momentary meditation on these three aspects of God's flood-like work should elicit a gush of praise from us toward Him! Marveling at this water-picture produces awe and gratitude in those who cry out for deliverance, those who long for conviction leading to repentance and life, those who warn the unrepentant of the imminent danger of God's judgment, and those who eagerly await the final flood of God's righteousness, which will cleanse the world of sin forever.

Gushaholic's Prayer

Thank You, God, for sharpening my understanding and appreciation of You through the water-picture of a flood. Please use the various facets of this picture to hydrate my heart. Amen.

Gushercises

1. Recall a time when you experienced God like a flood of deliverance.
2. Recall a time when you experienced God like a flood of conviction.
3. Recall a time when you experienced the joy that comes from re-realizing that God has spared you from His flood of final judgment through your faith in Jesus Christ.
4. What can you do to help these water-pictures nourish your soul daily?

13

Like a River

You visit the earth and water it;
You greatly enrich it;
the River of God is full of water;
You provide their grain,
for so You have prepared it. Psalm 65:9

In our minds, we all occasionally tend to "shrink" God and His capacity to satisfy our supreme thirst. It's hard for us to continually conceive of a Being who gushes as a never-ending Source of spiritual vitality. These lapses in our impression of God are actually lapses in our belief. God Himself, of course, remains unchanged. But in our disbelief we can rob ourselves of much-needed hydration. We also show that we think God is a liar! That's because God clearly and repeatedly reveals Himself in the Bible as a rich, opulent, lavish, plentiful, generous, luxurious, prolific, abundant, copious, teeming, bountiful, profuse, and eternal Hydrator. Hopefully, we're beginning to see and believe this, fellow voyagers! Gazing at the biblical water-picture of God like a river will continue to nourish our belief.

Luxuriously Life-Giving

To help us conceive of God's lavish, life-giving gush, let's consider the Amazon River, by some standards the largest river in the world. The Amazon River supports an unparalleled abundance of life in its 2.7 million square-mile basin. That's nearly thirty percent of South America's total land mass. From its various tributaries and channels, the Amazon gushes more water into the ocean than any other river in the world — more than seven million cubic feet per *second*. This super-abundant, life-giving, nutrient-rich river supports over one third of the earth's species, many of which live in the world's richest, most biologically diverse, tropical rainforest.

Because of the Amazon River's richness and size, determining the exact number of plant and animal species in and around it is impossible. Some sources estimate that there are over 2,100 species of fish, including the piranha and the arapaima, the world's largest freshwater fish. There are over 300 species of mammals, including jaguars, squirrel monkeys, tapirs, and capybaras. In addition, the Amazon Basin is home to over one third of the world's bird species, including the toucan and the macaw. More than 600 reptile species and another 600 amphibian species — including the poison dart frog and the anaconda — creep, crawl, slither, or jump around the area.

Although the list above may seem like a lot of animal life, it represents less than ten percent of the species supported by the Amazon River — because more than ninety percent of all the animal species in the area are *insects*! A single square mile of Amazonian rainforest can be home to over 50,000 insect species. One Peruvian national park boasts 1,300 butterfly species (more than four times the number of butterfly species in all of Europe). Some of the more famous insects in the Amazon Basin include the rhino beetle, the leaf-cutter ant, and the majestic blue morpho butterfly. This jaw-dropping assortment of fauna thrives in an astonishing web of plant life that includes over two-thirds of the flora species of the entire world.[1]

The luxuriously fertile, life-giving Amazon River and its basin provide an excellent illustration of the "River of God" mentioned in Psalm 65:9, quoted at the beginning of this chapter. A superlative spiritual parallel to the physical Amazon, God's "River" offers inexhaustible soul-resources for our hearts' fertility as we dwell in and around Him. In relationship with Him, we can find every "species," or facet of human vitality, fulfilled in one way or another: hope in the midst of despair, joy in sadness, peace in conflict, forgiveness in sin, healing in brokenness, wisdom in confusion, order in chaos, and even more. In one word, we are "blessed." This is how God describes it in Jeremiah 17:7–8.

> Blessed is the man who trusts in the LORD,
>> whose trust is the LORD.
> He is like a tree planted by water,
>> that sends out its roots by the stream,
> and does not fear when heat comes,
>> for its leaves remain green,
> and is not anxious in the year of drought,
>> for it does not cease to bear fruit.

Constantly Life-Giving

But even if we believe that God is like a *luxurious* river, we may sometimes doubt that He's like a *constant* river. For example, we may fear that He'll dry up because we feel we've sinned too flagrantly or too often. For help with this particular battle of faith, let's remember for a moment that the Bible was written by God primarily through people who lived in very dry, often scorched, places. They had good reason to fear actual physical dehydration caused by fluctuating water supplies. Most rivers were wadis — streambeds dried by the sun's merciless onslaught. Wadis would remain dry until rains replenished them with flowing water.

Against this backdrop, we can see that Bible writers rightly celebrate the ongoing certainty of spiritual hydration offered by the God who compared Himself to a river that never dries up. Like them, we must take God at His Word. *God is not like a wadi!* Not even our sin can dry Him up, as indicated in Romans 5:20b — "But where sin increased, grace abounded all the more." Like a gushing river, God's goodness toward us never depends upon anyone or anything but Him. Confidence in God's autonomy frees us to plant ourselves in Him and to send our roots into Him with assurance that we'll find the spiritual nourishment we need. When we do this, our souls can "remain green" and "bear fruit" (Jeremiah 17:7–8), even in the hottest and driest conditions!

Nevertheless, in our occasional disbelief we act just like the ancient Israelites sometimes did — mistakenly thinking that God has suddenly become like a wadi. When that happens, we start to "uproot" ourselves from God. We begin to doubt that He can satisfy our supreme thirst, and we become lax in our devotion to Him. Then, driven by our ongoing need, we chase mirages that look like rivers but then evaporate into heart-parching wilderness. We'll even try to "replant" ourselves by river look-alikes by acting upon the belief that they can provide what we think God cannot.

Our folly starts with disbelief. Even though God has clearly told us that He's like a luxurious and constant river for our souls, we no longer trust that to be true. Then we believe that there are other "rivers" that can give us what we believe He cannot. We act on this redirected belief by sinking our roots (i.e., by investing our energy and hopes) into things like relationships, accomplishments, food, entertainment, sex, career, family, and health. Sometimes we even plant ourselves beside the false stream of religion by over-investing ourselves in moral effort, spiritual disciplines, and/or ministry in hopes that we'll find the soul-hydration we seek.

Praise God that our temporary disbelief, uprooting, and re-rooting does not change Him! He was, is, and always will be like a goodness-gushing river. No matter what we do or what happens in the world, He'll continue to flow in all His luxuriously life-giving opulence, beckoning us to experientially re-root ourselves in Him. That, in fact, has always been the big invitation and encouragement of the water-pictures of God as a river: to *stay rooted* in relationship with Him as the inexhaustibly nutrient-rich riverlike God. As voyagers in the Christian life, we often need to turn back toward God and reaffirm our rootedness in Him (i.e., repent; see Chapter 8). There's undeniable biblical precedent that when we do that, His gush will spiritually revive us (see Psalms 105:41 and 107:35–37, and Isaiah 41:18).

Life Between Two Rivers

God is so passionate about our seeing His riverlike qualities that in the Bible He "bookends" human history with two rivers that easily make the Amazon look like a dirty back-alley trickle. The first river is in Eden (Genesis 2), and the last is in heaven (Revelation 22). Both rivers picture God's personal grandeur and the magnificent opulence that flows from His being, along with His desire for us to live in eternal bliss amid all those blessings. Even now, as we live *between* those two rivers in human history, we can experience significant soul-satisfaction in relationship with God.

In the beginning, God created Adam and Eve, and then He placed them in Eden, a land that gushed with abundance of every kind, including perfect communion with God. This epicenter of opulence was a reflection of God's character and was particularly embodied in an overwhelmingly rich and nameless river that flowed out of Eden as the *source* for four other mighty rivers (Genesis 2:10): Pishon, Gihon (literally, "to burst, gush, or bubble forth"), Tigris (called "the great river" in Daniel 10:4), and Euphrates. These four rivers that originated in Eden, formed a 1,200-mile arc of water-rich, nutrient-rich land that stretched from the Persian Gulf to the Mediterranean Sea — an area we've come to call "the Fertile Crescent." Eden and its nameless source river pictured God as One who is comprehensively hydrating and who desires that His people live in blessed nearness to Him (see Psalm 65:4).

Unfortunately, Adam and Eve sinned and were cast out of Eden — away from the great nameless source river, and away from perfect communion with God. Thankfully, God gives us another river — the final bookend that promises good news when God brings the present epoch of human history to an end. That river reveals God's intention to return us to unending, Eden-perfect opulence — with God at its center. Here's how our eternal abode is described at the end of God's story (the very last chapter in the Bible, actually) in Revelation 22:1–4.

> Then the angel showed me the river of the water of life, bright as crystal, flowing from the throne of God and of the Lamb through the middle of the street of the city; also, on either side of the river, the tree of life with its twelve kinds of fruit, yielding its fruit each month. The leaves of the tree were for the healing of the nations. No longer will there be anything accursed, but the throne of God and of the Lamb will be in it, and His servants will worship Him. They will see His face, and His name will be on their foreheads.

We'll discuss the magnificent delights of this end-time water-picture more fully in Chapter 27. For now, notice God as the source of this river ("flowing from the throne of God"). Notice also the indescribable and perfect joy of living with God and in His pure, riverlike gush ("no longer will there be anything accursed"). The river-picture of heaven shows the full realization of God's perfect intention.

We live between these two rivers — between Eden and heaven. Part of God's purpose in giving us these bookend rivers is to convince us of the good that He intends to gush *toward* us and *for* us. It's our privilege as Christian voyagers to learn to abide as river dwellers via relationship with God in His hydrating gush. Though we will not have *total* hydration until we experience the God-river in heaven, we can still have *substantial* hydration here on earth by abiding in God, who remains a luxurious and constant river for our souls.

Daily "Planting"

As I've said previously, the summer of 2012 brought searing temperatures and drought to much of the Midwest, where I live. I remember one day that summer taking a walk in a riverless city park and noticing that the giant sycamore trees looked withered. They'd prematurely lost so many of their leaves that they looked the way they usually look in autumn. They were obviously distressed.

A week or two later I was walking in a different park — one by the Meramec River near my home. As I plodded along in the scorching heat, I was struck by the appearance of another sycamore tree. But this tree, having been planted by a still-flowing, nutrient-rich river, was vibrant, green, flourishing, and fruitful. There were no withered leaves on its branches. The contrast between this tree and the withered ones in the city reminded me of Jeremiah 17:7–8 (earlier in this chapter) and Psalm 1:3, below.

> He [one who delights in God] is like a tree
>   planted by streams of water
> that yields its fruit in its season,
>   and its leaf does not wither.
> In all that he does, he prospers.

The water-picture of God as a river suggests this question to Christians: Where are we "planting" ourselves daily? That is, where are we seeking the satisfaction of our supreme thirst (Chapter 4)? Fortunately, the drought of 2012 passed. And one Day for Christians, the grand, comprehensive drought caused by sin will end, too. But in the meantime, we get to experience substantial hydration by planting our hearts and minds intimately in God. Only in relationship with Him can we "feast on the abundance of [His] house, / and [receive] drink from the river of [His] delights" (Psalm 36:8).

Gushaholic's Prayer

God, forgive me for "uprooting" myself from You by disbelieving that You are a constant, luxurious River for my soul. Forgive me also for "planting" myself beside "rivers" that aren't rivers at all — by believing that they can provide what I thought You could not. Thank You for always extending Yourself like a luxuriously rich, heart-nourishing river to my thirsty soul. Help me to continually enjoy the benefits of being firmly planted in intimate relationship with You. Amen.

Gushercises

1. Explain something you learned or relearned about God from this water-picture.
2. How do you tend to "uproot" from God and "plant" yourself beside false rivers? Let your answer be part of your turning back to the God who, like an ever-flowing river, invites you to return to Him for hydration.
3. Wade through the waterlogged text of Ezekiel 47:1–12. Assume you're Ezekiel and the Lord is leading you through the same tour described in that text. Meditate on the rich biblical imagery, and then describe your experience as personally as possible.

Buoy IV

The God of Gush

We're making good progress on our voyage. So far, we've experienced and clarified our supreme thirst, heard God's lavish invitation to the thirsty, practiced returning to Him (repenting), and begun soaking in Him as He's described in some prominent biblical water-pictures.

Because the pivotal issue in the Christian voyage is knowing God as He truly is, we must *continue* soaking in Him. As we sail around Buoy IV, we'll learn more about God's gushing nature as it's revealed in some over-arching biblical themes, many of which form a long string of theological rainclouds that span both the Old and the New Testament. Like parched sailors, let's come above deck and let God's drenching character soak us all the way through to our hearts.

14

The God Who Gushes

> *⁹You visit the earth and water it;*
> *You greatly enrich it;*
> *the river of God is full of water;*
> *You provide their grain,*
> *for so You have prepared it.*
> *¹⁰You water its furrows abundantly,*
> *settling its ridges,*
> *softening it with showers,*
> *and blessing its growth.*
> *¹¹You crown the year with your bounty;*
> *Your wagon tracks overflow with abundance.*
> *¹²The pastures of the wilderness overflow,*
> *the hills gird themselves with joy,*
> *¹³the meadows clothe themselves with flocks,*
> *the valleys deck themselves with grain,*
> *they shout and sing together for joy.*
> Psalm 65:9–13

It's become popular in recent years for municipalities to build elaborate public water parks for the enjoyment of their citizens. In the summertime heat, these playgrounds are a wonderland of refreshing, watery delights. They're a veritable cornucopia of hydration, offering a creative assortment of heat-quenching happiness: water slides, lazy floating rivers, pools of various shapes and sizes, sprinklers, showers, and even a big bucket that occasionally tips over, drenching those beneath its lip. Children gladly spend all day at these water parks — slipping, sliding, splashing, diving, floating, swimming, and playing. It's a physical gush-fest that tends to produce gleeful hearts and minds.

Sopping soul-hydration that comes from continually believing in the God of Psalm 65, quoted at the beginning of this chapter, is the spiritual equivalent of the dripping body-hydration that comes from frolicking daily in one of these physical water parks. Use of the physical to point to the spiritual — a legitimate interpretive principle — presents our opulent God as One who gushes at us from every direction in order to ensure our souls' supreme well-being.[1] What's more, He *beckons* us to dive into Himself — to believe that He is, indeed, the God described in these verses. That's a main reason why He inspired David to write this psalm! God wants us to frolic by believing in the incredibly hydrating picture of Him as the Water Park Extraordinaire. So let's put on our spiritual bathing suits, poise ourselves for belief, and take the plunge.

Repentance and Nearness

In St. Louis, water parks provide relief from summertime heat. In the same way, the water park of Psalm 65 benefits only those who feel the spiritual "heat" and dehydration caused by our desert home, our dehydrating enemy, and our own sin. King David reveals that he's feeling this heat in Psalm 65:3. Though the details of his confession are unknown, it's possible that a drought — spiritual and physical — may have occurred as a result of the sins he admits. Like David, we must remember that our repentance doesn't merit God's gush of grace, mercy, and forgiveness. It does, however, open our hearts to experience all these reviving joys. So, like David, we need to once again turn away from our scorching false water parks and turn to our only *true* Water Park: God.

Immediately upon making this turn, the repentant Christian is doused by the first spray for his dry, cracking heart: God's nearness. This is the joy of pleasant relationship with God that causes David to say, "Blessed is the one You choose to bring near" (v. 4). It's a nearness that hydrates the soul. It's a nearness that says, "Yes, you sinned. But I still love you! I still gush toward you with my grace (i.e., unmerited favor, help, and affection), both personally and lavishly! I still want you to be with Me. I will not condemn you or reject you. In fact, I will bring you to My side where you can receive My forgiveness and healing."

God's happy nearness is the merriment-causing blessing that echoes throughout this psalm as indicated by the repeated use of "You" (i.e., God) to open many of the psalm's phrases. Verse 10 brims with this joy, exulting, "You water.... You settle.... You soften.... You bless." This main point is as clear as a water park is wet: God's primary blessing is glad nearness to Him. To see this preeminent truth is to see through each attraction at the water park (e.g., the big bucket) to appreciate the water itself as that which hydrates. To embrace this truth by faith is to recognize that it's God's personal, loving closeness to us — not the means He employs to bring Himself near — that makes the difference to our hearts.

The gushing nearness of God described in verse 4 also opens repentant Christians to experience the power of God that subdues chaos. Verse 7 points this out, using several water metaphors: "[It is God] who stills the roaring of the seas, / the roaring of their waves, / the tumult of the peoples." To grasp this verse's meaning, we need to understand that in biblical parlance, a roaring sea symbolizes anarchy and pandemonium. The word "roaring" and its repeated use signal intense mayhem, like the din caused by clashing armies. We all have felt this roaring, either spiritually or physically — or perhaps we have felt this roaring in both ways at the same time.

But God can subdue (*shabach*) all that bedlam. He can certainly do it physically by quelling life-threatening weather, subduing a rebellious teenager, removing an abusive boss, preventing a deadly fall, or eradicating a horrible disease. Jesus vividly demonstrates His power to *shabach* physical mayhem when He calms a wild sea in Luke 8:24.

> And [Jesus' disciples] went and woke Him, saying, "Master, Master, we are perishing!" And He awoke and rebuked the wind and the raging waves, and they ceased, and there was a calm.

It's even more likely that His nearness has brought a mysterious calm to your heart, despite continued chaos in your circumstances. In this sense, we recognize that God *shabachs* the most intense soul-chaos by — you guessed it — His happy nearness (verse 8). He often brings this inner soul-calm even when He permits external circumstances to continue to rage in our lives.

This is particularly true when persecutions flare against us as a result of our Christian convictions. The 1563 classic *Foxe's Book of Martyrs* records many inspiring instances of God's *shabach*-ing work in the hearts of His people. The account of Dr. Rowland Taylor, a parish clergyman in England who was tried and convicted of believing, living, and preaching the gospel, is one of many sobering examples. Like many in the sixteenth century who sealed their faith with their own blood, Dr. Taylor exhibited the internal soul-calming nearness of God amid the most severe circumstances.

> At the last they set to fire; and Dr. Taylor, holding up both his hands, called upon God, and said, "Merciful Father of heaven, for Jesus Christ my Savior's sake, receive my soul into Thy hands." So stood he still without either crying or moving, with his hands folded together, till Soyce with a halberd struck him on the head that the brains fell out, and the corpse fell into the fire.[2]

We should not be startled by the apparent extremity of this example. It showcases the same serenity produced by God's *shabach*-ing, soul-calming nearness displayed in Stephen's response to his stoning in Acts 7:54–60. Such stonings still take place today. They take many forms — from the literal killing of Christians in some countries to the verbal abuse from a coworker or family member who's offended by our beliefs. Whatever circumstantial stonings we face, we can be sure that God is still capable of *shabach*-ing our hearts by His nearness and love in the midst of them. This internal peace is just one of the many wonderful benefits of our relationship with the God of Psalm 65.

Water, Water Everywhere

We'll continue soaking in God by exploring His drenching lavishness as revealed in verses 9–13. Consider each word below, taken from these verses, to be like a water jet to our parched souls. Our hydration depends, in part, upon letting their rich meaning deeply impact our hearts.

We do this by believing that these words actually describe God and the way He blesses those near to Him. When we do believe, we may just find ourselves knocked off our spiritual feet, swimming with joy in the opulent goodness of our amazing God. So read the words slowly and trustingly, letting the gush of their spiritual water soak your soul. Remember: These words describe God's posture toward *you* as a Christian![3]

1. Visit (*paquad*): God pays attention to, and is concerned about, your well-being.
2. Enrich (*ashar*): He makes you spiritually wealthy.
3. Provide (*kun*): He gives you everything you need for spiritual hydration.
4. Prepare (*kun*): This is the same Hebrew word that is translated "provide" above. By repeating the verb, God adds His exclamation point to His actions. He *really* wants you to know that He *very* actively gives you all you need to stay spiritually healthy.
5. Water (*ravah*): God saturates or drenches you with spiritual nourishment.
6. Settle (*nacheth*): God robustly subdues your heart to receive His hydration. The NLT gets it right by rendering this phrase as "melting the clods." This image shows rain softening the dirt so that a field can receive seed.
7. Soften (*mug*): God dissolves your spiritual hardness so that you can receive His hydrating goodness. This idea works in concert with *nacheth*. Together, they amplify the fact that God works hard to make you ready to receive Him and His gush.
8. Bless (*barak*): God gives His authoritative approval to your spiritual well-being and confers His power and presence to ensure your hydration.
9. Crown (*atar*): God bestows royal honor on you by taking lavish care of your spirit.

Who or what else in this vast universe supports our spiritual well-being so gushingly? Nobody! Nothing! God — and God alone — is holistically concerned about us and provides for our soul's hydration. Belief that these actions describe God evokes our delight in Him. And in our delight, we're like the children who trustingly and enthusiastically give themselves over to the water's refreshment as experienced through the flume, slide, pool, and big bucket in the water park. The more the children immerse themselves in these activities, the more they're refreshed by the water that the various attractions were designed to deliver. By the end of the day, the kids may be prune-fingered, but they're also joyful and satisfied.

The meaning of the words themselves is only the first thing about this psalm that signals God's supremely hydrating capacity, however. The fact that they all exist in such tight proximity in one psalm enhances their power to thoroughly soak us in God. They show us that God isn't a water park with only one attraction or even with many attractions spread out over one hundred miles. He's an expansive Water Park that abounds with the most amazing hydration attractions in the world. Everywhere we turn, there's God working to satisfy our souls. He's inescapably hydrating to those who truly experience His nearness.

Another aspect of this list that enhances our experience of the God it describes is the water pressure with which the concepts are delivered. Four of these verbs (*water, settle, bless*, and *crown*) appear in the Hebrew text in their most robust form. God isn't just lazily watering our hearts. His settling power isn't just a trickle. No way! He's saturating, drenching, flooding, inundating, and soaking with great zeal and delight.

A third aspect that increases our hydrating experience of God in these verses is that many of the verbs describing His actions are modified to their superlative degree (we'll read more about our superlative God in the next chapter). He enriches the earth *greatly*; the river of God is *full* of water; He waters its furrows *abundantly*; He crowns the year with His *bounty*; His wagon tracks *overflow* with *abundance*. It's a veritable gushfest of God's opulent provision. God didn't *need* to add these modifiers. He did so because He really wants us to know that He's a gushing God toward those who continually repent and trust in Him.[4]

God intends that Psalm 65's gushfest cause joy to emanate from the core of our being — even to gush out so it's apparent to those around us. He paints several water-pictures in verses 11 through 13 that describe the effect of His nearness on those He loves (that's us, in Christ). He puts it this way in verse 11: "Your wagon tracks overflow with abundance" (or as the NASB renders it, "Your paths drip with fatness"). This is the image of a cart so loaded that its delightful cargo is spilling over, leaving a luxurious trail of blessing. We, fellow voyagers, are His "wagon tracks." As God makes His presence known in our hearts, good stuff pours off Him, causing us to overflow with spiritual richness!

In verse 12, God goes on to say that His nearness causes the wilderness to "drip." This simple word-picture confirms that God's presence turns the vast and previously barren expanses of our hearts into fields that sustain life and even support growth. This verdant result is explicitly described in verse 13, where God pictures lavish fields so covered in flocks and grain that they shout and sing for joy at the abundance. These rich images describe the results of a life lived in intimacy with the God who gushes spiritual goodness in epic proportions toward His people.

Just trying to comprehend and appreciate a God who gushes so richly and who causes such abundant joy may lead us to stagger and stutter in worship. The sheer intensity and density of these water pictures create a heart-quenching situation of mind-blowing proportions. Believing and experiencing these truths leads to spiritual ecstasy. These truths literally displace our other thoughts, or properly, "drive us out of our mind," as the literal meaning of the Greek root for ecstasy (*ekstasis*) indicates. When we experience God's nearness as He's described in all the elements of this psalm, it's appropriate for us to be delighted, awed, astonished, elated, thrilled, excited, pleased, and enraptured. Or — in one word — *hydrated*.

The Big Question

The big question in this chapter, as in many other chapters of this book, is about belief: Do we believe, *at this moment*, that God is the God of Psalm 65? Do we believe — in the midst of our hardness and skepticism — that God can *soften* and *settle* our hearts to receive Him as He truly is? Do we believe — despite our fears of being abandoned or forsaken — that He *visits* us to take care of us? Do we believe — against our glaring record of need and thirst — that He can and will *enrich*, *provide*, and *water* us with the forgiveness, love, security, and significance we crave?

All these are good questions that challenge our faith. God is so expansive and so lush and so hydrating that it's normal for us to have trouble embracing the wonder of who He is. Sometimes we're like eager children who've just entered a million-acre water park that's chock-full of the most amazing water attractions on the planet. God's sheer opulence may raise doubts and fears that actually keep us from diving in. "This is just too good to be true!" we may say under our breath, cowering on the side of the pool.

But it *is* true, dear children. God *really is* as gushing as Psalm 65 describes Him to be. Let's ask Him to help us take Him at His Word. To do that, let's pray a personalized version of Ephesians 3:14–19 from the New Jerusalem Bible. As you read it, make it your own.

> This, then, is what I pray, kneeling before You, Father, from whom every fatherhood, in heaven or on earth, takes its name. In the abundance of Your glory may You, through Your Spirit, enable me to grow firm in power with regard to my inner self, so that Christ may live in my heart through faith, and then, planted in love and built on love, with all Your holy people I will have the strength to grasp the breadth and the length, the height and the depth; so that, knowing the love of Christ, which is beyond knowledge, I may be filled with Your utter fullness.

Gushaholic's Prayer

Pray the prayer that God gave us through the apostle Paul in Ephesians 3:14–19 for yourself.

Gushercises

1. Do you believe, *at this moment*, that God is the God of Psalm 65? Why or why not?
2. Describe other word-pictures, besides a water park, that illustrate God's powerful and comprehensive gush toward you. Ideas: You as a mud-caked car and God as a car wash, or you as a food-encrusted plate and God as a dishwasher.

3. Create a piece of art (e.g., a photograph or a painting) that expresses the meaning of one or more words or images of Psalm 65. As you create it, focus on God, and let the whole process and the final product be an act of worship to Him.
4. How do the truths about God presented in this chapter make you feel?

15

Our Superlative God

*If He withholds the waters, they dry up;
if He sends them out, they overwhelm the land.* Job 12:15

Everybody loves superheroes. At least box office receipts would indicate so. Between 1978 and July 2011, sixty-four superhero movies grossed a total of $6.7 billion in the United States and $13.5 billion worldwide.[1] That's *billion* with a *b*! We've been inundated with *Batman, Superman, Spiderman*, the *Fantastic Four*, the *X-Men*, the *Incredibles, Iron Man, Thor, Captain America*, the *Green Lantern*, and more. What's the appeal, do you think? Cool costumes? Hairstyles that can hold up under Mach 1 speeds? The ability to spring to action at a moment's notice without first downing a double cappuccino?

As a culture, we're fascinated with excessive power coupled with virtue. We go to the theater again and again to see these superheroes use their "superpowers" for the good of ordinary schleps like you and me. To superheroes, this union of power and virtue is matter-of-fact. It's just who they are. In this way, every comic-book superhero that possesses extraordinary powers is a reflection of the ultimate Superhero: God.

The matter-of-fact power of God gushes from Job's rather blunt confession quoted at the beginning of this chapter. Job's statement acknowledges God's absolute power over the waters, where "waters" represents both chaos and vitality. This superlative essence of God, combined with His absolute goodness, brings voyagers like us tremendous joy and peace. We are, after all, the beloved objects of all God's superlatively good work in the world. In this chapter, we'll soak in the matchless aspects of the God who invites us to enjoy ongoing relationship with Him for the satisfaction of our supreme thirst.

Welcome to Superlative City

God is the ultimate Superhero — the ultimate Fount of infinite power and goodness. By definition, He's excessive and incomparable. He's also one hundred percent morally virtuous (i.e., holy). It's fitting, then, that we call God a *huperballo* hero, not just a *super* hero. This incomparably lofty title comes from the Greek word *huperballo* (pronounced hoop-er-*ball*-o). It's a *superlative*, which raises the word it's modifying to a degree that's "excellent, unmatched, unbeatable, untouchable, best, matchless, outstanding, exceptional, incomparable, without equal, unparalleled, beyond compare, top, consummate, unrivaled, supreme, unique, peerless."[2] *Huperballo* literally means "hyper-thrown." It's the fusion of two Greek words: *huper* ("hyper," or "over") and *ballo* ("throw"). The full Greek definition is to "throw over or beyond, excel in throwing; in the New Testament, as expressing a degree beyond comparison — go beyond, surpass all measure, go beyond all comprehension."[3]

God is the Superhero of superheroes. Superman is strong, but God is *huperballo* strong. Batman is vigilant, but God is *huperballo* vigilant. Spiderman is just, but God is *huperballo* just. Any superhero is virtuous and self-sacrificing on behalf of the weak, but God is *huperballo* virtuous and self-sacrificing. Whereas any superhero displays any truly good quality, God displays that quality perfectly and immeasurably.

Huperballo is used only five times in the Bible — each quoted below — and always with reference to the work or attributes of the *Huperballo* Hero toward Christians. The English rendering of the word, along with the word or words it's modifying, has been italicized. The information in brackets gives the context for these verses. Let's marvel at the superlative beauty of God's gush to us as Christians:

> Indeed, in this case, what once had glory [the Old Testament law code and sacrificial system] has come to have no glory at all, because of *the glory that surpasses it* [Christ, the fulfillment of the law and the last, perfect sacrifice for sin].
> 2 Corinthians 3:10

[I, Paul, pray that you may] know *the love of Christ that surpasses knowledge*, that you may be filled with all the fullness of God.
Ephesians 3:19

[One of the reasons God redeemed us in Christ is] so that in the coming ages He might show *the immeasurable riches of His grace* in kindness toward us in Christ Jesus. Ephesians 2:7

[Fellow believers outside Corinth glorify God] while they long for you and pray for you, because of *the surpassing grace of God* upon you. 2 Corinthians 9:14

[I, Paul, pray that you know] what is *the immeasurable greatness of His power* toward us who believe, according to the working of His great might that He worked in Christ when He raised Him from the dead and seated Him at His right hand in the heavenly places, far above all rule and authority and power and dominion, and above every name that is named, not only in this age but also in the one to come.
Ephesians 1:19–21

Huperballo Glory, Love, Grace, and Power

The four attributes of God highlighted as *huperballo* in these texts are His glory, love, grace, and power. As if we were examining Superman's superpowers, let's take a more specific look at exactly how these texts say that God is "excellent, unmatched, unbeatable, untouchable, best, matchless, outstanding, exceptional, incomparable, without equal, unparalleled, beyond compare, top, consummate, unrivaled, supreme, unique, and peerless."[4] If you want to have some hydrating fun, substitute some of the synonyms in these definitions for the original word in the verses above.

1. Glory (*doxa*): radiance, brightness, splendor, majesty, grandeur, power, honor
2. Love (*agape*): affection, benevolence, goodwill, concern, devotion

3. Grace (*charis*): favorable attitude, kindness, favor felt and displayed
4. Power (*dunamis*): strength, ability, faculty, might

If God is going to be *huperballo* in any four qualities, don't you agree that those are four of the best? Absolutely! Because He's *huperballo* in these ways, Christians can be sure that God will always and forever be able to abundantly satisfy our supreme thirst.

"Sippy-Cup" Christianity

God's *huperballo*-ness radically confronts our tendency toward what we could call "sippy-cup" Christianity. Sippy cups are cups we give to toddlers so they can get restricted sips of liquid and hopefully avoid a massive spill. We act like sippy-cup Christians when we sadly misperceive God's gush of glory, love, grace, and power as something He delivers in meager portions, thus causing us to take only teensy-weensy sips of it. "We'd better take just a little of God now and save some for tomorrow," we think to ourselves. "We don't want to use Him up." Those who feel extensively dehydrated and needy, who come from strict upbringings, or who dealt or deal with constant shortages in different aspects of life may struggle with this parching misconception.

The challenge for sippy-cup Christians is to believe that God is *huperballo* toward *them* in a spiritual/relational sense. This sets up a classic confrontation with the lies championed by our desert home, the devil and his minions, and our dehydrating flesh. Those parching enemies scream at us, "What? Are you *crazy*?! God can't really help you or forgive you or heal you. Sure, He's powerful, but He's not *that* powerful. Sure He's gracious, but He's not *that* gracious. What? Did you really think He's as opulent as that book *Gush* says He is? Get real!"

Lies!

Crying out to God and admitting our parching misconceptions of Him is a great way to open our hearts to His *huperballo*-ness and to destroy our sippy-cup delusions about Him. To help us do this, hear God's invitation from Psalm 81:10 — "Open your mouth wide, and I will fill it." Note the lavishness of the words "wide" and "fill." These aren't sippy-cup terms. They amount to a *huperballo* invitation from the *huper-*

ballo God, who undeniably possesses the superlative glory, love, grace, and power to completely forgive us of all our sins, endow us with indelible dignity, and provide us immeasurable relational security with Him in Christ forever and ever.

Niagara Falls

Niagara Falls, on the border between Ontario and New York, is 180 feet high. Experts tell us that during the wettest time of the year, six million cubic feet of water flow over the crest line (edge) of the Falls every minute at a rate of about thirty miles per hour. That's about a million bathtubs full of water every minute![5] Every day, enough water gushes over Niagara Falls to meet the water needs of all the households in the United States. This gush goes on day after day, year after year, and decade after decade. It has done so for centuries. Niagara Falls is truly a superlative, *huperballo* gush.

As stunning as those facts may be, experiencing the Falls firsthand is even more incredible. Perhaps my friend's description of his visit to the Falls will help us. Back in 2010, he boarded the famed *Maid of the Mist* Niagara Falls tour boat, which takes visitors very, very close to the Falls. His description of the event was vivid: "It was deafening. The water was boiling around us. There were waves ten feet tall. The sheer power — wow!" He continued with enthusiasm, "I've seen a few things in my life, but this was *amazing*."

Niagara Falls illustrates the *huperballo* gush of God flowing from His superlative glory, love, grace, and power. As we draw close to Him, God intends the magnitude of these truths to wash the ridiculous, sippy-cup images of Him out of our hearts. He wants the hands that were previously clinging to our paltry misconceptions to open and fly up with praise as we shout, "This God is *amazing*!" This is the movement from dehydration to hydration.

The essence of this movement is belief nourished by proximity. Just as it's easier to embrace the *huperballo*-ness of Niagara Falls when we're close to that marvel, so too is it easier to embrace God's *huperballo*-ness when we're close to Him. This once again takes us back to the core of God's desire for His people: intimate relationship with Him. And what a difference that closeness makes! In fact, as we bask in the *huperballo* beauty of God, we'll likely begin to experience several hydrating effects in our lives.

Our Response

We probably all agree that to truly come into contact with this *huperballo* God will affect us *somehow*. Actually soaking in relationship with God will deepen our experience of that relationship. Yet to try to describe the response to relationship with God is similar to trying to predict what someone might feel upon witnessing a sky-adorning meteor shower or a horizon-swallowing sunset. Not only is each person's experience personal and unique — each person's experience is likely to defy description. Still, it's helpful to articulate a few main aspects of our thoughts and feelings when we soak in relationship with God as the Ultimate Superhero.

First, we'll be awestruck. We'll feel awe, not just because God is so powerful, but also because He's so powerful *and so good* toward us *personally*. Knowing God in this way is likely to prompt an overwhelming combination of wonder and reverence that will leave us gladly breathless. This breathlessness is one of the purest forms of worship we can offer to God. To be gladly dumbfounded by who He is forms the essence of real adoration. It's the root of all the outward actions we typically associate with worship, including prayer, singing, dancing, lifting our hands, confessing, listening to His Word, crying, and bowing down.

Spontaneous astonishment with the *huperballo* nature of God is also one of the cleanest ways to break our fascination with desiccants and the vanity of this world. We'll find that nothing compares with the supernatural "high" of knowing this God. The more intimately we become acquainted with Him, the more sin will lose its appeal. Who yearns for the muddy glow of a streetlight after gazing upon a blazing, sky-filling sunset? Who longs to swim in a sewer after joyfully experiencing the ocean?

Regarding issues of the heart, we might ask a series of deeper questions. Who needs moment after moment of fleeting physical pleasure after imbibing God's *huperballo* glory? Who craves the approval of others after tasting the *huperballo* love of God? Who must have the forgiveness of *people* after gulping the *huperballo* grace of God? Who absolutely must be strong and in control after drinking the *huperballo* power of God? Each of these questions challenges us to ponder God's *huperballo*-ness and grow in astonished spiritual hydration.

Second, we'll be humbled. Prideful chest-pounding melts in the presence of this indescribably powerful God. We'll feel appropriately and joyfully small — the way we feel when walking through the Rocky Mountains or a forest of giant redwood trees. After all, who walks up to a 14,000-foot peak and says, "*I'm* the big deal around here!" No one who's sane, that's for sure. Better yet, our *huperballo* God isn't some towering, but impersonal, slab of rock. He's the personal *huperballo* God, whose power is measureless and who loves *His people* specifically and beyond comprehension.

Being humbled relieves us of our sinful and desiccating illusions of vain self-importance, control, power, and responsibility. It helps us gladly say, "It's good to be taken care of by God." This helps us relax in the face of challenges and hardships. "Why worry?" a God-soaked Christian can muse. "I'm small, yet beloved. My Father knows I'm weak. But He's not! And He loves me! So I know He'll exert His immeasurable power to protect and care for me. What a relief that I don't need to grab for control or personal grandeur."

Third, we can feel secure in our relationship with God. Knowing that God's love and grace are inexhaustible reduces the fear that He might leave us due to our occasional bouts with desiccant eating. Of course, we still hate our sin, as we should, and we still repent regularly throughout our Christian life. But we can feel relationally safe with God, and we can know that even our sinfulness won't weaken His love for us. *Huperballo* grace is *insurmountable* grace. And insurmountable grace means that nothing can separate us from the love of God, which is in Christ Jesus (Romans 8:39).

Instead of fearing that God will abandon us in our sin, we can imagine our sin as flaming pebbles that are easily engulfed by the watery deluge of Niagara Falls. This is the sense we get from 2 Corinthians 9:14, which reminds us that "the surpassing [*huperballo*] grace of God [is] upon [us]." The grace-glue bonding us to God is just too abundant and too strong. It's *huperballo* strong and abundant! We can't dissolve it. Nobody can. So we're secure in relationship with Him forever. Hallelujah!

Fourth, we can feel incredibly valued. This is one amazing *huperballo* God who loves us. Yes, *us*! Forget not being picked for the fourth-grade kickball team. Forget not being asked to the senior prom. Forget being passed over for that job or promotion. The *huperballo* God has chosen us in Christ! While we may grieve lesser, human rejections, their sting is washed away in the gush of being chosen and being loved by the most magnificent Person in the universe. The embrace of this King makes the frown of a peasant much less hurtful.

All these spiritual benefits are ours for the taking, fellow voyagers. God constantly gushes these things and invites us to soak in them, in Him. Our challenge is to repent by letting go of our sippy-cup misperceptions of God and embracing (i.e., saying "Yes" to) the God who is *huperballo*. This is our blessed privilege, not so that we're constantly re-saved, but so that we may continually re-experience the wonderful soul-hydration God offers our hearts in ongoing intimate relationship with Him through Christ.

Gushaholic's Prayer

God, You're amazing! I'm astonished by the *huperballo* nature of Your glory, love, grace, and power. Please help me let go of my sippy-cup misperceptions of You and embrace You as You truly are: *huperballo*! Thank You, Lord. Amen.

Gushercises

1. Explain the meaning of the word *huperballo*.
2. Describe the four attributes of God that are called *huperballo* in the Bible.
3. How do you demonstrate sippy-cup Christianity?
4. Describe how drawing close to God (as the *huperballo* God) can increasingly wash away your sippy-cup delusions about Him, and increase your heart's hydration.

16

God, the Gushing Rock

[And God said,] "Behold, I will stand before you there on the rock at Horeb, and you shall strike the rock, and water shall come out of it, and the people will drink." And Moses did so, in the sight of the elders of Israel. Exodus 17:6

As we've seen many times in this book, the Bible often uses physical images or events to illustrate spiritual truths. The verse above is part of an amazing physical story, related in Exodus 17:1–7, that has profound spiritual applications. This true and extraordinary account features God as the *huperballo* Hero who comprehensively quenches His people's thirst. In many English translations of the Bible, the word *gush* is frequently used to indicate God's action in this story.

To first grasp the story's physical meaning, let's replay the scene as if it's a black-and-white movie. Then we'll add color, and finally high definition 3-D, to the same movie to see the sharp, vivid, soul-nourishing details of its hydrating spiritual truths. As we watch, let's imagine that we see ourselves in the Israelite crowd. Let's draw biblically warranted parallels between this dramatic historic event and the spiritual reality of finding our supreme thirst increasingly quenched by God in Christ.

In Black and White

The movie starts with a blurry focus on the blazing sun, and pans to heat waves rising from a parched, desolate desert landscape. Then the picture slowly shifts to a massive dust cloud in the distance. Moving closer to the cloud, we see a rag-tag mob — over a million strong — of weary men, women, and children mingled with livestock and a multitude of beast-drawn wagons loaded with possessions. We get a wider picture of the situation through a slow-motion collage of images: a woman shielding her newborn from the hot desert sun, a man squeezing the last drops from a wineskin, a dehydrated grandmother lying limp on a lurching oxcart. The soundtrack is hollow and dry, including only sullen sounds of beasts groaning under their burdens, weary children crying, and wooden wagon wheels creaking.

As the horde stops to set up camp, we hear shouts in the distance. We find ourselves just outside Moses' tent, watching a growing throng of parched and angry people. "There's no water!" they shout, fists in the air. "You've brought us here to kill us!" Some pick up stones and roll them around in their hands, eager for their leader's blood.

A quick glimpse inside Moses' tent reveals a man facedown in the dust. Trembling, he pleads, "O Lord, what shall I do with these people? They're almost ready to stone me." His cries continue as the shouts outside increase. Finally he rises, resolute now that he has heard from the Lord. At this, the soundtrack shifts to a confident, yet subdued, symphonic melody. God, the Hero, has entered the scene.

The music picks up tempo as Moses bursts from his tent and makes his way through the miraculously quieted crowd. People look at each other with lingering anger and uneasiness. "What is he up to now?" they whisper to one another, some still gripping stones and others thumping their empty water jars with nervous anticipation. Finally, Moses, with several bearded, nervous elders, approaches a large rock. Facing the rock, he takes his staff in his hand, raises it above his head, and strikes the rock with violent force.

The blow echoes across the silent multitude. Nothing happens. A parching desert gust furls Moses' robes. The elders look at each other nervously. A desert jackal lets out a thin howl.

Then, with a sound like a peal of distant thunder, the ground begins to rumble and shake as the rock quakes spasmodically. Along a growing crack, large chunks of stone explode as if loosed by dynamite. The elders and others standing nearby quickly shield their eyes from the rocky projectiles. From this eye-shielded perspective, we see a rock strike a man's cloak, leaving what looks like a wet spot on it. With dazed curiosity the man lowers his drenched garment-clad arm, revealing a close-up of the stricken rock, which now has a growing number of water jets streaming from its cracks and holes. The strident springs continue to increase until, with a dramatic musical crescendo, a torrential geyser erupts from the fissure.

At first the crowd is too astonished to move. Then, as the massive gush surges out, some people cheer and shout. Others run to fetch water jars. Still others are happily swept away in the deluge God sent to hydrate the nation. People on the fringes dance or fling themselves into the flow, gulping and laughing. The scene ends with a lofty, God's-eye view of the refreshing flood spreading rapidly through the million-plus throng. Once again, God has watered His desperately thirsty people in opulent fashion.

Part of our response to the black-and-white version of this story is to acknowledge the lavish and gracious nature of God's provision. Just think about its opulence: enough pure water to hydrate over 1.2 million people and all their livestock in the middle of the desert! This is no trickle, folks. This is the Fountain (Chapter 9) gushing with sumptuous provision for His people. And let's not forget that God does all of this *despite* the people's (and often, our own) angry cries for blood and their grumbling against His chosen leaders.

Even this most basic version of God the Gushing Rock elicited praise from God's people for centuries after it happened. It's often referred to as a vivid example of God's unmerited kindness. Let's add our praise to these choruses before we move on to the color version of this hydrating story.

> He [God through Moses] struck the rock so that water
>   gushed out
> and streams overflowed.
> Can He also give bread
>   or provide meat for His people? Psalm 78:20

> He [God] opened the rock, and water gushed out;
>   it flowed through the desert like a river. Psalm 105:41

> They did not thirst when He led them through the deserts;
> He made water flow for them from the rock;
> He split the rock and the water gushed out. Isaiah 48:21

In Color

1 Corinthians 10:1–4, paraphrased below, colorizes the black-and-white scene we just considered. By adding pigment to Exodus's black-and-white *physical* facts, we begin to see the *spiritual* delights to which they point. We start to understand that God deluges us spiritually in Christ the Rock just as He deluged Moses and Israel materially by causing torrents of water to flow from a literal rock in the desert.

> I, the apostle Paul, want you fellow Christians to know that our spiritual fathers, the Israelites, "all drank the same spiritual drink. For they drank from the spiritual Rock that followed them, and the Rock was Christ."

These verses, like others in the New Testament, reveal that many stories and symbols in the Old Testament were "types" (i.e., foreshadowing illustrations) of Christ and His work. In this case, we see God connecting the gushing rock of Exodus 17:1–7 with the Incarnate Rock, Jesus Christ. He tells us that the physical gush from that scene points to the spiritual gush that comes to us through Christ.

As God's people suffered physical dehydration in a physical desert, we suffer spiritual dehydration in a spiritual desert. As the rock gushed physical water to their bodies, Christ gushes spiritual water to our souls. As God's people drank from the superabundant water that poured from the physical rock, we drink from the opulent spiritual water that pours from the spiritual Rock, Christ. In both cases, the supply was/is opulent, and the satisfaction received by enjoying that supply is opulent, too.

Though not explicitly mentioned in 1 Corinthians 10, there's deep spiritual significance in the fact that God instructed Moses to "strike" the rock to cause water to gush out. The spiritual meaning of that action finds a strong thematic parallel in God's plan to strike Jesus for our spiritual nourishment. The colorization of this black-and-white truth takes place in Isaiah 53:4–6 and 10–11.

Surely He [Christ] has borne our griefs
    and carried our sorrows;
yet we esteemed Him stricken,
    smitten by God, and afflicted.
But He was wounded for our transgressions;
    He was crushed for our iniquities;
upon Him was the chastisement that brought us peace,
    and with His stripes we are healed.
All we like sheep have gone astray;
    we have turned every one to his own way;
and the LORD has laid on Him
    the iniquity of us all....
Yet it was the will of the LORD to crush Him;
    He has put Him to grief;
when His soul makes an offering for sin,
    He shall see His offspring; He shall prolong His days;
the will of the LORD shall prosper in His hand.
Out of the anguish of His soul He shall see and be satisfied;
by His knowledge shall the Righteous One, My Servant,
    make many to be accounted righteous,
    and He shall bear their iniquities.

Jesus, the Incarnate Rock, was struck just as Moses' physical rock was struck — at God's command. In Jesus' case, the blow consisted of His being humiliated, beaten, and crucified to pay the penalty we deserved for our sins. In Isaiah 50:6, Jesus' response to this striking is envisioned before it actually happened: "I gave My back to those who strike, / and My cheeks to those who pull out the beard; / I hid not My face / from disgrace and spitting." Jesus knew He'd be struck before it ever took place, and He willingly embraced His Father's plan to accomplish our salvation and subsequent hydration. In fact, Jesus refers to Zechariah 13:7 in Matthew 26:31 just before being struck to open the gush of God for His people.

The color version of the Incarnate Rock's being struck is much more graphic and lengthy than is its black-and-white counterpart in the Old Testament. The Old Testament allusion is described in just one verse (Exodus 17:6), while the New Testament version is told in full color and in multiple chapters in all four Gospels. Here are a few verses from the color version. (Note that "He" and "Him" in these texts refer to Jesus. Emphasis added.)

> When He had said these things, one of the officers standing by *struck* Jesus with his hand, saying, "Is that how You answer the high priest?" John 18:22

> Then Pilate took Jesus and flogged Him. And the soldiers twisted together a crown of thorns and put it on His head and arrayed Him in a purple robe. They came up to Him, saying, "Hail, King of the Jews!" and *struck* Him with their hands. John 19:1–3

> Then they spit in His face and *struck* Him. And some slapped Him, saying, "Prophesy to us, you Christ! Who is it that *struck* You?" Matthew 26:67–68

> And they spit on Him and took the reed and *struck* Him on the head. And when they had mocked Him, they stripped Him of the robe and put His own clothes on Him and led Him away to crucify Him. Matthew 27:30–31

In High Definition 3-D

The striking of Jesus culminates in His crucifixion and death. This is where the Bible moves us past the black-and-white scene of Exodus 17 and past the color scene of 1 Corinthians 10 to the high definition, 3-D scene of Mark 15:33–34, 37.

> And when the sixth hour had come, there was darkness over the whole land until the ninth hour. And at the ninth hour Jesus cried with a loud voice, *"Eloi, Eloi, lema sabachthani?"* which means, "My God, My God, why have you forsaken Me?" … And Jesus uttered a loud cry and breathed His last.

In these words, Jesus, the Rock, testifies to the agony of being struck by His Father as payment for the sins of God's thirsty, sin-wracked people. God's judgment of those sins is depicted by darkness coming over the whole land. Jesus was struck as His Father's fury for our sins replaced His loving, gracious posture toward His Son for the only time in all eternity. Jesus was struck with a blow so spiritually and physically violent that all words fail to describe it. At the end of that excruciating hit, Jesus died, causing the torrential spiritual gush of God's grace and mercy to burst forth from the Rock Incarnate.

Isaiah 53:5, Mark 15:38, and John 19:34 — passages from both the Old and the New Testament — refer to the torrential flood of forgiveness, grace, and mercy that became available to us, through relationship with God, because the Rock (Christ) was struck in payment for our sins. It's a spiritual gush that's pictured by the physical gush in Exodus 17. In the color, high definition, 3-D clarity of the New Testament, we see that it's all about Jesus Christ! He's the Rock! He was struck! He gushes! And it's through faith in Him and in His being struck for our sins that we receive His forgiveness and can eternally soak in the God who gushes!

Soaking in Silence

Have you ever watched a movie so powerful that you just sat motionless in your seat after it ended? Mel Gibson's *The Passion of the Christ* was like that for me and for many of my friends. When it was released in 2004, I took a group to see that movie. We prepared for it beforehand, and planned to discuss it afterward. But our discussion had to wait, because after the final credits, we all just sat there — astonished.

In that film, Jesus Christ the Rock was struck with staggering cinematic clarity (i.e., the movie was rated R for violence). It was all there — the betrayal, arrest, beatings, disfigurement, mocking, scourging, blood, black eyes, humiliation, sweat, crucifixion, and death. The curtain was torn in two (Mark 15:38). A soldier pierced Jesus' side after His death so that water and blood gushed from it (John 19:34). With unparalleled clarity, Christian viewers understood in a new way how Jesus "was wounded for our transgressions; / He was crushed for our iniquities; /

upon Him was the chastisement that brought us peace, / and with His stripes we are healed" (Isaiah 53:5).

We must soak in these truths, friends — silently if need be. Living as hydrated Christians means that, one way or another, we constantly allow ourselves to be ravished by the high-definition, 3-D version of the Rock, stricken, then gushing. To soak in these truths is to revisit them, ponder them, marvel at them, and above all, *believe* them. Just as physical exercise strengthens our muscles, this spiritual activity strengthens our faith. We must constantly exercise our faith by "picking up" these truths and (re)affirming the picture of God painted in this story.

Our "work" of faith — to believe the amazing truths we've examined in this chapter — can be bolstered by acknowledging our thirst as we did around Buoy II. This is the spiritual parallel to placing ourselves in the dusty, ravaged Israelite rabble tromping through the desert. Let's stand before the Rock with our spiritual tongues sticking to the roofs of our mouths, eager for His gush to erupt. Let's bring all our deepest needs — for forgiveness, intimacy, meaning, value, and love — to be filled by the One who was struck for our hydration.

Gushaholic's Prayer

Incarnate Rock, thank You for Your willingness to be struck for me! I marvel at Your sacrifice, and I worship You for the gush Your sacrifice brings. Please hydrate my heart with You as You are described by these truths. Amen.

Gushercises

1. How can you regularly exercise your faith by "picking up" and reaffirming the truths presented in this chapter?
2. Create a work of art (e.g., a song or a drawing) that ponders and/or explains any part of the scenes we've discussed in this chapter. As you create, consider your own response to the fact that God gushes toward you through the Stricken Rock, Christ.
3. In the next week or so, read all four Gospel accounts of Jesus' being struck (Matthew 26–27, Mark 14–15, Luke 22–23, John 18–19). Journal your thoughts and feelings.

17

Being God's Beloved, Part I

For the LORD takes pleasure in His people. Psalm 149:4a

Do you feel special? Wanted? Valued? Rejoiced over? At peace with God despite your sin? Forgiven? Happy in relationship with Him? What do you depend upon to experience these ultimate joys in your heart and mind on a daily basis?

Hopefully, we're beginning to see that voyagers like us (Christians who turn from their sin and receive Christ as their Lord and Savior; see Appendix A) must go directly and only to God Himself to satisfy all these facets of our supreme thirst. We've seen that God constantly and lavishly offers Himself to us through faith in Christ, and He rambunctiously invites us to enjoy ongoing, soul-hydrating relationship with Him. In the next two chapters, we'll dive more deeply into this blessed lifestyle by swimming in the sparkling, pure, unfathomably deep blue sea of our divine belovedness as Christians.

If there were a soundtrack to the theme of our belovedness, it might be God singing "I Only Have Eyes for You." This song has delighted listeners since it was written in 1934 by composer Harry Warren and lyricist Al Dubin. It has been recorded by many artists, including Al Jolson, Frank Sinatra, Ella Fitzgerald, Billie Holliday, Art Garfunkel, and Bette Midler. Its popularity is likely due to its gushing theme: belovedness. And while the writers and various artists who've covered the song were probably singing of mere human love, the lyrics can also be redemptively interpreted as a beautiful rendition of God's smitten-ness for His beloved people in Christ.

> My love must be a kind of blind love.
> I can't see anyone but you.
>
> Are the stars out tonight?
> I don't know if it's cloudy or bright.
> I only have eyes for you, dear.
>
> The moon may be high.
> But I can't see a thing in the sky.
> 'Cause I only have eyes for you.
>
> I don't know if we're in a garden.
> Or on a crowded avenue.
> You are here. So am I.
>
> Maybe millions of people go by.
> But they all disappear from view.
> And I only have eyes for you.[1]

Of course, it isn't as if God *can't* see anyone else in the world. It isn't that He doesn't know the weather, can't see anything else in the sky, or doesn't know His proximity to gardens, avenues, or crowds. The quintessentially hydrating truth is that He *gladly chooses* to see His people — both corporately and individually — as the special objects of His love. We Christians are unique in this way. Because of Christ, God is smitten with each one of us! It's almost embarrassing how much God loves us. He doesn't want us to be embarrassed by His love, though. Instead, He wants us to embrace it and experience the heights of hydration. His passionate love for us is so important to Him that He repeats it over and over in the Bible.

Let Us Count the Ways

In Psalm 149:4, quoted at the beginning of this chapter, God says quite bluntly that He "takes pleasure in His people." Did we get that? It means that God is happy, satisfied, and gratified with us. It's a word heavy with positive emotion. God *feels* pleasure, even *delight*, at the thought of us. He also calls us His "treasured possession" in several places, including Exodus 19:5, Deuteronomy 7:6 and 26:18, and Deuteronomy 14:2, quoted below:

> For you are a people holy to the LORD your God, and the LORD has chosen you to be a people for his treasured possession, out of all the peoples who are on the face of the earth.

Being "treasured" means that God considers us precious, prized, dear, exquisite, and priceless. The NLT helpfully renders the phrase as "He has chosen you to be His own special treasure." As if that weren't enough, God amplifies our value at the end of the verse by clarifying that He selected us "out of all the people who are on the face of the earth." As we mused in Chapter 5, God is like Blake Remington zeroing in on Sally Mae Pew out of all the other people in the gymnasium. Only in God's case, it isn't a bunch of high schoolers in a gym; it's everybody who has ever lived, lives now, or will live in the future. Wow! *You* are so treasured by God.

Do you remember what it was like to get picked from two dozen fifth graders at your elementary school to be on the kickball team? Did that make you feel special? If it did, then just soak in the radically sweet idea that from among everyone in the *whole world,* the God of the Universe picked *you* to be with Him as a cherished son or daughter *forever!* Can being picked by anyone else from any other crowd for any other honor ever compare to this extraordinary privilege? Nothing else could even come close!

Or maybe you remember *not* being picked for the kickball team. Maybe you grew up feeling rejected or insignificant. In that case, it might be very difficult for you to enjoy the gush of God's choosing you and calling you His "treasured possession." Perhaps the label "worthless" has hardened your heart to this truth the way too much dirt clogs the pores of a sponge, keeping it from soaking up water. Maybe the world, the devil, and your own flesh compact that dirt by whispering, "*You?* You've *got* to be kidding! Why would anybody — let alone God! — pick *you* for such a lavish honor?"

Those are lies! If you're a Christian, God considers you His special treasure. He says so Himself. Our ability to enjoy this magnificent *fact* is at the heart of our lives as Christians. Remember: God seeks parched people — even parched people who have a *hard time* believing He considers them precious (Chapter 6). Our battle is one of faith. God yearns for us to believe on a daily basis that we are who He says we are: His beloved. God's declaration is rightly paraphrased this way in Romans 12 by *The Message* (a biblical paraphrase): "The only accurate way to understand ourselves is by what God is and by what He does for us, not by what we are and what we do for Him" (v. 3).

God reiterates His exuberance over us in texts like Deuteronomy 7:7 and 10:15, in which He says that He "set His love" on us. Once again, God expresses His gladness at attaching Himself to us. He *wants* to be joined to us. He associates pleasure with His choice in 1 Samuel 12:22, "Because it has pleased the LORD to make you a people for Himself." This theme is picked up and intensified in the New Testament in Ephesians 1:3–10. Verses 4 through 6 are quoted below with emphasis added to highlight God's delight in choosing us:

> For He [God the Father] chose us in Him [Christ, the Son] before the creation of the world to be holy and blameless in His sight. *In love* He predestined us to be adopted as His sons through Jesus Christ, in accordance with *His pleasure and will* — to the praise of His glorious grace, which He has freely given us in the One He loves (NIV).

This passage overflows with God's bliss over us and over His decision to adopt us. One way He emphasizes this is by using the Greek word *eudokia* in verses 5 and 9. It expresses a "feeling of strong emotion in favor of something."[2] In layman's terms, this means that God *really* enjoyed choosing us. You could say that God had a smile on His face and a song in His heart when He chose us! Actually, God says this exact thing when reflecting on His love for His people in Zephaniah 3:17.

> The LORD your God is in your midst,
>   a Mighty One who will save;

> He will rejoice over you with gladness;
>   He will quiet you by his love;
> He will exult over you with loud singing.

In this light, it's easy to accept the fact that God freely and lavishly gives us the things He lists in Ephesians 1:3–7: every spiritual blessing, holiness, blamelessness, predestination to adoption, His glorious grace, redemption, and forgiveness. Jesus, too, states this idea plainly, in Luke 12:32 — "Fear not, little flock, for it is your Father's good pleasure [*eudokia*] to give you the kingdom."

Beloved

Have you ever been near a disgustingly in-love couple that rubs noses and calls each other syrupy pet names? "Oh, pumpkin muffin," one says. The other coos, "Yes, sweet boopsie?" "Can you please rub my nose some more, smootchums sugar bear?"

Well, God's pet name is even more intense, while also being devoid of infatuated, unthinking sentimentality. It's "beloved ones." That's right. God is so enthralled with us that His Holy Spirit refers to us this way through every single inspired New Testament letter writer. The actual word is *agapetoi* (and its linguistic cousins). It means "those who are 'beloved, dear, very much loved not only with a great love, but with a unique love, one in a unique class of love.'"[3] That's *us*, beloved! God calls us His "beloved ones" at least thirty-seven times in the New Testament letters.

1. Paul's letters: Romans 9:25, 11:28, 12:19; 1 Corinthians 4:14, 10:14, 15:58; 2 Corinthians 7:1, 12:19; Ephesians 5:1; Philippians 2:12, 4:1; Colossians 3:12; 2 Thessalonians 2:13; 1 Timothy 6:2
2. James's letter: James 1:16, 1:19, 2:5
3. Peter's letters: 1 Peter 2:11, 4:12; 2 Peter 3:1, 3:8, 3:14, 3:17
4. John's letters: 1 John 2:7, 3:2, 3:21, 4:1, 4:7, 4:11; 3 John, verses 2, 5, 11
5. Jude's letter: verses 1, 3, 17, 20

6. The letter to the Hebrews (unknown human author, yet same divine Author as the letters listed above): Hebrews 6:9

Can we Christians believe the supremely hydrating fact that God has declared us His beloved ones in Christ? Can we believe it *daily*? It's quite natural to blush at this idea. It might even make us squirm. Those with a history of abuse or victimization might feel downright sick. But it's true, beloved. It's true. This is God's name for Christians. So if you're a Christian, it's His name for *you*. (If you're not sure you're a Christian, see Appendix A right now!)

God wants us to root our sense of value in this divinely declared name. He wants us to form our identity around it. He wants us to measure all else in life, including life's ups and downs, by this supreme "up." He wants us, in so doing, to experience the stability of heart that comes from being indelibly declared His beloved. Like a delighted starfish, we're to cling to the immovable piling of God's love for us as His beloved ones in Christ. We do this even as God secures Himself to us by His own divine power in Christ.

Early Christians were so steeped in their identity as God's beloved that many of the New Testament letter writers greeted or referred to Christian friends by that title. The apostle Paul calls the following believers "beloved": Tychicus (Ephesians 6:21, Colossians 4:7), Luke (Colossians 4:14), Epaenetus (Romans 16:5), Ampliatus (Romans 16:8), Epaphras (Colossians 1:7), Onesimus (Colossians 4:9, Philemon 1:16), Philemon (Philemon 1:1), Stachys (Romans 16:9), Persis (Romans 16:12), and Timothy (1 Corinthians 4:17, 2 Timothy 1:2). John calls Gaius "beloved" in 3 John, verses 1, 2, 5, and 11. Peter calls Paul "our beloved brother" in 2 Peter 3:15.

As modern Christians, we can add our names to that list, beloved. Through faith in Christ, we're loved by God as dearly and as uniquely as any of those listed above. When Paul, James, Peter, John, and Jude wrote to God's "beloved," their greeting includes us as modern-day believers in Jesus Christ!

So let's revisit the questions we asked at the beginning of this chapter. Do you feel special? Wanted? Valued? Rejoiced over? At peace with

God despite your sin? Forgiven? Happy in relationship with Him? What do you depend upon to experience these ultimate joys in your heart and mind on a daily basis? As we've seen in this chapter, you must depend on God's declaration of your belovedness in Christ, fellow Christian!

The truth is, we *are* special, wanted, valued, and rejoiced over. The only real question is whether we believe daily what God has declared about us in Christ. As we soak in the stupendous truth that God looks upon us as His beloved, we might be inclined to whisper to our own hearts, "I get it, but how can I remain God's 'beloved' when I still occasionally sin and do bad things? I get the idea that I'm beloved because God's declared it, but how can He declare it when my moral performance fluctuates so much?" Those are great questions! In the next chapter, we'll explore the answers — much to our delight and in praise of the God who calls us His beloved.

Gushaholic's Prayer

Thank You, Lord, for declaring me Your beloved in Christ! I love this name! Please help me to believe that I am who You've declared me to be. Amen.

Gushercises

1. What has happened or is happening in your life that's keeping you from resting in God's declaration that you're His "treasured possession"?
2. How can you expose your heart to the lavish, heart-nourishing truth of your divine belovedness on a daily basis?
3. Spend some time praising and thanking God for so clearly and frequently repeating the wonderful assertion about who you are in Christ.

18

Being God's Beloved, Part II

He has blessed us in The Beloved. Ephesians 1:6b

The truth is that we Christians often don't look, feel, or act like God's beloved. We definitely don't merit this title by our own behavior, either in modeling virtue or in avoiding vice. The world, the devil, and our own desiccating flesh are quick and relentless about pointing this out. So how and why can God, the Great Knower of All Things, continually call us His beloved? How can He not revoke that declaration every time we sin, or at least when we commit "big sins"?[1]

The wonderful answer is that our belovedness is a gift from God through Christ throughout the Christian life. Belovedness never was and never will be a result of anything in us, anything done by us, or anything *not* done by us. It's given to us by God because of our union with Christ, who's The Beloved One. Because God calls Jesus *The* Beloved One, and because we're united to Jesus by faith, God also calls us His beloved ones. We're beloved, because Jesus is The Beloved and the Bible says we're "in Him."

We can be sure that Jesus Christ really was and is The Beloved of God.[2] His Father publicly declared it at least two times during Jesus' public ministry: at Jesus' baptism (Matthew 3:17) and at His Transfiguration (Matthew 17:5). The declaration was "This is My Beloved Son, with whom I am well pleased." There's no doubt that Jesus was and is the apple of God's eye. And "in Him," we are, too. In fact, it's reasonable and necessary for us to embrace the idea that God's declaration over His Son is also His declaration over us, since we're "in Him." We embrace this idea by believing it's true, resting our hearts on it, and acting on it in our lives.

The idea of receiving benefits based on our relationship with another shows up various places in everyday life. For example, suppose Dave works for a company that provides health insurance to its employees. Dave obviously receives that insurance. He gets it as an employee of the company. But suppose that Dave's family also receives health insurance from the company, even though none of *them* are employees of the company. The family receives health insurance only because of their familial relationship to Dave, their husband/dad. Because they're "in Dave" (i.e., "in relationship or family union with Dave"), the health insurance that he gets comes to them as a "gift."

Our "benefit" of belovedness works the same way. Christ gets the title "The Beloved One" and its benefits, because He is the only begotten Son of God. We Christians receive our belovedness and its benefits only because of our association with Christ, our Savior and Lord. Because we're "in Christ" (i.e., "in relationship or family union with Christ"), we receive as a true gift the title and benefits that He possesses because of His position as God's Son.

Unlike Dave's family members' receiving health insurance, however, our belovedness in Christ is a sheer gift; it requires no "payment" from us in any way. It can't be earned or deserved by anything we do. While it's true that faith is necessary to be "in Christ," even that faith isn't earned or deserved; it doesn't depend on our words or deeds. You could say that Christ paid the price, including the copay and all other necessary contributions, required for us to receive the title of God's beloved ones and all the accompanying benefits. He did this by living a perfect life and by giving His life on the cross as the payment for our sins so that we could be reconciled to God (Matthew 5:17; Romans 3:21–26, 8:3–4; Galatians 2:20; Hebrews 2:17; and 1 John 4:10).

A Gushing List of "Benefits"

For our increased hydration as God's beloved, let's soak in the benefits we receive as signaled by the phrase "in Christ" (*en Christo* in Greek) in the New Testament. That phrase is used by God seventy-six times to saturate us with joy in our relationship with Christ. It signals that we receive benefits from God because of our relational link to Him through Christ, much as Dave's family receives various health insurance benefits because of their relational link to the company through Dave. The question that shines over each individual item, and the list as a whole, is this: Do we believe, rest, and act upon what God has declared over us in Christ? With that question in mind, consider that as beloved ones through faith in Christ, we are …

1. redeemed by God in Christ (Romans 3:24)
2. alive to God in Christ (Romans 6:11)
3. recipients of eternal life in Christ (Romans 6:23; 2 Timothy 1:1)
4. freed from God's condemnation in Christ (Romans 8:1)
5. set free in Christ from having to earn God's favor by keeping God's law (Romans 8:2; Galatians 2:4)
6. inseparable from God's love in Christ (Romans 8:35–39)
7. one with other Christians in Christ (Romans 12:5; Galatians 3:28)
8. sanctified, or cleansed, in Christ (1 Corinthians 1:2)
9. given God's grace (unmerited favor) in Christ (1 Corinthians 1:4)
10. given whole life (material/immaterial) in Christ (1 Corinthians 1:30, 15:22)
11. given wisdom in Christ (1 Corinthians 1:30, 1 Corinthians 4:10)
12. received by God at death in Christ (1 Corinthians 15:18; 1 Thessalonians 4:16)
13. led by God in Christ (2 Corinthians 2:14)
14. new, redeemed spiritual creatures in Christ (2 Corinthians 5:17)
15. reconciled to God in Christ (2 Corinthians 5:19)
16. justified (declared righteous) by God through faith in Christ (Galatians 2:16; Philippians 3:9)
17. recipients of God's rich blessings and promises in Christ (Galatians 3:14; Ephesians 1:3, 2:7, 3:6)

18. adopted as beloved sons and daughters of God in Christ (Galatians 3:26)
19. given God's immeasurable riches of His grace and kindness toward us in Christ (Ephesians 2:7)
20. created in Christ Jesus for good works (Ephesians 2:10)
21. brought near to God in Christ (Ephesians 2:13)
22. chosen to be loved and redeemed by God in Christ (Ephesians 3:11)
23. conduits of God's glory through all generations in Christ (Ephesians 3:21)
24. encouraged in Christ (Philippians 2:1)
25. given God's mind, especially that which produces humility, in Christ (Philippians 2:5)
26. encouraged to gladly give up on trying to earn God's love in Christ (Philippians 3:3)
27. beckoned to reflect God's pure and virtuous life in Christ (Philippians 3:14)
28. guarded in heart and mind in Christ (Philippians 4:7)
29. supplied in all our true needs in Christ (Philippians 4:19)
30. exhorted to give thanks to God in all circumstances in Christ (1 Thessalonians 5:18)
31. recipients of God's grace and power in Christ (1 Timothy 1:14; 2 Timothy 1:9)
32. recipients of faith and love in Christ (2 Timothy 1:13)
33. strengthened by grace in Christ (2 Timothy 2:1)
34. saved and made wise for salvation through faith in Christ (2 Timothy 2:10, 3:15)
35. called to eternal glory in Christ (1 Peter 5:10)

This isn't your general list of dental, vision, and overall health benefits, fellow voyagers! There's no other list like this list! It is, to coin a new term, "gushalicious!" I know that lists in books can sometimes seem boring. But I urge us to slowly ponder the opulent nature of what this list describes. Truly resting in any single one of these items can cause our hearts to sing. Taken together, there's no end to the joy, praise, and peace we might experience. Embracing this list by faith is enough to launch our hearts into hydrated ecstasy! This reminds us that God consistently asks, for our own ongoing hydration, if we believe that we are His beloved in Christ.

Sealed in Christ

Because we live in a world where nothing seems permanent, the indelibility, or permanence, of God's declaration may make that declaration especially hard to believe and enjoy. Who, after all, loves us unchangeably? What good thing truly lasts? "Certainly not God and His declaration of love!" say the world, the devil, and our own desiccating flesh. Well, stand firm, fellow Christians, because here comes another nourishing gush: God's declaration of our belovedness in Christ is completely irrevocable.

This is another huge difference between being connected to Dave and being connected to Christ. In Christ, nothing — not even our death — can void our belovedness in Him. Our belovedness and the benefits that come from it in Christ are infinite, eternal, and indestructible. Here's how God puts it in 1 Peter 1:3–5.

> Blessed be the God and Father of our Lord Jesus Christ! According to His great mercy, He has caused us to be born again to a living hope through the resurrection of Jesus Christ from the dead, to an inheritance that is imperishable, undefiled, and unfading, kept in heaven for you, who by God's power are being guarded through faith for a salvation ready to be revealed in the last time.

And here's another amazing prooftext for this truth, from Ephesians 1:13–14.

> In Him [Christ] you also, when you heard the word of truth, the gospel of your salvation, and believed in Him, were sealed with the promised Holy Spirit, who is the guarantee of our inheritance until we acquire possession of it, to the praise of His glory.

The Greek word for "sealed" in Ephesians is *sphragizo*, which means "to secure, confirm, authenticate, hide, place beyond doubt, or signify ownership." It hearkens to a time when people sealed letters by pressing a signet ring into melted wax. Its Greek grammatical form (aorist indicative passive) tells us that God does the sealing when we trust in Christ. So once sealed in Christ by God, we can never be unsealed. No person or thing can break this seal — not the world, not the devil, not even our own flesh. Our belovedness in Christ is permanent, fellow voyagers!

There are many places where God reminds us that His declaration of our belovedness, our eternal life, and our adoption in Christ is everlasting. Believing these verses and resting our souls upon them will help us guard our hearts from destructive doubts about God's love and about His goodness toward us. This belief is especially important in the wake of our own sin — when we tend to (erroneously) think that we may somehow have forfeited our belovedness. When we sin, our enemies (the world, the devil, and our own flesh) may be more likely to attack our belief in God in general and our belief in our eternal belovedness in particular.

> I give them eternal life, and they will never perish, and no one will snatch them out of My hand. John 10:28
>
> As the Father has loved Me, so have I loved you. Abide in My love. John 15:9
>
> There is therefore now no condemnation for those who are in Christ Jesus. Romans 8:1
>
> For I am sure that neither death nor life, nor angels nor rulers, nor things present nor things to come, nor powers, nor height nor depth, nor anything else in all creation, will be able to separate us from the love of God in Christ Jesus our Lord. Romans 8:38–39
>
> He [God] has said, "I will never leave you nor forsake you." Hebrews 13:5b, quoting Deuteronomy 31:6, 8

It's no wonder that God's people throughout the ages, upon experiencing their rock-solid belovedness to God, have been compelled to spontaneous acts of joyful praise. Passages like Psalm 100 and Ephesians 3:14–21 are two among hundreds of great examples. When we believe these unrivaled truths, it's entirely appropriate for us to gleefully erupt with the apostle John as he affirms our belovedness in Christ with this excited declaration:

> How great is the love the Father has lavished on us, that we should be called children of God! And that is what we are!
> 1 John 3:1a (NIV)

Living as God's Beloved

For many people, the experience of being God's beloved — and of the resulting joy — remain elusive at best. This may be particularly true for those who've been victims of abuse or betrayal — or among those who had emotionally cold or absent parents. It may also be true for those whose lives and accomplishments have been devalued or minimized. It's beyond the scope of this book to deal comprehensively with such wounds. However, here are some basics to help us all soak in the gush of our belovedness to God and to move toward healing, if healing is needed.

First, know that it's completely normal for all Christians to fluctuate in embracing and enjoying the gush of our belovedness. *Uninterrupted* awareness of our unique status as objects of God's special love awaits us in heaven. Recognizing that in this life we won't always be aware of God's love for us keeps us from setting unrealistic expectations for our feelings — and being repeatedly disappointed. Forgetting that fluctuation is normal sets us up for heartache, since our hopes will constantly be dashed by reality. We're leaky pots in this life (2 Corinthians 4:7), which means that we can't perfectly contain such exhilarating truths. Instead of letting that idea depress us, we can let it set us free from the tyranny of impossible standards.

Second, we must avoid letting our subjective experience of our belovedness displace our assurance of the objective reality of our belovedness. Oftentimes we can *feel* unloved (subjective experience) by God when, in fact, we *are* loved (objective fact) by Him. Our belovedness in Christ is noncontingent; it doesn't depend upon our acknowledgment, or even our perception, of His love. His love for those in Christ is an absolute fact; our experience of it is not. The objective solidity of God's declaration should be to us like the North Star — a permanent fixture to which we refer and by which we navigate in the changing seas of our emotional life.

Third, it's good to acknowledge that the enemy works hard to steal our joy as God's beloved. The world, the devil, and our own flesh know they can gain a major foothold by duping us into believing that we're no longer secure in God's love. They know that this basic belief is the foundation of our Christian life. So expect fiery darts designed to elicit doubt and fear in this regard. Know, too, that those darts cannot extinguish the objective fact of God's love for those in Christ. Remember that His love is indelible, and rest upon the certainty of His power to keep His own declaration despite any opposition.

The Plunge of Faith

A main remedy for our doubts and fears over our belovedness is to give God the credibility He deserves as *God* in making such a declaration. We must trust His Word and let the truth of His declaration permeate our sense of identity, value, dignity, and relational security with Him, others, and ourselves. This is a daily exercise of faith. We must daily plunge our hearts and minds into the radical flow of these hydrating truths and let them soak there for the satisfaction of our supreme thirst.

I tried to physically emulate this plunge in an attempt to get a picture suitable for the cover of this book. I did so by visiting Boiling Pots, a series of cascading waterfalls and churning pools on the Big Island of Hawaii. I gave a friend the camera, slid into one of the natural rockbound "pots," and swam over to one of the smaller waterfalls. Then I tried to brace myself under the gush that torrentially surged over my body. It wasn't easy, which is why one of those pictures does *not* adorn the cover of this book (though it did appear in several pre-publication drafts)!

Still, my physical attempt to stand under the gush at Boiling Pots is a good illustration of our need to "stand" under God's gush of calling us

His beloved. It isn't easy. Slippery spiritual moss and jagged rock make the task difficult. The current of God's love — so powerful and rich that it's often happily staggering — increases the challenge. This is the blessed daily "work" of faith for God's beloved — to believe that we are who God has declared us to be in Christ.

Gushaholic's Prayer

God, please help me to stand by faith under the waterfall of Your divine declaration that calls me Your beloved. Amen. (Note: You might want to read, personalize, and meditate on Paul's prayer from Ephesians 3:14–19 as part of your prayer.)

Gushercises

1. Describe a situation in which you received some sort of benefit(s) simply because of your relational connection to a friend or family member. Ponder how this instance illustrates how you receive the blessing of being declared God's beloved because of your relational connection to Christ.
2. What benefits of being "in Christ" listed in this chapter stand out to you? Why?
3. What keeps you from believing that you're permanently declared God's beloved in Christ?
4. How can you grow in your joyful awareness of being God's beloved in Christ?
5. Praise God for being the kind of Person who'd declare you His beloved in Christ as a free gift!

Buoy V

Life in the Gush

We're making good progress on our voyage. So far we've re-examined our thirst, heard God's lavish invitation to the parched, and soaked awhile in Him by looking at several water-pictures and other amazing truths about Him as a lavish, soul-hydrating God. We've been challenged to believe what God has revealed about Himself and what He's declared about us (i.e., that we're His "beloved ones" in Christ) for the increased satisfaction of our supreme thirst.

Now we're ready to talk about the daily reality of living with the God of gush. Our goal around this buoy is to get help navigating the ups and downs of our ongoing Christian voyage this side of heaven, and to whet our appetites for a promised future of gush everlasting.

19

Relationship and Radiance

Let us press on to know the LORD. Hosea 6:3a

Do you tan, or do you burn? Whatever the case, one thing's for sure: Your skin changes when it's exposed to the sun. You don't change it yourself; it *is changed*. More precisely, we could say that our skin's relationship with the sun results in our skin's transformation. We tan or burn by remaining in the sun's presence. We either turn a rich, chocolaty brown, or glow like a freshly boiled lobster. No matter the color, relationship with the sun results in our skin's transformation, either for good or for ill.

Spiritually, things work the same way. Our relationship with and exposure to God's S-O-N (Jesus) results in transformation of our hearts and character. We don't change our own hearts. As we spend time with God, our hearts *are changed* by Him. We could say that God's S-O-N gushes a soul-hydrating flow that, through constant exposure, washes our hearts and transforms us from the inside out. This is God's design for our ongoing lives as His beloved, where the emphasis is on relationship with Him.

Radiant Results (~1500 B.C.)

> When Moses came down from Mount Sinai, with the two tablets of the testimony in his hand as he came down from the mountain, Moses did not know that the skin of his face shone because he had been talking with God. Exodus 34:29

Moses had a divine suntan. We see it happening in the text above, where Moses "had been talking with God" (relationship) so that "the skin of his face shone" (resulting radiance). To say it more poetically and succinctly, Moses' relationship with God resulted in radiance! Let's see how this worked for him and learn how this transformation also works for us as Christians.

The relational cue in this text is that Moses "had been talking with God." The Hebrew word used here is *dabar,* which means "to speak or converse." It's used twice in Exodus 33:11 — "Thus the LORD used to speak to Moses face to face, as a man speaks to his friend." This talking isn't mere chitchat with God; it's heavy-duty relating. We know this because the word is used twice (repetition signals emphasis), and both times appears in a form (Piel stem in Hebrew) that indicates intensity. These conversations with God were deep, significant, active, and personal. The result? Radiance.

We, too, are changed when we *dabar* intensely with God. To get a hint of this, just imagine spending one hour in deep conversation with someone incredibly famous, loving, powerful, virtuous, and intelligent. Maybe it's a world leader, a scholar, or a Christian thinker from today or from years gone by. Don't you think you'd be changed as a result of that one hour? Well, God dwarfs every human figure as far as prestige, love, power, virtue, and intelligence are concerned. He's *huperballo,* remember? Having a real talk with Him will *definitely* transform us.

What's the result of Moses' relationship-through-intense-*dabar*-ing with God? His face "shone" (*qaran*), which means "to send out rays." Elsewhere in the Bible, this word is most often translated "horns" in order to symbolize strength radiating outward. In fact, that translation was used in the version of the Bible read by the artist Michelangelo. That's why he placed two horns on Moses' head in his famous sculpture of the man.[1]

Michelangelo's horned Moses helps us understand the deeper meaning behind the physical shining of Moses' face. The outward radiance (symbolized by horns on the head) was a sign of the inward radiance (strength of God) that Moses experienced as a result of deep friendship with God. Moses was made spiritually, emotionally, and relationally strong by abiding in God's presence and interacting with Him. He didn't make *himself* strong, he *was made* strong. Moses didn't improve *himself*, he *was improved* by God. He beamed with the radiance of *God's* power, not his own. This is how relationship with God results in transformation.

It's interesting that God adds the detail that Moses didn't even know he was transformed and radiating. The text reveals that he "did not know that his face shone." This phrase beautifully highlights the idea that radiating God isn't something we can conjure or grab. Much of the time, it isn't even something we perceive. We can't acquire it through our own strength. Nor do we have to! Life in the gush of God *results in* transformation. And as was the case with Moses, this process hinges on our relationship with God.

Radiant Results (~A.D. 55 and Beyond)

Moses had such a divine tan that he makes a significant appearance about 1,500 years later in the pages of the New Testament.

> Now the Lord is the Spirit, and where the Spirit of the Lord is, there is freedom. And we all, with unveiled face, beholding the glory of the Lord, are being transformed into the same image from one degree of glory to another. For this comes from the Lord who is the Spirit.
> 2 Corinthians 3:17–18

This text expands on a detail we haven't yet discussed concerning Moses' relationship with God: Moses wore a veil when he related God's words to the people, but *not* when he talked with God (Exodus 34:34). Moses' veillessness with God is an incredible sign of intimacy. It meant that there were no barriers between him and God when they met. It meant that nothing came between them. It meant deep friendship as explained in a verse we've already enjoyed in this chapter, Exodus 33:11a — "Thus the LORD used to speak to Moses face to face, as a man speaks to his friend."

In Moses' day, and in many modern cultures, veillessness between people signals immeasurable intimacy. Without a doubt, around 1500 B.C., Moses was the *only* human who could appear veilless in God's presence. In that light, 2 Corinthians 3:18 reveals something overwhelmingly amazing. It points out that *all* Christians now have this amazing privilege because of Christ. Because of Christ, we can go veilless with God!² We can be at "liberty" with Him (verse 17, NASB)! This means that we, too, can "talk with God face to face, as a man speaks to his friend." Wow!

This is hydrating news because, like Moses, our being transformed *depends upon* our "beholding the glory of the Lord." The Greek verb used here is *katoptrizo,* which describes contemplative gazing at a great marvel. Like Moses' *dabar*-ing, this contemplation is intense — not superficial or fleeting. Just as the suntan we get depends on the intensity of the sun's rays and the degree of our exposure to them, so the degree (quality and quantity) of our spiritual transformation depends on the intensity of the S-O-N's relational radiance and the degree of our time interacting with God in that radiance. Of course, we know that the S-O-N always shines brightly toward us; *we* are the variable. The big question is whether we're scurrying in and out of intimacy with God, merely "catching Him on the fly," relating to Him with six-word text messages — or we're contemplatively gazing at Him in intimate fellowship.

It's important to note that we're gazing, contemplating, and marveling not at ourselves, but at God's glory (*doxa*). You may remember glory as one of the four attributes of God described as *huperballo* — marvelously surpassing every measure (Chapter 15). Glory has to do with radiance, brightness, splendor, majesty, grandeur, power, and honor. God embodies these qualities immeasurably. We can reflect them robustly as indicated by the thrice-repeated use of *doxa* in 2 Corinthians 3:10. We can gush God's glory as we behold — that is, relate to — God, the Glorious One.

The transformation described here is literally a metamorphosis in us (*metamorphoo*). It means we're transfigured, changed in appearance, and/or changed in inward nature or character. A suntan, in which our skin is changed in appearance, is the same kind of metamorphosis. Another example is a caterpillar being *metamorphoo*'d into a butterfly. Both of those examples involve a physiological metamorphosis. God's emphasis, however, is our *inward* transformation — spiritual, intellectual, and emotional — which then results in both inward and outward relational radiance with Him, others, and ourselves. God fuels this inward heart-metamorphosis as we gaze upon and contemplate Him.

When it comes to reflecting God's glory and all of His other moral attributes, our job is mainly to relate to Him and let Him do His work. The text reinforces this idea, because the main verb in this verse, *metamorphoo,* appears in the passive voice. That's God's way of saying that we're being acted upon by Him, not performing the work on ourselves. Or we could say that *our* main work is to let God do *His* work in us, especially as we relate intimately with Him. The NLT's rendition of the end of this verse helps us understand this point: "And as the Spirit of the Lord works within us, we become more and more like Him and reflect His glory even more."

How's Your Relationship with God?

The heading above poses a huge question. It's similar to asking about our relationship with the sun in the context of getting a tan. This question, however, asks how we're doing with the Son as we look for a divine Son-tan — that is, as we look for His character reflecting within us and radiating from us. This is an extremely important question for Christians seeking the hydrated life. So — how are things between you and God?

It's important for us to acknowledge that all relationships can at times be difficult — even our relationship with God. Maybe you picked up this book precisely because you've been struggling with God. If that's the case, know that everyone sometimes has difficulty *dabar*-ing and *katoptrizo*-ing with God. Even a quick recollection of the most prominent people in the Bible confirms this reality. A brief survey of the psalms reveals that David wrestled greatly in relationship with God. Moses and Paul, whose experience and writing we've examined in this chapter, also grappled at times with God.

A good relationship with God doesn't mean a perfect or pain-free relationship with Him. In fact, the most mature Christians may wrestle with God more deeply and frequently than others do! The goal isn't flawless pleasure, but persistent honesty. Ongoing honesty with God is what typically yields the sweetest relational richness with Him. The same is usually true in committed, loving human relationships. Our best relationships are typically those in which we feel safe to be honest, and in which commitment, grace, and love help us grow together.

We can be encouraged by the fact that God passionately pursues relationship with us. He *wants* to spend time with us. The amazing fact that Jesus came, lived, died, and rose again so that we could spend eternity with God is the supreme proof that He wants to spend time with us. Sometimes we'll have to fight the lies of our enemies who taunt, "God's tired of you. You're just not a very good friend to Him, you know. You keep failing Him. He's probably going to 'un-friend' you soon and get some new, better friends."

Sometimes our enemies will say, "You're just too busy to spend that kind of time with God." Combat these lies with the many truths of the preceding chapters, especially the idea that needy and parched people are precisely the ones that God seeks for His own. Expose the deception that time spent with God is wasted time. It's never wasted time! It may not be enjoyable time. We may not consider it productive time. But it's never wasted time. We often fall into those traps because of our brokenness or our self-centered ideas of what makes a relationship worthwhile.

When our relationship with God becomes difficult, we need to remember that the main point of our relationship with Him isn't really the divine suntan He provides. Sure, that's good and important. But the *main* point of our relationship with God is *to know God*. This is the difference between being in a relationship with someone for what we can *get* from them and being with someone to *know* them. Sometimes these lines are blurry, because when we get God, we always get amazing spiritual stuff along with *Him*. As we mature, we'll long to simply know God better and better. So let's enter veilless into God's presence and freely enjoy Him! Let's get ready for a divine suntan!

Gushaholic's Prayer

God, thank You for wanting a relationship with me — even *me*! I'm amazed! I want a good relationship with You, too, that transforms me into Your likeness. Please help me to live out this desire. Amen.

Gushercises

1. So really — how is it going with God?

2. Be a modern-day Michelangelo! Try to artistically convey Moses standing before Israel — wearing a veil, yet radiating God. Imagine the spiritual implications of this idea for you and your life with God, yourself, and others.
3. How does knowing that God is super-interested in you help you move toward Him in relationship?
4. What do you find to be the key ingredients of your best human relationships? Many of those elements also characterize a good relationship with God. How might you apply those key ingredients to your relationship with God so that you can converse with, and marvel at, Him?

20

Going with the Flow

I [Jesus] am the vine; you are the branches. Whoever abides in Me and I in him, he it is that bears much fruit, for apart from Me you can do nothing. John 15:5

It's 1184, the era of the Christian Crusades as portrayed in the Ridley Scott film *Kingdom of Heaven*. We join the story as the new "Christian" king of Jerusalem, Guy (pronounced "gee") de Lusignan, is about to ride out and fight the Muslim sultan, Saladin. The problem is that Guy is prideful and trusts in his own strength to win the victory and grab the glory.

Enter Balian, a handsome and virtuous new knight in Jerusalem. He rides up to the king's war-advising assembly just in the nick of time. They're about to put the final touches on their idiotic battle plan, with lots of presumptive self-congratulation and bravado. In a cloud of dust, Balian dismounts from his horse with a firm "No." He continues, "If you must have war, [Jerusalem's] army cannot move away from water. You have a chance to hold the city. But if you move out against Saladin [into the desert], this army will be destroyed, and the city left defenseless."[1]

Vainly dismissing Balian's wise advice, Guy marches with his army into the desert. The next few moments are a visual montage of dehydration: heat waves, a baking sun, the scorching desert, and staggering soldiers. Suddenly, a cavalry rider drops his spear and faints from heatstroke, falling off his steed. Others drag their weapons and reel to and fro. Balian's prediction is coming true.

Saladin, spying his enemy's dust cloud in the distance, commands his army to attack. The dehydrated Christian force offers little resistance. Saladin easily defeats them and takes their prideful king as prisoner. It turns out that you really shouldn't take your army away from water.

It's All About Relationship

Without an ongoing connection to water, Guy's army was ineffective, fruitless. In the end, they suffered and were later destroyed. In John 15:1–11 Jesus tells us that the same thing is true in our spiritual lives. He says that apart from an ongoing relationship with Him — the Fountain of Living Water — we'll be fruitless. He says that we'll suffer spiritually and even watch our intimacy with God wither. We may remain Christians in the technical sense (forgiven, saved, and among God's beloved), but our spiritual lives and experience will be empty. This emphasis on relationship builds on what we learned in Chapter 19 — that our ongoing communion with God is absolutely essential to our lives in the gush. In this chapter, we'll learn more about our role in that relationship.

The premium on ongoing intimacy with God is highlighted in John 15:1–11 by the tenfold repetition of the word *abide* (*meno*). To abide (*meno*) in God means "to dwell, lodge, or remain in a close and settled union" and "to be intimately intertwined"[2] with Him. Jesus used this word to describe His own relationship with His Father in John 14:10. More than anything else, *meno* is a relationship word.

To *meno* in Christ is absolutely essential to the hydrated and fruitful life. Jesus says that if we don't *meno* in Him, we can do nothing (v. 5). He doesn't mean that we can't comb our hair or bake lasagna or get on the Internet. He means that without dwelling in a tight relationship with Him, we won't be able to do anything of lasting spiritual value. In other words, we'll be useless in God's kingdom. *Nothing* is a stark word. It signals just how much is at stake in our *meno*-ing.

Jesus also says that when we do *meno*, we'll be pruned to bear more fruit (v. 2), will bear much fruit (v. 5), will experience a fruitful prayer life (v. 7), will glorify the Father (v. 8), will prove to be God's disciples (v. 8), and will experience God's joy in us so that our joy may be made full (v. 11). Friends, that just about covers it. That list identifies practically everything we should want as Christians — for ourselves, for God, and for others. Enjoying the realities listed also means increased satisfaction of our supreme thirst. And Jesus says it's all a result of *meno*-ing.

Golden Hoses

By now, I'd expect us to ask, "If so much is at stake in *meno*-ing, then how do we do it?" Good question! In John 15, Jesus wraps the lesson in a metaphor about a vine and its branches. Since most people reading this book probably don't have a grapevine, however, let's use a more modern metaphor: a hose and a faucet. There are a few gaps in the substitution, but the main ideas flow nicely.

Let's consider Jesus as the Faucet (Vine) and ourselves as the hose (branches). As a hose, our ability to spray water (our fruitfulness) is totally dependent upon our connection to the Faucet, right? When was the last time you saw a hose spraying water *without being connected* to a faucet? Never! So it's true that without *meno*-ing in the Faucet, we can do nothing, just as John 15:5 says. But if we keep a wide, clean, and tight connection to the Faucet, we hoses can be employed for all kinds of good things. The water from the Faucet can flow through us, enabling us to wash cars, water flowers, and turn Slip 'N Slide into a child's backyard plaything. That's why this chapter is titled "Going with the Flow." It signals that we're to let God flow through us via an intimate, ongoing connection with Him through Christ.

Our life and fruitfulness as hoses depend completely on the Faucet, which is the Source of life itself and the Source of all God-honoring fruit (John 5:21, 6:33 and 63; Acts 17:25 and 28; Romans 4:17 and 11:36; James 1:17). Jesus, our Faucet, is the Source; we're the recipients and conduits. We're participants in bringing forth God's fruit, but we definitely don't originate that fruit. John points this out by saying that we bear (*phero*, used five times in John 15:1–11) fruit instead of producing (*poieo* or *ergazomai*) it. In context, bear (*phero*) means that we "carry" *someone else's* produce. In this case, we bear *God's* fruit. Not our own — God's. As a hose bears its faucet's water, so too do we as golden hoses bear God's fruit. And doing that depends upon our relationship with Him.

I titled this section "Golden Hoses," in part because of the incredible honor we have in even being connected to God, the Faucet.[3] He's done all the work in connecting us to Himself: "Already you are clean because of the word that I have spoken to you" (v. 3). He calls us His beloved ones (Chapters 17 and 18). We're honored because we get to bear God's fruit to our own souls, a subject we'll discuss in greater depth in Chapter 22. We're also privileged because we get to gush God and His fruit to a dehydrated and dying world. God pursues us for this purpose, graciously and consistently pressing into us like the gentle push of water pressure coming from a faucet through a hose. In so doing, God releases us from self-help Churchianity and from living the Christian life in our own strength. Hallelujah!

Relationship 101

We golden hoses have a role to play in responding to God's miracle of connecting us to Himself in Christ. Thankfully, God gives us some helpful instruction in John 15:1–11 about how to do this.

First, we need to enter into a relationship with Jesus. We need to get connected to the Faucet, and Jesus pursues us for that very reason. Verse 3 signals that pursuit: "Already you are clean because of the word that I have spoken to you." "The word that I have spoken to you" encompasses Jesus' teaching about who He is and what He's done as Lord and Savior. The disciples who were hearing these words were already Christians, which means that they had already embraced Jesus' words and were therefore already connected to Him. If you aren't sure about your connection to Jesus, please turn to Appendix A to be sure you're connected. The rest of Jesus' training won't make sense unless you're first connected to the Faucet.

As Faucet-connected Christians, we must soak in the Bible, or what this text calls "My words" (v. 7). The irony here is that in the book of John, Jesus *is* the Word. So to say we must soak in the Word/Bible means that we must soak in Jesus, a living Person. We can do this, in part, by not treating the Bible the way we'd treat a vacuum cleaner manual, for example (i.e., impersonal and merely instructional). Instead, we should treat it like a very personal love letter written by the divine Lover of our souls. Reading, singing, pondering, studying, memorizing, and applying the Bible all help us experience close union with God. When we pay close attention to the Bible's words, we're connected to God and are allowing Him to reveal Himself to us.

We must also abide in Jesus' love for us (verse 9b). What a wonderful command this is! Jesus is telling us, "I really want you to experience My love for you!" He uses "love" three times in this one verse to stress just how important experiencing His love for us is to our life in His gush. In 1997, Bob Dylan wrote a song (also recorded by Garth Brooks, Adele, and others) titled "Make You Feel My Love." We can redeem the lyrics as one of the most beautiful expressions of Jesus' desire for us to abide in His love for us.

> When the rain is blowing in your face
> And the whole world is on your case
> I could offer you a warm embrace
> To make you feel my love.
>
> When the evening shadows and the stars appear
> And there is no one there to dry your tears
> I could hold you for a million years
> To make you feel my love.[4]

We can experience God's love in countless ways. They don't always have to be "religious" ways either. Sure, we experience Him in Bible study and during Sunday worship. But the Bible expands the possibilities for widening the connection between us and the Faucet. For example, God says in Psalm 19:1 that we can experience Him by marveling at creation: "The heavens declare the glory of God, / and the sky above proclaims His handiwork." The most widening advice of all in this regard comes from Philippians 4:7–8. In this passage, God encourages us to look *everywhere* for marks of His presence and goodness so that His peace will abide in us:

> And the peace of God, which surpasses all understanding, will guard your hearts and your minds in Christ Jesus. Finally, brothers, whatever is true, whatever is honorable, whatever is just, whatever is pure, whatever is lovely, whatever is

commendable, if there is any excellence, if there is anything worthy of praise, think about these things.

Another part of maintaining a clean connection with God — and therefore a robust flow from Him to us and through us — is our keeping His commandments (v. 10). Because our enemies (the world, the devil, and our own flesh) tend to twist this aspect of life in the gush, let's be sure of what Jesus is *not* saying. He's *not* saying, "If you obey My commandments, I will love you." No! God's love for us *never* depends on our obedience — *ever*. It depends only upon Christ and our being in Him by faith. Obeying His commandments is a way for us to say, "I love You, God." Simply drawing closer to Him in this way provides an opportunity for us to experience His love of us. Perhaps an illustration will help.

Marriage, for Example

Suppose two couples — Bob and Bette, and Joe and Jane — get married on the same day. They take vows, exchange rings, and sign papers to make their marriages official. In the eyes of God, the state, and the wedding guests, they're married. From that point forward, the only variable is their *experience* of marriage. And their experience of marriage depends in large part upon how they obey God and serve each other.

As the years go by, Bob and Bette make it their joyful aim to obey God and serve each other. Of course, they do this imperfectly, but as a general lifestyle, their marriage is characterized by love and joyful obedience. Bob graciously leads, cherishes Bette, serves her, communicates with her, provides for her, and shows affection toward her. Bette endeavors to be a godly responder to her husband's leadership, serves him, and shows affection toward him. Generally speaking, Bob and Bette's love toward each other in joyful obedience to God yields a happy and peaceful marriage experience for them and for those around them.

Now let's look at Joe and Jane. Over the years, they haven't seemed very interested in obeying God or in serving each other. Joe needlessly spends long hours at work, then comes home to plop down in front of the TV for the entire evening and nag Jane about the food she cooks, the house she keeps, her appearance, and their kids. Jane calls Joe a lousy failure whenever they're out with friends, lets her health go to pot, and suspiciously questions Joe's every decision. Generally speaking, Joe and Jane's lack of love for each other in brash disobedience to God produces a miserable and chaotic marriage experience for them and for those around them.

The couples in both of these scenarios remain equally married in a technical sense. God, the state, and the people around them consider them contractually bound together — regardless of the *quality* of their marriage. It's only their *experience* of marriage that's radically different. That experiential difference is the result of their ongoing love toward each other in obedience to God. Because Bob and Bette exhibit love toward each other, they enjoy a better marriage *experience*. Because Joe and Jane don't exhibit love toward each other, they suffer in their *experience* of marriage.

It's the same with God and us. Once we put our trust in Jesus Christ for eternal life (Appendix A), we're "married," or bound, to God. Even this is a gift from God rather than a result of our obedience. Once we're joined to God, our experience of that union — and more particularly, our *experience of His love for us* — depends in large part on our obedience. Notice that His love for us doesn't change; only our *experience* of His love changes. Because God loves us and wants our experience of Him to be as rich as possible, he implores us in John 15:10a to obey Him: "If you keep my commandments, you will abide in my love."

Consider the second part of John 15:10 as an example that makes even Bob and Bette's marriage look inferior: "just as I [Jesus] have kept My Father's commandments and abide in His love." Wouldn't we say that Jesus was bound to God the Father? He was! And why did Jesus have such an amazingly excellent experience of that union? Because Jesus kept His Father's commandments perfectly. Even Jesus' experience of His union with God the Father depended upon His obedience. It's the same with us as Christians regarding our experience of God's love.

Of course, we're not Jesus, and we can't obey God perfectly as He did. Consequently, our relationship with God this side of heaven will never be exactly like His. However, Jesus' obedience and His experience of His Father's love is still a helpfully gorgeous example of how obedience leads to a joyful relationship with God. That's the thrust of verse 10, actually, given the grammar of that text.

The great news is that God is a "Spouse" who always pursues us in love. He calls us His beloved (Chapters 17 and 18), and continually showers us with kindness and goodness. We never have to worry about His leaving us or forsaking us (Hebrews 13:5). His love for us never depends on our love for Him! These astonishing truths help us to enjoy Him and obey Him all the more. Once we get a taste of a sweet, abiding relationship with God, we're even more motivated to maintain a strong connection with Him so that His love can flow into and through our hearts.

Relief in Relationship

In the summertime, I often visit the St. Louis Zoo in Forest Park. On really hot days, they place oscillating mist machines around the zoo to blow cool fog into throngs of hot zoo-goers. I enjoy sidling up to one of those machines, usually amid a mob of sweltering kids, to cool down.

For many dehydrated Christian voyagers, hearing the truths in this chapter might seem like standing in front of that cool mist machine. It should be incredibly refreshing to hear that we no longer have to produce Christian virtue on our own or out of our own strength. It's wonderful news that we're golden hoses, and that we're blessed bearers of God's good things as we focus on our relationship with Him. I can just hear all the parched, self-help junkies joining me in a collective sigh of relief.

It should also be a glorious joy to know that a big part of relating to God is simply knowing that He loves us so much. All Christians become Christians by apprehending that God loves them — despite their sin — because of the life, death, and resurrection of Christ. The great news of John 15 (and many other texts of the Bible) is that the entire Christian life is lived in that same amazement. We're to know and enjoy God's gracious love *throughout* our Christian lives.

This chapter and the previous one have focused on our relationship with God. That's because life in His gush is absolutely, positively centered on continuing intimacy with the God who pursues parched people.

As we continue around Buoy V, we'll hear this theme over and over again.

Gushaholic's Prayer

God, thank You for connecting me to You as a golden hose and for constantly pouring into me. I want to have a great, wide, clean connection with You! Please help me to soak in Your Word, abide in Your love, and obey Your commandments so I can enjoy You and bear Your fruit. Amen.

Gushercises

1. We sometimes fall into the trap of thinking it's our job to originate fruit instead of bear God's fruit. What does this look like in your life?
2. How does it make you feel to know that you don't have to originate fruit in your life, but that you get to focus on your connection to God and bear His fruit?
3. Although God's love for us never depends on our obedience, our obedience *can* affect our *experience* of God's love. How has your experience of God's love risen and fallen based upon your obedience?
4. Read John 15:1–11. What other insights from that text can help you in your relationship with God? I'll give you one hint: God's threat in verse 6 is meant to graciously remind us that relationship with God is *everything*.

21

The Law of the Gush

Water will gush out in buckets. Numbers 24:7a (NLT)

The sports drink manufacturer Gatorade constantly streams the message that taking their "thirst-quenching" liquid into your body yields higher performance out of your body. One ad campaign asked, "Gatorade: Is it in you?" That question was accompanied by images of athletes dripping green, orange, blue, and other Gatorade-colored sweat. The premise is simple: If you drink Gatorade, you'll sweat Gatorade. Another campaign coached, "Win from within." Again, the premise is that if you take their sports drink into your body, you'll get winning performance out of your body.

Apparently, regarding athletic performance, whatever comes in, goes out. If it's Gatorade in, it's Gatorade-like (i.e., heightened, winning) athletic performance out. This is a physical illustration of an unchangeable spiritual dynamic: Whatever we allow into our hearts will eventually gush out of our hearts. If it's God in, it's God out. If it's sin in, it's sin out. "What comes in, goes out" is a universal axiom that's true in both the physical and the spiritual worlds.

A life lived in the gush of God is a life that's synchronized with this basic premise and is lived in relationship with Him according to His Word. The beauty of living this way is pictured many places in Scripture, including Numbers 24:7, quoted at the beginning of this chapter. That text is a testimony of the fruitfulness of God's people who are drinking in His opulent blessings. As the people of Israel let God into their lives, they're pictured as buckets that overflow. Isn't that what we want our lives to look like, fellow voyagers?

We've all experienced this on a spiritual or moral level. We know that when we consistently and thoughtlessly imbibe violence through movies, other media, video games, or real people, we tend to express violence in our thoughts and behavior. We know that when we look at pornography (drinking through our eyes), we tend to radiate lust and treat others as mere sex objects. We know that listening to gossip (drinking through our ears) and reading gossip rags is likely to transform us into people who *spread* gossip. We know that consistently watching virtue-bashing, grumble-slanted morning, afternoon, and evening news programs often results in morally tangled, discontented thoughts that we sometimes voice.

On the other hand, we know that when we restrict the inflow of those kinds of things, both our inward and outward lives tend to grow more peaceful and virtuous. We know that consistently and wisely letting godly stuff into our hearts typically means that more godly stuff will come out of our hearts and be evident in our lives. For example, we know that regularly attending a healthy church, hearing good preaching, enjoying virtuous entertainment, and reading wholesome books generally cause us to exude godliness. We know that taking in the fellowship of godly friends tends to cause godliness to grow in and gush out of us.

The law of the gush is very simple: What comes in, goes out. Like gravity, it's always at work, whether or not we're aware of it at any given time. Just as life goes better when we recognize the law of gravity and act in such a way that people stay safe and property remains intact, so does life go better when we acknowledge the law of the gush — using it for God's purposes and choosing to take in things that are pleasing to Him. Obviously, disregarding either of these laws can have disastrous consequences. In addition, our desert home, our dehydrating enemy, and our desiccant-loving flesh can make harmonizing with the law of the gush *in godly ways* very difficult. That's why God makes us aware of this law and warns us to guard our hearts against these dangers.

Guard Your Heart

> Keep your heart with all vigilance,
> for from it flow the springs of life. Proverbs 4:23

This warning affirms how serious the law of the gush is to our well-being. God tells us pretty bluntly to "keep" (*natsar*) our hearts. Some other translations of this verse render that verb as "guard." The action depicted is that of a sentinel watching over a fortress, garden, or house to keep intruders out and to let well-wishers in. Thinking of a muscular bouncer at a really popular club or event will give you the idea. That's who we're to be with our own hearts.

The phrase "with all vigilance" intensifies the alertness God desires of us in this matter of "keeping." A more literal translation of this phrase would be "With all/whole guarding, guard your heart." God warns us to do this with vigor, because He knows that our hearts are sponges that absorb and convey whatever we let into them, for better or for worse. So God says, "Post a guard! Stay awake! Come on, let's go! Keep dehydrating sin-toxins *out*! Let *Me* in! Your inward and outward vitality depends upon it!"

Think for a minute about something very precious to you. Maybe it's your child, your house, your health, or a family heirloom. The more precious that thing is to you, the more you'll guard it, right? For example, I see people guard (*natsar*) their child by carefully evaluating the child's diet, car seat, pediatrician, clothing, toys, books, nap time, snacks, schedule, and diaper brand. They do this for the sake of the child's life. Because they want a healthy child, they try to keep bad stuff out while letting good stuff in.

We're to do this same thing with our own hearts.

God wants us to experience and exude *life*. The word *life* used in Proverbs 4:23 is comprehensive. The highest use of this word refers to God Himself and anything congruent with Him. It describes true, holistic vitality, encompassing all aspects of the human experience: physical, spiritual, emotional, relational, financial, social, intellectual, and even more. Looked at another way, *life* suggests anything not dead or death-like. The law of the gush says that God's brand of life will come in and go out of us to the degree that we let life in and keep evil out.

Drinking Is Believing

A good next question might be "Okay, if part of guarding our hearts means letting God in and keeping evil out, then how does that work?" A big part of the answer comes in John 7:37–38, a passage we've examined before.

> On the last day of the feast, the great day, Jesus stood up and cried out, "If anyone thirsts, let him come to Me and drink. Whoever believes in Me, as the Scripture has said, 'Out of his heart will flow rivers of living water.'"

Do you see the law of the gush in this text? Jesus invites us to let Him in by believing in Him (the gush-in). As we believe, rivers of living water will flow out of our hearts (the gush-out). Thus, the primary "work" of our ongoing Christian life is to *keep believing in Jesus*.[1] The emphasis on ongoing belief is solidified in this text because Jesus' invitation to "come" and "drink" appears in the present tense in the original Greek. This means that He's inviting all people, believers and those who are not yet believers, to continually come and to continuously drink Him in the present moment — one moment after another after another.

It's interesting how John 7:37–38 parallels God's invitation in Isaiah 55:1–3 (Chapters 5 and 6). Both texts are stellar invitations from God to come and drink Him *continually*. These actions are metaphorical ways to describe our need for an ongoing gush-in connection with God. In John 7, when God invites us to drink (*pino*) Him, He means that we're to soak up, absorb, or consume[2] Him in relationship. Obviously, in this case we're drinking not a liquid, but a Person! In these texts and many others, God is getting at the root of our need: to vibrantly let Him come *into* our lives so that He will lavishly gush *out* of our lives.

And how do we "drink" Jesus, the Person? We believe that Person. We trust that Person. We share life with that Person and communicate with Him. We listen to and follow that Person when He speaks to us in His Word. We gladly receive that Person's forgiveness. We let that Person's declaration of our belovedness define us. We hear that Person's heartbeat, and let our hearts synchronize with His. We depend upon that Person in ways He's said we can depend upon Him. We live our lives as a response to that Person.

When we let Jesus in by drinking Him, we're letting the purest, sweetest gush — far surpassing our ability to conceive it — into our guarded hearts. And Jesus says that when we drink Him, a pure, sweet, godly gush will come *out* of our hearts (i.e., "Out of his heart will flow rivers of living water").

Guarding the Golden Hose

The image of us as golden hoses (Chapter 20) perfectly illustrates the law of the gush. The hose is our heart. It's both a reservoir for and a conduit of *whatever* gushes into it. If a hose is hooked up to a barrel of toxin, then toxin will fill that hose and gush out of its nozzle. However, if the hose is hooked up to the tap on a pure mountain spring, pure mountain-spring water will fill it and gush out of it. Like other hoses, our hearts *automatically* store and send out whatever flows into them.

The pristine flow of God into and out of our hearts is corrupted, at least temporarily, when we sin. Even if we're primarily enjoying God but go off on a short toxin-spree, our flow — and therefore our hose's storage and output — become tainted. Who wants to drink from a hose that usually carries pure spring water, but sometimes conveys sewage? What would the inside of that hose look like and smell like, even though it *usually* carries spring water? Even a little toxin can contaminate a hose for a long time.

Some of us know this all too well. One careless night of drunkenness can lead to years of pain through a traffic fatality, jail time, a forfeited license, and deep regret or sorrow. One illicit sexual indulgence can cause the difficulty of disease, an unplanned pregnancy, divorce, financial hardship, relational friction, and emotional angst. One hit of methamphetamine can lead a person into a lifelong cycle of addiction and recovery, or can even cause death. One year of clubbing instead of going to church can dry up a soul for years. One too many years of workaholism can leave a family in ruins. One selfish, inappropriately angry word can cripple a relationship for months.

Be warned that the world, the devil, and our remaining flesh are constantly tempting us to forsake the gush-in of God for the gush-in of sin. They'll connive for months just to push us into a momentary toxin-fest, because they actually take pleasure in the devastating results. The rock band Creed wrote a great song titled "Beautiful," which reveals our enemies' wily ways. The song is about a man who indulges in a lustful woman's enticements. It's a rock 'n' roll testimony to God's warning in Proverbs 1–7 about drinking from the well of ungodly sexual permissiveness. The song's refrain affirms the law of the gush by revealing the temptress's craftiness and the deadly result for the one who lets her come into his heart:

> Beautiful is empty
> Beautiful is free
> Beautiful loves no one
> Beautiful stripped me.[3]

Living It Out

Ensuring that the law of the gush works in our own lives for God's glory requires vigilance from us. But it's a vigilance that God makes easier by His strong, constant flow of goodness and grace to us. He's *huperballo*, remember? He's always robustly inviting us to come to Him for satisfaction, remember? We're His beloved ones in Christ, remember? Consequently, we're like hungry people who need to eat lots of good food to keep our hearts fit, and who are standing in front of the world's healthiest, cleanest, most lavish, and most succulent buffet with a hearty, even urgent, invitation to eat all we want. In Psalm 37:3, God actually invites us once more to Himself as the ultimate Buffet for those who want to synchronize with Him according to the law of the gush.

> Trust in the LORD and do good;
> Dwell in the land and feed on His faithfulness.
> (NASB's alternate translation)

Still, enjoying life by this law doesn't happen by accident. We have to recognize that the law is true, and we need to take deliberate steps to be sure that the things we allow into our hearts are things of God. As we do this, we must also acknowledge that we won't do it perfectly and that our lapses in no way diminish God's love for us. We can do nothing to earn, maintain, or lose the gift of His love and our resulting belovedness (Chapters 17 and 18).

In fact, it's our security in Christ and His indelible declaration of our being His beloved ones that inspire and empower us to cherish our own hearts and to strive, in the strength He supplies, to guard them. Believing in God — and letting His grace and truth gush into our hearts — is the main thing we can do to ensure that the law of the gush *blesses* both ourselves and others. Letting our hearts soak in God is a natural deterrent to parching desiccants that constantly compete with God for gush-in access to our hearts. As we receive God's gush-in more and more robustly, our hearts can brim with a gladness that faces temptation with a relaxed "No thanks. I'm already full." Here are some specific examples designed to help us figure out what it means to synchronize with the law of the gush for godliness in our lives.

Maybe you struggle with the alluring, but toxic, gush-in of materialism. As a bouncer posted at the door of your own heart, you might need to restrict activities that open this tempting gush-in — strolling around the mall, watching shopping networks on television, or surfing product websites. You might want to unsubscribe from the gush-in of merchant emails, and cancel the torrent of catalogs to your U.S. mailbox — thus protecting your heart from this onslaught. At the same time, you might open your heart to receive the gush-in of God's opulent provision for all your most important needs (forgiveness, eternal life, value, etc.). You may also gladly receive God's gush-in of wisdom on themes like material stewardship, needs versus wants, and your eternal inheritance in Christ.

Maybe you wrestle with gossip and slander. If so, you might restrict the toxic gush-in of gossip-heavy magazines, TV shows, and Internet sites. You may try quelling your participation in social networking sites, where gossip and slander often flow like sewage down a drainage tunnel. At the same time, you could open yourself to the pure, clean gush of God's glorious gospel, in which you hear God's voice telling you the juiciest morsels of all time: "I love you. You are mine. I will never leave you nor forsake you." You might also open yourself to the healthy gush-in that comes from serving and dignifying others.

Maybe you grapple with the rancid flow of self-contempt that endures long after you've confessed a particular sin. In that case, you may want to restrict the toxic gush-in of influences (e.g., hypercritical people) that embody this type of soul-bashing. You may need to limit the time you spend detailing and confessing your sin, especially if that time is spent vainly repeating yourself in an attempt to somehow pay penance for your wrongdoing. At the same time, you might open your heart to reading, pondering, singing, studying, and memorizing the contempt-swallowing gush of God effected by Scriptures that clarify His verdict of "no condemnation for those who are in Christ Jesus" (Romans 8:1). You might also seek out people, churches, books, music, art, employment, and living situations where a godly gush of affirmation, forgiveness, and mercy flow freely to your soul.

The examples could go on and on. The main point is that the law of the gush is real and active. It calls us to the vigilance involved in keeping toxic gushes out and letting godly gushes in. It's at work all the time, whether we acknowledge it or not. So let's acknowledge it! Let's identify how we need to guard our hearts, and do so in the strength and joy of Christ. Also, let's continually receive God's perpetual and *huperballo* gush-in of love, grace, power, and glory. As we do, we'll increasingly enjoy the holy pleasures of living according to the law of the gush.

Gushaholic's Prayer

Lord, thank You for so clearly describing how my heart works — by revealing the law of the gush to me. Please inspire and empower me by Your grace and joy to guard my heart. Help me to keep bad stuff out while letting You come into and go out of my heart continually. Amen.

Gushercises

1. In your own words, describe the law of the gush.
2. How does the law of the gush show up in your life in a negative way?
3. How does it show up in a positive way?
4. How can you guard your heart more diligently? Be as specific and practical as you can in your answer, which should include both keeping evil out and letting godly things in.
5. Are you having trouble acknowledging the law of the gush in your life? Read Matthew 23, asking the Lord to break through to you.
6. Of the flows and gushes in your life, which would you like to see transformed by God?

22

Gush-Out Trifecta
Part I: To God and Self

We love because He first loved us. 1 John 4:19

Let's pretend that we're that kid who's spent the whole day frolicking around the luscious water park described in Chapter 14. Between the untold liters of water we've willingly (and unwillingly!) swallowed — along with an entire day soaking and playing in water rides of every variety — we're thoroughly waterlogged by the late afternoon when our mom calls to us that it's time to go home. Still dripping, we reluctantly tear ourselves away from our hydro-delights and make our way to Mom, leaving a gushy trail of wet footprints in our wake. We don't *try* to make those footprints, they just happen naturally, because we're still drenched from head to toe from a day immersed in liquid.

This simple illustration pictures the law of the gush: water in, water out. Or, to reframe 1 John 4:19 quoted at the beginning of this chapter, we could say, "We gush because He first gushed to us." In a spiritual sense, when we relate intimately with God, we'll tend to leave wet, God-like footprints everywhere we go. We don't even need to *try* to leave those footprints, because they just tend to happen. In this chapter, we'll explore the nature of the footprints we leave behind as a drenching gush-out trifecta: gushing back to God, to ourselves, and to others.

Gush-Out to God: Praise

> Because Your steadfast love is better than life,
> my lips will praise You. Psalm 63:3

It's only natural that we'd automatically gush out praise to God for opulently forgiving, loving, and hydrating our parched, weary, sinful selves. It's as natural as spontaneously kissing the feet of someone who just drenched us with water because they saw that we were on fire. There were many instances when God threw buckets of forgiveness on King David when he was on fire, including times when he had ignited those fires himself as a result of his own sin. God has drenched *us* to save us from such "fires," too.

The verse quoted above closely follows David's intense confession of sin and spiritual thirst that we studied in Chapter 4. There's no doubt that the greater a person's peril — and the more that person is aware of his peril — the more he'll gush back praise to the one who rescues him. That's one reason why it's so important for us to feel the weight of our supreme thirst and to be honest about it with ourselves and with God. That admission sets the stage for a more exhilarating experience of God's quenching, forgiving grace (the gush-in), which in turn sets the stage for a more robust gush-out of praise to Him.

David's praise (gush-out) is rooted in a profound personal experience of forgiveness and deliverance (i.e., hydration) by the God whose "steadfast love [gush-in] is better than life." Did we hear that? Better than *life*! Life is the most spectacular thing anybody could ever pour into us, right? It is! But what God gushed toward David, and what He gushes toward us, is *better* than life! And because it is, David spontaneously gushes out praise to God.

Notice, too, that David gushes praise back to *God*, not to God's steadfast love. There's a difference. God, not His blessings, must be the object of our entire gush-out of praise. We know this is right, even from mundane experiences. If someone refills our water glass, we thank the *person*, not the water or the glass. Though we're glad for the fresh water, we thank its giver. So it is with our gush-out of praise. We can be glad for God's blessings, but we're to thank *Him*.

The word David uses for praise is an intensive form of the Hebrew word *shabach*, which can mean "to laud, praise, commend, congratulate, or exhibit mirth for something as the best." This is a beautiful, content-rich word for David's gush-back to God. It's full of emotion as well. David's whole person is *shabach*-ing God! This insight helps us understand what praise is and helps us give it to God. The word acts like a nozzle that adjusts our praise-spray in appropriate ways.

Nonetheless, we all experience times when praise to God seems forced or dry. Unfortunately, when that happens, many of us try to whip up excitement merely by changing external factors. For example, we might look for a church with a more lively worship style. Or we might seek other changes in our circumstances that we think will elicit our praise to God. While these external changes may have some value, the law of the gush and David's example reveal the deeper issue. They show us that praise is the natural gush-out caused by our ongoing gush-in of God, accessed through intimacy with Him.

It's ironic that even though we want to express gratitude to God and want to praise Him, we often neglect our relationship with Him. Often, circumstances and worries stifle our primary captivation, causing our praise to plummet. When our gush-out of praise to God is meager, it's time to examine our intimacy with Him. More specifically, we might ask Him for a deeper awareness of our thirst and His quenching rescue. We might ask Him to renew in us a sense that His salvation is "better than life" (Psalm 63:3). As we re-experience our dire need, rehear His amazing invitation, and resoak in His supremely hydrating Person, our praise tends to gush forth with fresh intensity.

Gush-Out to Self

> As the Father has loved Me, so have I loved you. Abide in My love. John 15:9

Experiencing God's love for us (gush-in) should also cause healthy love for ourselves (gush-out). This is the next evidence of a person in sync with God's intent for us in the law of the gush. "Abide in My love" (John 15:9) is God's splendid way of saying that He wants us to continuously experience, embrace, and enjoy His love for us in the gospel. He wants us to enjoy His joy over us (Nehemiah 8:10). He wants us to thrill at His gladness in pronouncing us His beloved ones in Christ. He wants these amazing truths to swish around *within us* so that we ourselves enjoy them as the source of our gush-out of love to ourselves.

Too often we skip over this important aspect of living in the gush, rushing right on to God's command to love Him or others. "I can't spend time loving myself," we think nervously. "I might become selfish." But the healthy self-love (gush-out) that comes from experiencing God's love for us (gush-in) doesn't lead to selfishness. As we'll soon see, it leads instead to love, joy, peace, patience, kindness, goodness, faithfulness, gentleness, and self-control *toward ourselves* in godly ways.

Healthy self-love based upon our experience of God's love for us is so essential to our biblical worldview that it's frequently mentioned explicitly or implicitly as the foundation for loving others. In Galatians 5:14, God tells us that "The whole law is fulfilled in one word: 'You shall love your neighbor as yourself.'" If we were to amplify the meaning of this verse, we might hear God saying, "Godly love for yourself is not only healthy for *you*, it's also what shows you how to love your *neighbor*. Healthy self-love is extremely important! I'm pointing you to it as a model of what it looks like to love others."

Think back to Chapters 17 and 18, where we discovered that God calls us His beloved ones. Do we think He does that only to push us to love others, saying, "Well, now that I've called you My 'beloved,' stop feeling happy in your own heart and get out there and forget yourself and love others!"? No! He calls us His beloved ones, in part, so that we see and love ourselves correctly. In fact, one of the main reasons that He tells us in John 15:1–11 to abide in Him is so we can derive full personal enjoyment of being His beloved. He wants us to be saturated with Him so that we can live full, joy-filled lives, which include love for ourselves.

> These things I have spoken to you, that My joy may be in you, and that your joy may be full. John 15:11

The gush-in in this verse is God's own joy over us, which flows into our hearts by faith. God wants that joy to splash around inside us and lead us to the gush-out of full joy. This is an intense, holy, righteous, clean, and beautiful love for ourselves, rooted in God's love for us. This is what a healthy gush-out of self-love looks like.

As Christians, *we are God's beloved*! Let's enjoy that fact without shame or guilt. Let's let God's gush of love bring us deep internal blessing, godly pleasure, and joy. One way to do that is to examine the fruit of the Spirit (Galatians 5:22–23) for the purpose of healthy, gush-out self-love. Each statement in the list below was built from the meaning of the Greek word for the quality. The statements were written as personal confessions to help us soak in the gush of healthy self-love.

1. Love: I can affectionately appreciate myself as an object of God's fondness in the gospel. I can extend myself the grace to treat myself well, despite my own failures and sins.
2. Joy: I can allow myself to take pleasure in my infinite value, which is based solely upon God's irrevocably calling me His beloved in the gospel. I can be glad that I am the focus of God's redeeming love and joy.
3. Peace: I can rest deeply in the tranquility God has established between me and Him through Christ. I can stop beating myself up and stop warring with myself over my sins and faults, because I know God loves me permanently just as I am, in Christ.
4. Patience: I can restrain myself when I want to lash out against myself for my failures and sins. I don't need to get easily angered with myself. Instead, I can be slow to anger against myself, because God is "slow to anger and abounding in steadfast love" toward me (Exodus 34:6).
5. Kindness: I can be sympathetic and compassionate toward myself, understanding my frailty and embracing my humanity. I can do this, because even God knows I'm made of dust and therefore is gentle with me (Psalm 103:14).
6. Goodness: I agree with God that I am "fearfully and wonderfully made" (Psalm 139:14). I can embrace the honor God bestows on me, and I can confer that honor on myself gladly and freely, and without shame or guilt.
7. Faithfulness: I can rejoice in God's loyalty to me and gladly affirm my indelible value to Him in Christ. I can

trust His work in me and be genuinely glad when I see His fruit show up in my life.
8. Gentleness: I can be friendly with myself. I can be considerate toward myself, giving careful thought to who I am and being particularly sensitive and accommodating to my own weaknesses.
9. Self-control: I can keep my God-given appetites in check so they don't destroy me. (The word used here [*egrateia*] especially pertains to sexual hunger.) I can be filled with God and His gush as a way to help control my other desires.

Gushing out to ourselves as this list suggests is in no way selfish, fellow voyagers. It's *healthy!* God *wants* us to do this. And we do it because God does all of these things toward us in Christ as His beloved ones. Perhaps this clarification of 1 John 4:19 will help: "We love [God, others, *and ourselves*] because He first loved us."

Strong Reactions

Of all the subjects we've covered so far in this book, this idea of appropriate gush-out self-love elicited some of the strongest responses from manuscript readers. For me, it was one of the most difficult and most surprising sections to write. I found myself squirming, "I can't pen this much about the properness of godly, gush-out self-love, can I?" Amidst my squirming, I began to wonder why so many people, including me, get uncomfortable with this subject. I don't know all the reasons, but a few occurred to me immediately.

The first is illustrated by the posture of a church I visited several times a few years ago. They were conducting a multifaceted campaign (including, for example, sermons and service projects) called "Love God — Love Others." Those two phrases were displayed prominently in big white letters against the black velvet backdrop on the worship platform week after week. Then slowly it hit me. "What about godly, healthy 'Love Self?'" I wondered. "Isn't that part of God's passion, too?" I wondered even further, "If texts like Galatians 5:14 somehow make our love of others pivot on our love of ourselves, then maybe the reason we don't love others (or God) very well is because we don't really love ourselves very well."

As I visit different churches as part of my ministry, I'm struck by how often healthy, godly self-love is ignored in order to highlight our need to love God and love others. Many churches act as if they think God isn't interested in our being kind, good, and loving toward *ourselves*. Some faith communities even go so far as to give the impression that our only value as persons is our output in loving God and others. In exploring this disturbing omission, I realized that the roots of this problem may be that many Christians either are afraid to enjoy God's love for them or are ignorant of its appropriateness and beauty — its necessity even — in God's hydrating plan.

Another prominent reason for neglecting self-love seems to be the prevalence of abuse and brokenness in families and other primary relationships in our culture. It seems that few people have ever experienced the genuine warmth of heartfelt love. Few have felt what it's like to be delighted in regardless of their output, beauty, sexuality, or accomplishments. The result is that we often find the idea of self-love foreign or unwelcome. "I've never felt this before," goes the subconscious logic, "so how can it be a legitimate part of God's desire for me in relationship with Him?" With that, we scurry off to "do our Christian duty" in loving God and others, while leaving our own hearts gasping for part of the gush-out of His beautiful grace.

I'm sure there are many more reasons for our problems with healthy, godly self-love. Instead of musing in the abstract, perhaps it's best to simply ask, "How wet is this part of your heart?" Have you allowed God's gush to swish around inside *you* to thoroughly hydrate *your own* heart? The gushercises below will keep us from omitting the "Love Self" title from our own heart's backdrop. Let's not rush past our own supreme thirst in the name of loving God and loving others. Let's enjoy the *entire* gush-out trifecta, including love of ourselves, in response to God's lavish gush-in.

Gushaholic's Prayer

Thank You for gushing into my life, God! Help me gush out appropriately to You *and* to myself. Amen.

Gushercises

1. Describe how God has gushed into your life, especially spiritually, in the most important and eternal issues of your (eternal) life.
2. How can receiving God's gush-in to you elicit a spontaneous gush-out of praise to Him?
3. Express your gush-out of praise to God.
4. What keeps you from appropriately loving yourself as a proper gush-out response to God's gush-in to your life?
5. Revisit the list of gush-out-to-self fruit in this chapter. Describe how God's gush-in toward you can help increase the flow of the three fruits you have the most trouble experiencing.
6. As you wrote your response to question 1 above, did you find a spontaneous gush-out of praise rise in your heart? If not, revisit your response, add to it, ponder it, and soak in the amazing ways that God has been good to you.

23

Gush-Out Trifecta
Part II: To Others

Love the sojourner, therefore, for you were sojourners in the land of Egypt. Deuteronomy 10:19

So far we've learned about two aspects of the gush-out trifecta: loving God and loving ourselves. We've heard that these expressions of love are happy responses to God's lavish gush-in to us. Now let's look at the third aspect of this trifecta: loving others. Like the first two, this third facet also depends upon our letting the soul-hydrating, *huperballo* God gush into our hearts.

Deuteronomy 10:19, quoted above, is just one of many verses that describe both sides of this particular aspect of the law of the gush. In this verse, God bases Israel's active love for the sojourner (gush-out to others) upon the fact that the Israelites themselves were loved by God (gush-in) when they were sojourners in Egypt. We could paraphrase the verse this way: "Gush out to the sojourner, because I gushed in to you when you were sojourners." God's love for and rescue of Israel in Egypt is implicit in this text, but it's explicit in many other texts, including Deuteronomy 24:17–18 (emphasis added):

> You shall not pervert the justice due to the sojourner or to the fatherless, or take a widow's garment in pledge, but *you shall remember that you were a slave in Egypt and the* LORD *your God redeemed you from there; therefore I command you to do this.*

This command is for us as well as for the Israelites. Because God loved *us* as sojourners (i.e., when we were outsiders to Him), we also are to love sojourners (i.e., those who are currently outsiders to Him and/or to us). It's our own experience of being loved by God when we weren't yet part of His family that causes us to love those who aren't yet part of His family in Christ.

Here's the same idea from a slightly different view in Exodus 23:9.

> You shall not oppress a sojourner. You know the heart of a sojourner, for you were sojourners in the land of Egypt.

It's interesting that this verse puts things in the negative: "You shall not oppress a sojourner." Framing things this way reminds us of our nagging desiccant-loving ways, which are to ignore, isolate, or take advantage of anyone who isn't part of our group or clique. To keep us from following the rancid gush-in of our flesh, God wants us to remember that we weren't always part of His group — the "group" of the beloved in Christ. He also wants us to remember how He treated us in that state. He sought us to make us insiders and members of His family!

The New Testament–era equivalent to "you were sojourners in the land of Egypt" is the non-Christian's bondage to sin (Romans 3:9–20). God wants us, as His beloved ones, to remember what bondage to sin felt like. He wants us to remember the restless cycles of sinful indulgence that resulted in shame, guilt, emptiness of soul, and anxiety toward God. He wants us to remember the pain of being such a "sojourner" and to marvel at His hydrating grace that compelled Him to send His Son to rescue us: "But God shows His love for us in that while we were still sinners, Christ died for us" (Romans 5:8).

God didn't oppress us when we were sojourners who were lost in our sin. He rescued us! He sought us in order to save us and give our wandering, rebellious souls a home in Christ! He wants our hearts to be captivated with this tremendous gush-in so that we'll naturally and gladly love others and urge them to find their home in Christ, too. In this light it seems silly that we'd ever consider oppressing a sojourner, doesn't it? Doing so seems like trying to swim upstream in the happily gushing river of gladness caused by God's rescue of our own souls.

One way to understand the point God is making in these verses is to consider a time when you felt the pain of being socially ignored or isolated, along with a later time when you felt the joy of being invited or included. It could be feeling the pain of not being invited to one friend's party, but later experiencing the happiness of being invited to another friend's party. It could be the ache of sitting by yourself in church, along with the joy of someone asking, "Hey, would you like to sit with us?" It could be the sting of feeling left out of a group's secret conversations and inside jokes, along with the happiness of hearing their apology and later being invited to their next get-together.

God puts the principle this way in John 15:12b — "Love one another as I have loved you." In this text, Jesus' love for us is the horse in front of the cart labeled "love one another." Jesus' love is what causes and shapes our love for one another. And how does Jesus love us? He pursues us. He sacrifices Himself to pay the penalty for our sins. He adopts us into His family. He's patient and kind with us as He cares for us with grace and truth. We're to continually let this kind of love from God gush into our hearts, and then naturally gush it out toward others.

"Rescued Rescuers"

I've met many members of Alcoholics Anonymous (AA) who generally demonstrate this idea, even if they wouldn't articulate it the way we have in this chapter. These are folks significantly debilitated by alcohol addiction — perhaps even near death — who were invited or shuffled into an AA meeting. Through the general grace and truth extended by sober group members, these people were saved from physical death or devastation from alcohol. Months later, as recipients of a gush-in of "AA grace" from both the members and the methods of the organization, these rehabilitated members sometimes became "sponsors." A sponsor is someone who's been rescued through "AA grace," and who wants to gush out that same help to a struggling alcoholic.

This is a picture of how God intends the law of the gush to work in Christians and in Christian communities. First, He invites us into relationship with Him while we're spiritually dehydrated and heading toward eternal death. We receive His opulent grace in Christ and are eternally saved from God's wrathful condemnation for our sin. He wants us to continually experience His goodness in daily intimacy with Him. In the process, He wants us to gladly gush that same grace out to others who are dehydrated like we were. He wants us to look for those people, to seek and invite them the way He sought and invited us. He wants us to do this out of our joy for His endlessly inviting us to maintain our connection with Him.

Every soul needs God — and innumerable souls don't have Him. Physically and spiritually dehydrated and dying people *surround* us. They're in our schools, workplaces, cities, suburbs, neighborhoods, aerobics classes, nursing homes, cafeterias, churches, grocery stores, sports teams, families, shopping malls, social groups, and hospitals. What a break in the chain of grace to be so lavishly gushed upon by God — only to clog up that life-giving flow by fear, lethargy, or apathy while people are spiritually gasping and expiring all around us! Instead, let's get back in touch with the magnificent salvation God has wrought in our own hearts and, with joyful captivation, gush out His grace toward the parched people around us.

Sadly, Christian leaders often use guilt, fear, or manipulation to try to cajole congregants to love others. Or they run a program that merely teaches helping techniques without addressing the motives that drive involvement. That's like putting a brand-new gold-plated multi-spray nozzle on a hose that has no water pressure! The law of the gush is the answer to this dilemma. It says that when the water pressure (our experience of God's gush-in of love toward us in Christ) is good, then the spray coming out the other end (our gush-out of God's love toward others) will also be good. When it comes to loving others, this is how golden hoses (Chapter 20) like us work best.

For many years, I've worked to equip individuals and churches to live this out toward those in our culture in imminent physical peril, such as the unborn in danger of abortion, the infirm and elderly in danger of physician-assisted suicide and euthanasia, and human embryos in danger from research, fertility treatments, and other biotechnologies. Unfortunately, these arenas are rife with activists powered by all kinds of sub- or anti-Christian motivations. The bulk of my job, therefore, has been helping Christians understand that God wants us to defend the defenseless out of the joy that comes from knowing that He defended us when we were defenseless.

Day by day, I equip Christians according to the law of the gush: I help them to recognize, appreciate, and enjoy God's rescuing work in their lives through the gospel, and as they do, to let that same rescuing spirit gladly work through them and gush out toward others needing rescue. While it's true that not all of us were in danger of being aborted, we were all in danger of something much worse than that: eternal condemnation and God's eternal wrath for our sins. Jesus intervened and saved us from that fate.

> For while we were still helpless, at the right time Christ died for the ungodly. Romans 5:6 (NASB)

We must let our astonishment at what Jesus did for us propel us to love the unborn and anyone else in any kind of peril. This motivation leads to joyful, energetic, sustained, and gracious efforts on behalf of the defenseless. Many of the Scriptures highlighted in this chapter reinforce this motivation. Because He rescued us (gushed in), with grateful hearts we rescue others (gush out)!

This basic principle — that Christians are *rescued rescuers* — applies to many areas of the Christian life. We share the gospel with others (gush out), because God first shared the gospel with us (gushed in). We go to distant lands to help people spiritually and physically (gush out), because God did that for us in Christ by leaving heaven and coming to earth as a man (gushed in). We love our neighbor (gush out), because God became a neighbor to us and loved us (gushed in). We seek the isolated, dejected, and marginalized (gush out), because God sought us when we were all those things and even more (gushed in).

Loving others (gush-out) pivots on our astonishment with God's love for us (gush-in). What a clean and joyful dynamic this is! It sidelines guilt, anger, politics, duty, and all kinds of other lesser motivations for loving others. It roots our love for others in our astonishment and joy over God's love for us. It leads to lives that naturally pour out love for others. Let's see how this worked in the true story of my friend John.[1]

The Gush-Out Trifecta: John's Story

John was in his mid-thirties, living far from God and in comprehensive peril, when he was deluged with love by the God of gush. He'd been brought up in a deeply fractured and abusive home. His parents — based on their own upbringing, not by their design — had constantly provided a fare of emotional and relational abuse that John had no choice but to consume. Performance-based love was a cold dish often on the menu. As a child, when things would get really bad, John would harden his heart against this toxic incoming gush by hiding under the stairs. This was one of the many ways he learned to survive.

As an adult, without consciously meaning to do so and without even understanding what was compelling him, John gushed out various forms of abuse on himself, on others, and on God. For example, he tried to satisfy his thirst by swallowing desiccants: illicit relationships and extreme sports. Like the gush he had swallowed for so long, the gush he now spewed was bitter — the law of the gush in action. Finally, in a small European town where John had gone in pursuit of a girl — right in the midst of the desert created by his own and others' desiccating choices — God caught John and began flooding him with Himself.

The heavy downpour of God's gush to John continued month after month. Little by little, God graciously revealed to John the truth about Himself and about John's parched and hardened heart — and God began His opulently hydrating work. In that process, John turned into a man of praise. Praise just gushed from John! The fitness adrenaline junkie was now spontaneously saying, "I can't believe what my heart was made of, and that God loves me because of His amazing gospel!" The gush-out of praise back to God had begun.

John also began to gush God's love back on himself. Part of this came from God's connecting John to a group of other Christians, who were conduits of God's love to him in all his dehydrated brokenness. Oftentimes I'd sit down with him for coffee, and when we began talking about the love of God, John would begin to cry. He was literally gushing the tears of joy that God had shed over him, His beloved one in Christ. John experienced his thirst and the hydration of God as he wept, gushing out healthy self-love.

Several years after John was first overcome by the God of gush, he turned that life-giving spray on others. One of the major streams was his writing a book that told God's story in the context of his own story. The gush of God had washed away John's shame and had gladly compelled him to help others experience God's love and grace. His book was published in early 2010, and since then God has gushed waves and waves of His love for others through John.

The gush into, within, and out of John continues to this day. Only God knows where it will end! Lord willing, John's connection to God will widen like an ever-expanding golden hose, giving water to him and to others who live in a parched and scorching land. Altogether, John's life is an amazing picture of someone who's caught up in the gush of God and who hoses that gush back in praise to God, love to himself, and love toward others.

Can we see ourselves in John's story? The details of our lives are probably different, but I hope we see or long for the major themes we've explored: continuously experiencing God's gush for us and therefore gushing back to Him, ourselves, and others.

Gushaholic's Prayer

Lord, thanks that Your love is so powerful that I can't help but gush out praise to You, love for myself, and love for others. Please increase my capacity to receive You and to gush You out, especially as a "rescued rescuer" as I've seen in this chapter. Amen.

Gushercises

1. Recount the story of God's rescuing you from eternal condemnation by His grace and truth in the gospel. If you aren't sure what this means, you may not be a Christian. If you aren't sure you're a Christian, I plead with you to turn to Appendix A to learn more.
2. How might recounting God's rescuing you (gush-in) generate your concern for and action toward others in peril around you (gush-out)?
3. Who could you gush God's rescuing love out to this week? How could you do it?
4. How can you relate John's story to your own experience?

24

Mutiny, Drought, and Kisses

> *My people have committed two sins:*
> *They have forsaken Me,*
>   *the Spring of Living Water,*
> *and have dug their own cisterns,*
>   *broken cisterns that cannot hold water.*
>   Jeremiah 2:13 (NIV)

Nearly twenty-four inches of *Cosmopolitan*, *Vogue*, and *Glamour* magazines lean like the Tower of Pisa in the wicker basket next to Lisa's trendy sofa. Like little flags of caution, yellow sticky notes jut from between their pages, marking outfits, romance advice, hairdos, thigh-slimming exercises, and sex tips — all of which she hopes will someday get her what she craves: the man of her dreams. The trouble is that she's been employing this advice for years, and still lives in a studio apartment in downtown Chicago all alone. As age thirty looms on the horizon, the emptiness in her heart gets lonelier and lonelier.

Then one day while looking for a renegade hair clip under the sofa, she discovers her old Bible. Slowly she slides it into the center of the tiny room to see her name embossed on the dust-veiled cover. Memories of youth group, college Bible studies, and post-college church visits for Easter and Christmas flash through her mind. Compelled by a strange but undeniable urge, she opens the book to a place marked by one of the same yellow sticky notes that adorn her Leaning Tower of How-to-Find-Fulfillment-in-the-World magazines. The pages roll back to reveal the text of Jeremiah 2:13. As she reads the words of God, tears flood her eyes. Then, in a slow, tear-distorted glance at her pile of magazines, she softly utters the words, "O Lord, I am so thirsty."

Why?

Why would Lisa let her Bible gather dust while she accumulates a stack of worldly magazines full of dehydrating advice? Why would she ignore the one Person who can meet all her deepest longings for intimacy, meaning, love, and security — in favor of a wasteland of empty promises that can't consistently or comprehensively deliver any of those things? Why would she spend her hard-earned cash and devote countless hours to reading, marking, and employing the tactics from vanity rags instead of soaking in the life-giving words of God? The answer? Because Lisa is a recovering cistern-digger just as we are and just as God's people have been throughout the ages.

At least that's how God describes us in places like Jeremiah 2:13, quoted at the beginning of this chapter. This is one of many verses in which God expresses His bewilderment at this kind of behavior in us. He's taken aback because we've left Him and have gone to empty places to satisfy our cravings for personal value, meaning, love, forgiveness, grace, and the like. As we sail around Buoy V, it's important that we examine this hard part of life in the gush and explore how God invites us to grow out of it.

Through the prophet Jeremiah, God points out that Israel's sin began with their leaving Him as their Source of spiritual life. That is always the genesis of sin. We turn from God, insanely believing that soul-satisfaction is to be found elsewhere. We momentarily stop believing that God is our only true heart-nourishment. Though we seldom put it in these terms, all sin starts with a conversation within us that goes something like this: "You know, God, You're just not enough. Forgiving my sin really isn't all that exciting. Being declared Your beloved in Christ just doesn't bring me the sense of meaning I need. Fellowship with You doesn't bring me the sense of joy, security, and peace I'm craving. So I'll see You later. I'm going to look for satisfaction elsewhere, at least for a while."

Sounds pretty crazy, doesn't it? Sure it does. But we're all guilty of doing this *as Christians*. Sometimes we fight the impulse to do this several times a day. God's people have been struggling with this problem for millennia (Jeremiah was written between 626 and 586 B.C.). As Christians, we must see our sin as mutiny against God that's rooted in this type of temporary spiritual insanity. Viewing our sin in this way clarifies the most essential and foundational principle of our life in the gush: God is our only Fountain. Understanding our sin as mutiny against God reminds us that trusting in and relating to Him is our only hope of satisfying our supreme thirst (Chapter 4).

Revolted?

God is often appalled at our mutinous rebellion against Him as our only Satisfier and Fountain. He's practically incredulous about it, just as we would be incredulous if a dehydrated person refused a glass of cold water and grabbed instead for a cup of flaming Tabasco sauce. Let's listen to God's heart in these passages, and let our own hearts absorb how crazy we are to leave Him as our spiritual Spring. Remember that much of this language is metaphorical — physical examples pointing to spiritual truths.

> Why do you spend your money for that which is not bread,
> and your labor for that which does not satisfy?
> Isaiah 55:2a

> And now what do you gain by going to Egypt
> to drink the waters of the Nile?
> Or what do you gain by going to Assyria
> to drink the waters of the Euphrates? Jeremiah 2:18

> Their idols are like scarecrows in a cucumber field,
> and they cannot speak;
> they have to be carried,
> for they cannot walk....
> They [those who turn from God to other so-called sources
> of life] are both stupid and foolish;
> the instruction of idols is but wood! Jeremiah 10:5a, 8

Digging Broken Cisterns

Not only do we forget God and reach insanely for parching lies, but we actually build systems to fuel this crazy habit. Lisa was doing this by buying, building, reading, marking, and living according to a pile of magazines that she thought held the key to her heart's satisfaction. That is exactly what Jeremiah means when he says that we dig our "own cisterns, broken cisterns that cannot hold water" (2:13b). That phrase includes several convicting elements. First, a cistern can't *generate* water as a fountain can; it only *holds* water that's put into it. Nothing and no one but God is a Source that sends forth the life we crave.

Second, a *broken* cistern can't even *hold* water that's put into it! The sin-systems we set up are like cracked pottery that no amount of superglue (spiritual or otherwise) can make watertight. They have no capacity to retain the life-giving nourishment we crave.

Third, contrast the idea of our digging cisterns with the idea of God's watering us. When we dig cisterns, we wear ourselves out for something that can't possibly satisfy us. When we allow God to water us, He graciously gives us everything we need, requiring no meritorious work from us. As we've been discussing throughout this book, peaceful relationship with God is a free gift from beginning to end — a gift that's received by faith in Jesus Christ. When we consider these three elements together, it's easy to see how foolish we are when we rebel against God and create schemes that we think will provide soul-satisfaction.

A Wrecked Car

I dramatically experienced the sad phenomenon of digging a broken cistern early in my Christian life. I was about twenty-three years old and was advancing in my corporate career. I'd bought my first car — a shiny new Honda Civic, which was my pride and joy. For the first six months of my career, I lived in Los Angeles and didn't experience a single day of rain. Nonetheless, I washed my Civic every week and waxed it just about every month. I even had a car-waxing party to teach others how to wax *their* cars! I loved that car and poured my life into it.

One day, after visiting my parents in Chattanooga, I got into a car accident. The road was slick, and in order to avoid a jogger, I swerved, spun around, and went sideways into a ditch. Neither the jogger nor I was physically hurt, but I was shaken emotionally. Eventually I got out of the car to wait for the tow truck and my parents. As I stood there, I looked at my car. It was a twisted wreck. Cooling fluid was trickling onto the street like blood from a wounded animal. Broken glass littered the scene. It was obvious that the car was hopelessly wrecked, though it would be a few days before I'd learn that it was officially totaled.

As I stood looking at my car, my mind raced. I thought of the brand-new tires I'd just bought, and wondered if I'd lose all that money. I thought about the expensive stereo system I'd had installed, and wondered if I'd be able to remove the components and use them in another car. I thought of the brand-new coolant that was leaking onto the street and of the money I'd just spent getting a complete tune-up for the vehicle. I thought of how much time and effort I'd put into washing, waxing, and vacuuming the car.

I also thought about how vain all that effort had been. I knew it wasn't wrong to take good care of a car. What hit me was how much of my identity, sense of peace, and personal joy had depended on that car. In the wake of the accident, it became clear that I'd poured my life into what was now so obviously a broken cistern — a twisted, bleeding, broken hulk of metal, glass, and rubber. As I got into the back seat of my parents' car, I spontaneously began crying. I was overcome by the trauma of the accident and by the vanity of investing so much of my life in something that could never really satisfy.

How have you temporarily left God to dig broken cisterns? These cisterns — which the Bible also calls *idols* — come in all shapes and sizes. A cistern/idol could be a person — a spouse, lover, child, or friend. It could be a job. It could be a certain body type, specific intellectual achievements, financial goals, pleasure, a hoped-for lifestyle, ministry success, control, moral purity, acceptance into a social clique, political freedom, a house, making the team, a particular wardrobe, or a religious commendation.

Maybe you've dug a cistern of isolation that you think will keep your soul safe and make you happy. On the other hand, maybe you've surrounded yourself with people, parties, social commitments, Bible studies, and prayer gatherings, thinking that people hold the key to your heart's vitality. Perhaps you've immersed yourself in fantasy worlds — television shows, video games, cyber relationships, gossipy talk shows, romance novels, daydreams, or pornography — thinking these will satisfy your deepest needs. It could be that you've structured a rigorous regimen of physical health, including protein shakes, supplements, strict dietary rules, and daily personal training, in hopes that the broken cistern of your body will somehow give you the love, value, peace, and joy for which your heart thirsts.

Some of the things listed above (definitely not all of them) are just fine in their proper place and measure. But none of them will ever be a source or reservoir for the life we crave. Only God, the Spring — and a living relationship with Him — will fill that need. He's the only Fountain that can give us the love, value, peace, and joy we yearn for. To think or act otherwise is sinful mutiny on our voyage in God's gush.

Drought: God's Discipline

God is supremely interested in our spiritual well-being. He cares for every other part of our lives, too, but the state of our souls is His primary concern. So it probably isn't surprising that God graciously disciplines us in order to deter us from forsaking Him and digging broken cisterns. He sometimes does this by causing droughts in our lives — by withholding blessing and/or by causing or allowing pain. These droughts are designed by God in part to wake us up from our temporary spiritual insanity of cistern-digging and to move us to repentance. Here are some examples from Scripture. Notice how water (or lack thereof) plays an important part in these lessons.

> He turns rivers into a desert,
>   springs of water into thirsty ground,
> a fruitful land into a salty waste,
>   because of the evil of its inhabitants. Psalm 107:33–34

> And now I will tell you
>   what I will do to my vineyard [God's people].
> I will remove its hedge,
>   and it shall be devoured;

> I will break down its wall,
> > and it shall be trampled down.
> I will make it a waste;
> > it shall not be pruned or hoed,
> > and briers and thorns shall grow up;
> I will also command the clouds
> > that they rain no rain upon it. Isaiah 5:5–6

> [God said,] "You have polluted the land
> > with your vile whoredom.
> Therefore the showers have been withheld,
> > and the spring rain has not come;
> yet you have the forehead of a whore;
> > you refuse to be ashamed." Jeremiah 3:2b–3

Scripture is brimming with instances of God blessing His people with repentance-inducing drought. For more examples, read Isaiah 30, Jeremiah 25, Ezekiel 16, Nahum 1, and Haggai 1. Lest we think that God exercised this sort of discipline only in the Old Testament, look at 2 Corinthians 4:15–18, 1 Thessalonians 3:11–13, Titus 2:11–14, and Hebrews 9:13–14. You can probably add your own stories to these examples. Just think of a time when pain drove you away from sinful mutiny back toward God — where your heart belongs and is truly satisfied.

If we cherish God as our Fountain and only Source for our soul's well-being, we'll actually be glad that He works to cure us of our mutinous tendencies. We should be happy that He withholds rain and brings drought, leading us away from digging broken cisterns and pointing us back to Himself as our Spring of Life. Psalm 107 records a few instances where men gave thanks to God for doing just that. The godly author of Psalm 119 also praises God for bringing affliction that enlivened his need for and joy in God — "It is good for me that I was afflicted, / that I might learn your statutes" (v. 71).

In fact, mature Christians — aware that they're susceptible to bouts with temporary spiritual insanity — will *ask* God to do these very things. Again, the voyager of Psalm 119 praises God for this movement in verses 67–68:

> Before I was afflicted I went astray,
> > but now I keep Your Word.
> You are good and do good;
> > teach me Your statutes.

This same idea is taught in places like Matthew 5:1–12, Hebrews 12:4–13, and 1 Peter 1:1–9. It isn't that we're masochistic, fellow voyagers! We simply appreciate that God does whatever is necessary — even using, causing, or allowing pain — to draw us away from cistern-digging and to bring us back to Him, our Fountain.

Hope for Cistern-Diggers

The gushing good news of the gospel for Christians is that even our temporary God-forsaking, cistern-digging mutinies can't stop the gush of God toward us. God is completely and irrevocably committed to cleansing us of our desiccant-loving ways. He'll finish that job when we die or when He returns, whichever comes first. In the meantime, He pursues us even when we build contraptions that wind up doing nothing but hurting our own hearts. When I realized that my car was a cistern I'd poured my life into, God came to me to forgive me and heal me. Here's how He puts it in Jeremiah 3:22, a text that appears just after God indicts Israel for their broken cistern-digging in Jeremiah 2:13.

> Return, O faithless sons;
> > I will heal your faithlessness.

Though Israel is sometimes "faithless" — as we are — God still invites repentance through His Spirit in the gospel. In other prophetic books of the Bible, God pictures this healing as His turning deserts into pools of water and planting water-loving plants in them (see Isaiah 35, for example). It's a theme we've explored before: Gushing God invites parched people to get (re)hydrated. The nuance in focus here is that our parching has resulted from our own temporary spiritual insanity in forsaking God and building systems that we think will provide soul-hydration.

We talked much about repentance in Chapter 8. You may want to revisit that chapter if God is poking your heart in order to bring you back to spiritual sanity from a recent mutiny. Even if you have a shovel in your hands and are covered with the dirt that comes from digging your own broken cistern, run back to God. You'll find that God is already running toward you and has begun to deluge you with grace and love. He loves to passionately "kiss" returning cistern-diggers all over. As unbelievable as it sounds, that is exactly the picture in Luke 15:20, when God runs to His withered, cistern-digging prodigal son.

> But while he [His cistern-digging son] was still a long way off, his father saw him and felt compassion, and ran and embraced him and kissed him.

A more literal translation of the last six words of this verse is "and fell on his neck and kissed him." This stunning phrase is used two other times in the Bible (Genesis 33:4 and Acts 20:37) to picture overwhelming joy and intensely pure affection between people. But in this case, it's used to display *God's* affection toward a returning cistern-digger. In this awesome movement of grace, God is like an entire baseball team that ecstatically pours out of the dugout to lavishly swamp the pitcher upon winning the World Series. Only we haven't won the World Series. We've forsaken the team and lost the game. Nonetheless, through the amazing grace of Jesus Christ in the gospel, God opulently comes to us in our sinful failure when we make even the slightest turn of repentance.

So what are we waiting for? Return! Throw down your shovel! Fly back into the arms of God, who waits to smother you with the kisses of His hydrating love. As He embraces you, let the thirsty impulses that led you to start digging find satisfaction in the truly quenching gush of God.

Gushaholic's Prayer

Lord, it's true that I often commit mutiny against You. Thank You for the droughts You bring or allow that call me back to sanity. Please help me to return to You quickly and often. And when I do, smother me with your forgiving kisses. Amen.

Gushercises

1. What sorts of broken cisterns are you digging?
2. How is your disbelief in, or distrust of, God as your Fountain prompting you to dig?
3. What sorts of droughts are you experiencing?
4. How might those droughts be God's way of revealing your cistern-digging ways and driving you back to Him for real satisfaction?
5. Repent! See Chapter 8 for "turning instructions."

25

The Reality Sandwich

But we have this treasure in jars of clay. 2 Corinthians 4:7a

Back when I had just graduated from college and started my first job, I had a boss who'd frequently meet my innocent idealism with the balloon-puncturing phrase, "Doug, it's time to take a bite of the reality sandwich." At the time, that sandwich was always a bummer. The bites always seemed to go down hard. As I've grown more mature, I've learned that my boss was trying to help me. He wanted me to see things as they really are — to recognize the limitations of each of us, and of our company. He wanted us to operate realistically, not idealistically, so that we'd enjoy our work.

One of the most wonderful things about God is that He repeatedly presents us with a type of reality sandwich in Scripture and encourages us to bite it — often. He wants us to know the truth about ourselves, about Him, and about the world we live in. He wants us yet-to-be-perfected voyagers to see the limitations of living the Christian life. God offers us bites of the reality sandwich in order to graciously guard us from the many perils and sins associated with being out of touch with the realities of living a life of faith on this side of heaven.

So what's God's reality sandwich for us? It's simply this: The gushalicious life sometimes isn't so gushalicious.

Actually, we've taken bites of this reality sandwich before: In Chapter 24 we learned that we're still prone to mutiny against God. And around Buoy I we took several big bites of this sandwich by recognizing our supreme thirst and our continuing battle with a trio of dehydrating enemies. We learned that the world, the devil, and our flesh regularly inflame our deepest soul-cravings and that this is a *normal*, though often a painful, part of our life as God's beloved ones in Christ. The bite we'll focus on in this chapter has to do with our overall constitution — our ability to remain healthy and to withstand hardship so that we can maintain intimacy with God while fighting these enemies. One heart-reviving spice in this bite is that we remain beloved, yet leaky, pots in this life. This, too, is *normal*. So, for our joy and well-being, let's devour this bite of the sandwich together, shall we?

Beloved, Yet Leaky, Pots

The image of a leaky pot comes from 2 Corinthians 4:7, quoted at the beginning of this chapter. The Greek words (*ostrakinos skeuos*) are translated many different ways in English Bibles: "jars of clay" (ESV), "earthen vessels" (NASB), or "perishable containers" (NLT). By using this picture, God likens us to clay vessels (e.g., bowls or water jars), which were so abundant in biblical times and which were prone to leak or break. The idea is that we're frail, *even though we're God's beloved in Christ*. To be frail is to be made of delicate or weak materials and therefore to be vulnerable to injury, breakage, or damage. This frailty encompasses every part of our being. It means that we're subject to fracture physically, morally, spiritually, intellectually, and in every other aspect of the human experience.

    The image of a leaky pot also beautifully fits the water images we've been discovering in this book. Being a pot or a vessel reminds us that we don't *originate* life; God does. *He's* the Fountain, not us. The immediate context of this verse plainly reveals that the "treasure" God gushes (and that we leak out all the time) is His glorious desire for relationship with us through Jesus Christ. Furthermore, we're reminded that, despite God's immeasurable desire and ability to hydrate us, our present constitution keeps us from consistently gushing in and gushing out the wonderful intimacy He offers. We're just too frail.

    Swallowing this bite of the reality sandwich — that we're leaky pots — is both liberating and sobering. It's liberating, because it frees us from delusions about the gushalicious life. It rescues us from illusions of perfected strength and experience on this side of heaven. It reminds us of our limited ability in this life to remain in sync with the law of the gush. Recognizing this limitation deals a death blow to the perfectionistic impulses that so often oppress some Christians and people around them. It also liberates us from the contempt — both self-centered and other-centered — that accompanies the inevitable failure to meet unrealistic expectations.

The fact that we're leaky pots of clay is also sobering, because it reminds us that we absolutely, positively *must* remain under the Fountain if we have any hope of being hydrated. That coincides with what we learned about God being the *Who* and the *What* of His own invitation (Chapter 7). It's a vivid reminder of what we're learning around Buoy V: that relationship results in radiance and that we're to go with the flow of God's work in our hearts. In addition, recognizing that we're leaky pots sobers us to the dissonance in this life while fueling our longing for a future Day when we'll be resurrected without any leaks at all (2 Corinthians 15).

Embracing our leakiness doesn't mean we're to just let out a resigned sigh: "Well, I guess this is as good as I'm gonna get." It doesn't mean we're to shun any attempt to grow in godliness, or give up and sin "because I'm imperfect anyhow, so what does it matter?" Instead, it gives us the freedom to grow in virtue, knowing that God's love doesn't depend upon our becoming leak-free. It's like the joy of playing for a coach who wants us to improve, but who also knows our limitations, and values us regardless of our performance. We *want* to play for and improve for this coach, because he values us as we are. In the process, we also learn to love ourselves and others as we are.

Groaning

The liberating and sobering complexities of coming to grips with our leakiness invite us to take a second bite of the reality sandwich. This bite, which often closely follows the first bite, tells us that it's normal for leaky-pots like us to *groan*. A quick search for the words *groan* and *groaning* in the Bible reveals thirty-four occurrences (in the ESV). These occurrences are spread pretty evenly through the Old and New Testaments. From this, we learn that groaning is a normal part of every leaky pot's life on this side of heaven.

Groaning in the Bible literally means "to be sick, let out a deep sigh, or roar." It's a comprehensive word, often involving our entire being. On a more basic level, it's simply an expression of distress. Given this definition, groaning can take many forms and can be caused by many things. When we look up the words usually translated "groan" in the Bible (usually *shaag* or *anaq* in Hebrew, and *stenazo* in Greek), we see that the *heart* of *Christians'* groaning centers on interrupted intimacy with God — interruption either in themselves or in others. This is the groan that underlies all our other groans. Here's an example of what this looks like.

On a very simple and immediate level, I may groan when my neighbor's dog barks constantly between two and three in the morning when I'm trying to sleep. But this simple, surface-level groan opens up all kinds of other, more profound and uniquely Christian, groans. I groan that I haven't gushed in God's love to a degree that I naturally gush out love toward my neighbor in my thoughts, words, and deeds at two in the morning or at any other time. I groan that my fellowship with God is so easily interrupted by my own anger. I groan that my neighbor is so disconnected from God that he'd let his dog go on barking. I groan that all creation (including dogs) is out of sync with God and is under His curse as a result of the fall (Genesis 3). I groan for heaven, where there will no longer be any disconnection from God.

That's a lot of groaning, friends. And while the illustration of a barking dog may seem ridiculous, just think deeply about your own groaning for a minute. If you peel back the layers, I'm sure you too will find that dissonance with God is a foundational factor in all your groaning. This will be true whether the initial, surface-level groan is caused by your own sin, a physical disease, job loss, a flat tire, world strife, a manipulative friend, environmental disasters, white cat hair on black trousers, market crashes, traffic jams, family disunity, burned Pop Tarts, or a slow Internet. Ultimately, Christian groaning centers on the fact that there are problems between creation, others, us, and God. And this groaning is magnified, in part, because we're leaky pots.

Not only is this groaning *normal* for God's beloved in Christ; it's often *amplified* for us. That's because we're keenly aware of the forces (the world, the devil, and our flesh) that daily attack our relationship with God and try to create leaks in our hearts. We've also tasted the joys of God's "treasure" (intimacy with Him), which makes us roar more loudly when we see it drain away. Just as we feel alarm when a gash causes blood (essential for our physical survival) to gush from our bodies, so too will Christians groan when any enemy (the world, the devil, or our flesh) causes our souls' lifeblood — intimacy with God — to gush from our hearts. King David, a confirmed gushaholic, was a leaky pot who groaned this way in Psalm 38:8 — "I am feeble and crushed; / I groan because of the tumult of my heart."

The Gifts of Leakiness and Groaning

Maturing Christians like us won't run from, minimize, or medicate our leakiness or our groaning. We won't utterly despair when the gushalicious life isn't as gushalicious as we'd like it to be. Instead, we'll embrace leakiness and groaning as gifts with tremendous spiritual benefits. This won't stop all the discomfort, nor will it eradicate our proper longing for heaven. And this doesn't mean that we're to be spiritual masochists who delight in pain. It simply means that we'll thank God for reminding us of His soul-hydrating capacity, of the importance of staying intimate with Him, and of the certainty of the Day when all leaks and groans will end. Remaining mindful of God, despite our leakiness and groaning, gives us the opportunity to put His beauty on full display to a world that knows nothing of godly contentment in the midst of pain.

The apostle Paul demonstrates shades of this maturity in 2 Corinthians 12:7–10, paraphrased below based on our discussion in this chapter. (Remember that the verses in the Bible were written by the same apostle Paul who, only a few paragraphs earlier in 2 Corinthians 4:7, said, "we have this treasure in jars of clay.")

> God helps me remember that I'm a leaky pot. He shows me the joy of embracing myself as I am — as His beloved, yet leaky, child. He also shows me how wonderfully hydrating He is. He brought me from pleading with Him to patch my leaks to a point of thanking Him for them. He helped me see how my leaks drive me to stay close to Him, where I belong. For this reason, I'll actually gladly boast about my leaks!

Do *we* see our groan-causing leaks — frailties that diminish our ability to gush God in and out — as signs of God's goodness to us? Do we see them as blessings from Him that point us (back) to Him, where we can flourish? Do we see them as normal? Do we actually celebrate them, as Paul does, for their ability to build our relationship with God? This last question in particular may cause us to wince or at least to doubt the veracity of God's instruction through Paul in this text.

Yet in 2 Corinthians 12:9, the ESV, NASB, NIV, and NLT all use the word "glad" or "gladly" to describe Paul's boasting over his weaknesses. Because this seems like such an unnatural response to our weaknesses, a quick check of the Greek is helpful. There we find the superlative form of the adverb *hedeos*. As a superlative, it means that Paul is boasting very gladly, or with great pleasure or happiness. The New Jerusalem Bible captures this heightened enthusiasm by translating the phrase "It is, then, about my weaknesses that I am happiest of all to boast, so that the power of Christ may rest upon me." It's appropriate for us to have this same attitude about *our* frailties.

Sometimes being very glad about our weakness seems like insanity! The world, the devil, and our flesh certainly think so. They see no value in weakness, as touted by this slogan from Nike athletic equipment company: "The meek may inherit the earth, but they won't get the ball" (a corruption of Matthew 5:5). So we probably need some help swallowing these tough bites of the reality sandwich.

Help for Leaky Groaners

We'll be more inclined to "very gladly boast" about our leaks and groans if we hear God embracing them as part of who we are. This is simply another reminder of something we've already discussed: that God loves *parched* people and invites us to Him for hydration. Here's how He puts it in Psalm 103:13–14.

> As a father shows compassion to his children,
>> so the LORD shows compassion to those who fear Him.
> For He knows our frame;
>> He remembers that we are dust.

Did we get that? God is *compassionate* toward His beloved, yet leaky, jars of clay. Our constitution as "dust" in this passage is very similar to our constitution as "clay" in 2 Corinthians 4:7a. The dust of Psalm 103:14 particularly likens us to dry, loose earth that's easily thrown around — or anything pulverized, like ashes. Knowing we're like dust, God enters into, shares in, and helps us in our frailty. When the gushalicious life isn't so gushalicious — even because of our own sin — God compassionately cares for us. Compassion is a main feature in God's posture toward His people, especially when our weaknesses and sins have overtaken us. We see His compassion revealed in Psalm 78:37–38.

> Their heart was not steadfast toward Him;
> > they were not faithful to His covenant.
> Yet He, being compassionate,
> > atoned for their iniquity
> > and did not destroy them;
> He restrained His anger often
> > and did not stir up all His wrath.

This raises a series of essential questions. Can we embrace this reality about life in the gush? If God loves us as dusty, leaky pots, can we love ourselves as such, too? Can we love others made of dust? All these questions throw us back to the law of the gush, which makes our gush-out trifecta pivot on letting God gush into our hearts by faith. The degree to which we embrace God's gush-in of hydrating love for us as leaky, dusty, groaning pots will generally be the degree to which we embrace ourselves and others as leaky, dusty, groaning pots.

Still having a hard time swallowing? Then consider that God Himself became weak and groaned, in part to demonstrate compassion toward us. This truth is a radiant gem that's unique to Christianity. Our God isn't some ivory-tower deity who tries to relate to us lowly, leaky vessels from a safe distance. No! He *became* a lowly, leaky vessel when He became a man in the Person of Jesus Christ (and throughout His life, he remained absolutely sinless). This fact helps us embrace Him, which is to let Him flow into our hearts so we can responsively and freely love Him, ourselves, and others. Here's how He puts it in Hebrews 4:15–16.

> For we do not have a High Priest [Jesus Christ] who is unable to sympathize with our weaknesses, but One who in every respect has been tempted as we are, yet without sin. Let us then with confidence draw near to the throne of grace, that we may receive mercy and find grace to help in time of need.

It's radical that God Himself knew from experience that the gushalicious life often isn't that gushalicious! This stupendous fact keeps us from running for the spiritual makeup kit to try to cover up who we really are. It reminds us of how silly and unnecessary it is to paint rosy pictures of our lives when we pray. It means that when we come to God, we can throw away our self-help brand of leak-be-gone! We can come to Him "with confidence" *just as we are* and "receive mercy and find grace to help in time of need." Singer-songwriter Chris Rice puts it this way in his tune "Untitled Hymn."

> Weak and wounded sinner
> Lost and left to die
> Raise your head for love is passing by.
> Come to Jesus.
> Come to Jesus.
> Come to Jesus and live.[1]

One more reason to swallow this reality sandwich (that the gushalicious life sometimes isn't so gushalicious) is that God redeems our groaning to remind us of a coming Day when His beloved ones in Christ will be freed of all groaning. In this sense, God transforms our leak-caused groaning into a gift that points us forward and helps us persevere amid today's trials. God says it this way through the apostle Paul in Romans 8:23.

> And not only the creation, but we ourselves, who have the firstfruits of the Spirit, groan inwardly as we wait eagerly for adoption as sons, the redemption of our bodies.

The certainty of God's promise to bring this future gives us strength to keep opening ourselves to God's gush and letting that gush flow through us toward Him, ourselves, and others. We'll strive for this openness, knowing that God realizes how hard it can be. Sure, we'll groan. Yes, we'll fail. But we won't let those lapses destroy us. Instead, we'll let our groaning drive us to Him, where we can certainly receive His hydration to carry on. In fact, we'll even try to join our forefathers in the faith who, like Paul, celebrated groaning for this very reason!

Gushaholic's Prayer

So help me, Lord. Give me the grace, mercy, and help that You promise to me as I sometimes struggle to live the gushalicious life, especially when it isn't so gushalicious. I know You will. You promised. Thank You, Lord. Amen.

Gushercises

1. How do you feel about the idea that the gushalicious life is sometimes not so gushalicious?
2. How do you tend to leak? How have you groaned in your life, or how are you groaning right now?
3. How is your groaning uniquely Christian? This question asks you to consider your most fundamental, underlying groans.
4. How do you think God treats you in your weakness? How does this affect how you treat yourself and others?
5. Describe how our groaning is related to our longing for heaven. How does this show up in your life?

Buoy VI

Gush Everlasting

Our discussion about our continuing struggle with mutiny against the God of gush and with our remaining leakiness is a fitting send-off as we approach the last buoy of our journey: Gush Everlasting. Our struggle for lasting hydration in this life compels us to look forward to the next life. We're glad that in this life we can experience hints of life in the gush, but we also yearn for an eternal future centered around God and characterized by our complete and uninterrupted hydration from Him.

As we sail around Buoy VI, we'll look at God's promise of His eternal gush from a number of angles. We'll see that everyone lives in the gush of God forever, be it the bitter gush of hell or the sweet gush of heaven. We'll see that our blessed status as God's beloved makes our glimpse of each of these eternal ends increase our gush-out of praise to God, love for self, and love for others. We'll then conclude with some very practical insights to help us in our continuing voyage.

26

The Wrathful Gush of Hell

The LORD is my strength and my song,
and He has become my salvation;
this is my God, and I will praise Him,
my father's God, and I will exalt Him.
Exodus 15:2

It may surprise you to find a chapter on hell in a book like this. "How can talk about hell be refreshing?" you might be asking. That's a great question!

The answer is that knowing more about what we've been rescued *from* elicits greater appreciation of our rescue. That causes a greater gush-out of praise to God, and of love to ourselves and others. For example, if someone keeps you from stepping in a mud puddle, that's nice and you'll certainly be appreciative. But if someone dies while trying to pull you from a burning building and certain death — well, that's a whole other story. God's rescuing us from hell is more like the latter times ten to an infinite power.

Pondering hell's incomparable horror and God's having saved us from it is like adding a turbopump to our gush-out trifecta. It's like clicking "sharpen" on a blurry photo in an editing program, causing us to remark, "Wow, I never saw *that* before!" It's like watching the waters of a tsunami destroying your house and everything around it — from the arms of a Coast Guard rescue jumper who just pulled you from your rooftop.

Yes, greater appreciation of peril elicits a greater gush-out trifecta from those rescued.

That's what's going on in Exodus 15:2, quoted at the beginning of this chapter. It's the first verse in the song Moses and the sons of Israel sang to the Lord after He rescued them from the Egyptians. God had just drowned that archenemy in the Red Sea and delivered Israel safely to the other side. The nation's awareness of their imminent peril and the drama of God's rescue compelled them to sing a wonderful song to God, which you can read for yourself in Exodus 15.

Hell is infinitely worse than being recaptured, or even killed, by the ancient Egyptians. What kind of song will we sing when we realize what we've been saved from? Well, let's begin to find out.

What Is Hell?

In three words, hell is *aggressive eternal dehydration*. It's God's fiery eternal gush poured out on unrepentant sinners, the devil, and demons. It's described in both the Old and the New Testament. Let's look at one of the clearest passages in the whole Bible on this subject as we seek to adore the God who saved us in Christ (see Appendix A if you're not sure you're saved). Keep in mind that this text (Revelation 14:9–11) uses physical images to point to spiritual and relational realities.

> ⁹And another angel, a third, followed them, saying with a loud voice, "If anyone worships the beast and its image and receives a mark on his forehead or on his hand, ¹⁰he also will drink the wine of God's wrath, poured full strength into the cup of His anger, and he will be tormented with fire and sulfur in the presence of the holy angels and in the presence of the Lamb. ¹¹And the smoke of their torment goes up forever and ever, and they have no rest, day or night, these worshipers of the beast and its image, and whoever receives the mark of its name."

First we can identify those who are being tormented in hell. It's anyone who rejects Christ's invitation to the spiritually parched. These beings are referred to in verses 9 and 11 as those who "worship the beast and its image and receive a mark on [their foreheads] or on [their hands]." This strange phrase is shorthand in the book of Revelation for those who reject God and follow the dehydrating, wretched ways of the world, the devil, and their own sinful flesh. These people are entrenched in their rebellious ways and clearly hate God. That group included us — before Christ saved us. Like everyone else in the world, we have rebelled against God — and we sometimes still do rebel against Him. Outside of faith in Christ, we deserve the fate of any person who has not embraced Christ's rescuing work on the cross: hell.[1]

Next we see that unrepentant God-rebels are being made to drink something awful and are being tormented in various ways. They're being served God's wrath (v. 10), which is His *thumos*, His boiling rage. It's "full strength," which means that it's undiluted (*akratos*) and therefore as potent as it can be. We also read that this full-strength wine of God's wrath is served "in the cup of His anger." This means that God's fury is *delivered* with fury. It means that both the content (the wrath of God) and the delivery of that content are unimaginably violent.

Furthermore, verses 10 and 11 tell us that people are being tormented (*basanizo*) in hell. This means that they're being tortured, harassed, or distressed, which obviously involves intense pain. This is confirmed by Jesus' parable in Luke 16, which records the cries of a rich man who's experiencing hell:

> And he called out, "Father Abraham, have mercy on me, and send Lazarus to dip the end of his finger in water and cool my tongue, for I am in anguish in this flame."
>
> Luke 16:24

The torment is caused by the raining of "fire and sulfur" (v. 10). To the original hearers, this phrase would have conjured images of God's wrath gushing down upon the unrepentant cities of Sodom and Gomorrah (Genesis 19). In that scene, God rained "fire and brimstone," killing every living thing in those twin cities because of their wanton rebellion against Him. Yes, a fiery, horrible, excruciating punishment awaits God-haters in hell. And remember: It awaited us too, before Christ saved us.

We also see that all this torment and its resulting agony last forever (v. 11). The imagery here again hearkens back to Sodom and Gomorrah when, after God had rained fire from heaven, "the smoke of the land ascended like the smoke of a furnace" (Genesis 19:28b, NASB). In this case, constant smoking (i.e., smoke that "rises forever") indicates some degree of constant burning, thereby refuting the idea that hell means annihilation. This frightening point is reinforced by the fact that there's "no rest, day or night" for those in this hot gush of God's wrath and torment. It's truly "gush everlasting" in a form that's unimaginably horrifying and excruciating.

Our final observation is perhaps the most difficult. It's that God is the One doing all this tormenting. It *isn't* Satan, as many Christians believe. More specifically, it's the second Person of the Trinity, Jesus Christ, who in verse 10 is referred to by one of His titles, "The Lamb."[2] Jesus is accompanied by His "holy angels." This is no mere spectator's posture, as if God is only watching what's going on from a press box high up in the stadium of hell. It's an active presence, where God is the Actor, the Tormentor, and the Gusher of His own righteous wrath upon those who hate Him and have rebelled against Him.

God as the One gushing wrath in hell is reinforced by the possessives "*God's* wrath" and "*His* anger" (v. 10). God is the One that unrepentant sinners, the devil, and demons hate. God is the One who's offended by sin, not the devil. God is the One who's our Maker and Judge. So God is the One who deals out righteous punishment on unrepentant evildoers in hell.

Yes, greater appreciation of peril elicits a greater gush-out trifecta from those rescued.

Time Out

Before we go on, let me say something to you if you're not sure you're a Christian: You *can* be sure, and you *must* be sure. God cares *intensely* about saving you from the hellish eternal gush you deserve. He clarifies this craving strenuously with a rhetorical question in Ezekiel 18:23.

> Have I any pleasure in the death of the wicked, declares the Lord GOD, and not rather that he should turn from his way and live?

The phrasing of this question clearly demonstrates that God *wants* "the wicked" (including every human being who ever lived, lives, or will live) to turn from their rebellion toward Him. Furthermore, God says that His judgment will come suddenly and unexpectedly, and He urges us all to be ready (Matthew 24–25 and 1 Thessalonians 5). So please turn *right now* to Appendix A for help with this, the most important decision of your (eternal) life.

More Pictures of God's Wrathful Gush

Aside from the text we just explored, God describes hell in many ways in the Bible. As with so many other themes explored in this book, God uses water-pictures and water metaphors to help us understand what He means. One of the most common ways is His bringing temporal (earthly) judgment to people in the Old Testament as a warning against eternal judgment. This idea is presented as God's "pouring wrath" in Jeremiah 10:25.

> Pour out Your wrath on the nations that know You not,
>   and on the peoples that call not on Your Name,
> for they have devoured Jacob;
>   they have devoured him and consumed him,
>   and have laid waste his habitation.

Notice the similarities to Revelation 14:9–11. It's God doing the pouring. It's pouring that He's doing. It's His own wrath that He's pouring. And He's pouring it out on people who've rejected relationship with Him and who are living in rebellion against Him. All this pouring recalls the Flood, which is a dramatic water-picture of God's judgment and hell. This judgment-gush of epic proportions is described in Genesis 7:11–12.

> In the six hundredth year of Noah's life, in the second month, on the seventeenth day of the month, on that day all the fountains of the great deep burst forth, and the windows of the heavens were opened. And rain fell upon the earth forty days and forty nights.

Why did God do this? In Genesis 6:5–7, He reveals His exasperation with the evil of mankind and with their rebellion against Him. So he righteously judges and then totally destroys mankind in the greatest water-deluge the world has ever seen. Only Noah and his family are saved, along with pairs of animals, because they embraced the grace God extended to them (Genesis 6:8). Notice how God's description of the Flood, which prefigures the eternal, horrific gush of hell, perfectly fits the English definition of *gush*:

1. To flow forth suddenly in great volume
2. To emit a sudden and abundant flow, as of tears
3. To make an excessive display of sentiment or enthusiasm[3]

Another water-picture God uses to help us understand hell is that of a "lake of fire" (Revelation 19:20, 20:10, 14–15). Each time this metaphor is mentioned, a divine passive is used to indicate that God is the One putting God-hating rebels, the devil, and/or his demons into this place of torment. Like the "fiery furnace" of hell (Matthew 13:42, 50), the "lake of fire" is a place that violently attacks its inhabitants and continuously robs them of any hint of spiritual life. These images depict a place of super-aggressive, ongoing dehydration.

The Hot Gush and Christians

As hard as this chapter is, maturing Christians can't help but see its value. Taking in the facts just presented should stop our hearts with alternating horror and elation. This salvation that God has given to us is *extreme*. It's *huperballo*. In thinking about the cup of wrath we examined in Revelation 14:9–11, we should exult in ecstatic thanks to God when we recall that Jesus agonized over that cup (Matthew 26:36–46) and eventually drank it (Matthew 27:45–46; Romans 3:22–25; 1 John 2:2, 4:10). He did this *for us*, dear friends! Amazing! Tremendous peril averted must result in a tremendous gush of praise to God!

Disregarding hell and God's saving us from it stymies our life in the gush and severely stunts our spiritual growth. If we fail to acknowledge the magnitude of God's rescue of us, our spiritual life is likely to remain shallow and fruitless. God graciously warns us about the importance of this in Hebrews 2:2–3.

> For since the message [of God's rescue for sinners] declared by angels proved to be reliable and every transgression or disobedience received a just retribution, how shall we escape if we neglect such a great salvation?

We bloom in the soil of these radiant truths. Letting this God — the God who rescued us through faith in Christ from His hot gush of hell — flow into our hearts is a great way to amplify our gush-out trifecta.

We spontaneously flood torrential praise back to God the Son for His willingness to drink the cup of His Father's wrath that we deserved for our sins. We extol God the Spirit for opening our hearts to see and receive these magnificent truths. We marvel at the God who didn't leave us in our peril, but who came to rescue us. What an opulently kind and gracious God we have! He's our *Savior*! He has rescued us from an unfathomably awful fate. Praise Him! Praise Him! Make Him offerings of every kind! Gush your entire being back to God for saving you from hell by His love and mercy in Christ (Romans 12:1)!

We gush an astonished joy to ourselves, too, as we realize how privileged we are that God would choose us and rescue us from this fate! This joy intensifies when we affirm that He did this while we were yet sinners (Romans 5:6). His action confirms that we're infinitely precious to Him, so we should consider ourselves precious, too. It's as if God went into a building He knew would be set on fire eternally, looking particularly for us. Upon finding us, though we were playing with matches and gasoline, He considered us His "treasured possession,"[4] and brought us out alive. Wow!

Our soaking in these truths should cause us to naturally gush love toward others as well. By more clearly understanding the horrible eternal fate of those who reject Christ, we should be powerfully motivated to graciously shower them with Him. Knowing that the building of their lives is about to be engulfed in flames and having been saved by God from that peril ourselves, we are in a unique position to strenuously warn those who are ignorant of their certain doom.

Let us not live apathetic lives, my fellow gushaholics, hiding from people and refraining from sounding the alarm. Instead, let's gush God's invitation of mercy and salvation to everyone we meet so that as many people as possible will embrace His offer of eternal life in the sweet gush of heaven. Let's do this gladly, as those captivated with our Rescuer — who lived, died, and rose again to save us from His own righteous wrath for our sins.

Gushaholic's Prayer

Lord, thank You for saving me from hell! Grip my heart with this astounding truth, and let me opulently gush out praise to You, love for myself, and love for others. And, Lord, please use my gush-out, the gush-out of other Christians, and Your Holy Spirit to rescue <insert names here> from the fiery gush of hell. Amen.

Gushercises

1. Describe the biblical concept of the hot gush of God (hell).
2. How is this teaching affecting you?

27

The Sweet Gush of Heaven

For you will not abandon my soul to Sheol,
or let Your holy one see corruption.

You make known to me the path of life;
in Your presence there is fullness of joy;
at Your right hand are pleasures forevermore.
Psalm 16:10–11

I'm like a lot of people who schedule vacations well in advance. That way, I can anticipate time off in the months leading up to my trip. As the weeks go by, I'll often revisit online pictures of my destination and research fun things to do. As I make appointments in the intervening weeks, I smile when I see my vacation week already blocked off. Just knowing that I have a restful, fun trip coming up gives me joy and strength to deal with daily challenges of my everyday life. Anticipating the absence of hardship and the abundance of pleasure during these vacations is one of the main things that makes them so vitalizing — even before I leave home.

This is but a tiny representation of the great and final destination God has in store for His beloved ones in Christ: heaven. It's a classic "lesser–greater" illustration: If we gain joy and strength by musing on an earthly vacation (the "lesser"), then we can certainly gain *much more* joy and strength by musing on our heavenly destination (the "greater"). If thoughts of temporary relief from some of our hardships bolster endurance, then thoughts of *eternal* relief from *all* of our hardships should bolster *even more* endurance. If thoughts of tainted and momentary pleasure make us glad, then thoughts of *pure and eternal* pleasure with God should make us *immeasurably* glad! So in this chapter let's look at the "greater" picture of heaven, marveling at what God has saved us *to*.

After all, greater appreciation of heavenly delights elicits a greater gush-out trifecta from those certain to receive them.

In Psalm 16:10–11, quoted at the beginning of this chapter, King David reassures his own heart as he speaks to God. He finds strength by looking forward to the everlasting future pleasures of heaven. Considered as a whole, the psalm reveals that David is doing this — as we need to learn to do it — while embroiled in some sort of peril: "Preserve me, O God, for in You I take refuge" (Psalm 16:1). The delight David takes in his anticipation of heaven as a gift from God refutes modern misperceptions that it's a brightly lit place of benign harp playing and lazy, cloud-filled boredom. David rightly sees heaven as we're about to see it: as a personal gift from God that brings the *huperballo* joy and eternal delight of being in His presence. No wonder David gushes praise to God for the promise of heaven

It's impossible to fully describe heaven, especially in one chapter of one book like *Gush*. The Bible includes a lot of information about heaven, and much of that information expresses realities beyond our present intellectual and imaginative capacity. Nonetheless, within the context of our voyage so far, a sound, biblical definition is that heaven is *complete eternal hydration*. To soak in this wonderfully hydrating truth, let's look at two of the clearest passages about heaven in the whole Bible, Revelation 7:15–17 (referred to below as R7) and Revelation 21:3–5 (referred to below as R21).

> [15]Therefore they [those who embrace God] are before the throne of God,
> and serve Him day and night in His temple;
> and He who sits on the throne will shelter them with His presence.
> [16]They shall hunger no more, neither thirst anymore;
> the sun shall not strike them,
> nor any scorching heat.

> ¹⁷For the Lamb in the midst of the throne will be their
>   Shepherd,
> and He will guide them to springs of living water,
> and God will wipe away every tear from their eyes.
> Revelation 7:15–17 (R7)

> ³And I heard a loud voice from the throne saying, "Behold, the dwelling place of God is with man. He will dwell with them, and they will be His people, and God Himself will be with them as their God. ⁴He will wipe away every tear from their eyes, and death shall be no more, neither shall there be mourning nor crying nor pain anymore, for the former things have passed away."
>
> ⁵And He who was seated on the throne said, "Behold, I am making all things new." Also he said, "Write this down, for these words are trustworthy and true."
> Revelation 21:3–5 (R21)

Absolute Absence

The first aspect of complete hydration in heaven is the *absolute absence* of everything that *causes* or *results from* thirst and dehydration. That's because, as the New Living Translation puts it, "the old world and its evils are gone forever" (R21:4). This means that the world, the devil, and our desiccant-loving flesh will never be found there.[1] In addition, R7:16b tells us that the sun and scorching heat won't strike us in heaven. This means there will be nothing to beat us down, fall on us, or throw us down to cause brokenness, pain, sin, or death in any part of the human experience: physical, spiritual, emotional, relational, any part of our experience at all. Wow!

R7:16 says that there'll be *no* (a term emphasizing total exclusion) hunger or thirst (*dipsao*) of any kind, material or immaterial, in heaven. We've already learned that hunger and thirst can describe both the *causes* and the *results* of sin. As we learned in Chapter 4, thirst (*dipsao*) encompasses every human yearning, especially what we called our "supreme thirst," which is our yearning for right relationship with God. As Christians, we still fight corruption in our thirst for God, and we sometimes dig broken cisterns to try to satisfy our thirst in bouts of temporary spiritual insanity (Chapter 24). Heaven, however, is where the final bell has been rung on such bouts, exclaiming, "That fight is *over forever!*"

Perhaps the most breathtaking verse in the whole Bible regarding what's *absolutely absent* in heaven is R21:4 — "And death shall be no more, neither shall there be mourning nor crying nor pain anymore." Friends, this phrase sums up just about everything we groan about in this life. In it, God tells us that every single thing that's wrong here and now will be gone there and then. To amplify His point, God stacks ten negative particles or conjunctions in R21:4 and R7:16 (in the Greek text). He's saying there will be no, no, no, no, no, no, no, no, no, no evil causes or results in heaven. Wow! Let's imagine for a moment what it'll be like to swim in this amazing eternal gush.

Imagine, for example, a world without anything that causes pain in your relationship with God, yourself, or others. Imagine no more internal impulses to reject God and wander off into the desert to dig broken cisterns. Imagine never again experiencing the inward, desiccant-desiring fires described in Galatians 5:19–21 (Chapter 3). Imagine, therefore, never thinking, feeling, or acting in any way that contradicts God's moral standard and hurts or offends Him, ourselves, or others. Imagine no visible or invisible beings tempting you to gossip, cheat, lie, litter, lust, abuse, cower, steal, murder, or do anything else contrary to the will of God.

Imagine that there's nothing in any system (e.g., relational system) that will harm any part of you or introduce filth into your life. Imagine a world that doesn't grab for position and power at the expense of the weak. Imagine a reality that doesn't rely on manipulation, violence, fear, or sensuality to coerce or quell your thoughts, feelings, or behavior. Imagine an arrangement where neither personal possessions, nor body image, nor intellectual prowess, nor athletic achievements, nor religiosity, nor annual income, nor biological pedigree, nor popularity has any bearing whatsoever on your value in anybody's eyes, including your own. In short, imagine a world with no evil *causes* or *results* at all, forever and ever.

Yes, greater appreciation of heavenly delights elicits a greater gush-out trifecta from those certain to receive them.

Abundant Presence

Heaven is much more than the absolute absence of the causes and results of thirst, however. It's also — even more so — the *abundant presence* of supremely hydrating things. The first among these is God Himself as the One who will shelter (*skenoo*) us with His presence (R7:15, R21:3). This *skenoo*-presence of God is the uninterrupted, perfected realization of God's desire in coming to earth to redeem us in Christ: "And the Word became flesh and dwelt [*skenoo*] among us" (John 1:14a). *Skenoo*-ing in God's presence "expresses one of the most significant ways in which spiritual and human existence can be combined."[2]

One of the most radical things about God's *skenoo*-presence in heaven is that He'll dwell with us to continually ensure our unending, blissful, holy hydration. He'll preserve heaven's safety (R7:16). He'll guide us to springs of living water (R7:17b), which, incidentally, is God Himself, since He's the Fountain, remember (Chapter 9)? He'll heal all our wounds (R7:17c, R21:4). He'll make all things new (R21:5). In heaven, there'll be no more supreme thirst. Our heart's deepest desire will be for God alone, and *God Himself* will make sure that our desire for true hydration and joy in Him will be wonderfully and indescribably met.

Emphasizing that the main feature of heaven is a perfected relationship with God, R21:3b reveals that "God Himself will be with them as their God." This phrase couples an intensive pronoun (*autos*) with God's name (*Theos*), then repeats His name (*Theos*) to emphasize that *He's* the One who's going to be with us. This unique grammatical construction in the original Greek text is God's emphatically affirmative answer to questions we might excitedly and similarly ask when spying a celebrity in public: "Is that really *him*?"

On this side of heaven, we might be prone to ask the same sort of questions. "Is it really *God* who's going to be so near to us in heaven? I mean, will it really be Him *personally*?" Based on this and many other texts, God's answer has to be an excited, "Yes! It's *Me*! It's *Me* you'll finally and fully enjoy in heaven! It's *Me* — the One who loves you so much that I created you, chose you, called you, and redeemed you — and loved you all the way through your life!"

Yes, greater appreciation of heavenly delights elicits a greater gush-out trifecta from those certain to receive them.

A Water-Picture Perfected

Back in Chapter 13, we were hydrated by considering how God likens Himself and His work to a river. In part, we saw that at the dawn of creation one opulent, nameless river flowed from Eden as a source of the four rivers of the Fertile Crescent. We also saw that God intended Adam and Eve to live in the lush provision of that source in perfect fellowship with Him. Unfortunately, because of Adam and Eve's sin, we now see rivers both as spiritual testing grounds (e.g., Israel's crossing the Jordan River) and as places of divine blessing (e.g., John's baptizing people, also in the Jordan River). As canaries in a coal mine reveal changes in air composition, rivers in the Bible often reveal the spiritual condition of nations and individuals. Since Genesis 2, rivers have been either threatening or welcoming, based on the state of the intricate dance between humanity and God. Stability and enduring peace have been lost.

At the end of the Bible's story, however, the river metaphor reveals God's redemptive, heavenly gush. In Revelation 22:1–2, the last river in Scripture is described as a pure, life-giving flow of gushalicious proportions:

> Then the angel showed me the river of the water of life, bright as crystal, flowing from the throne of God and of the Lamb through the middle of the street of the city; also, on either side of the river, the tree of life with its twelve kinds of fruit, yielding its fruit each month. The leaves of the tree were for the healing of the nations.[3]

Feast your eyes on the consistent beauty of this heavenly river! It's especially marvelous to me, because I live in a "river city," St. Louis, Missouri, which is built on the west bank of "the Big Muddy." That's our affectionate name for the Mississippi River, an ever-changing ribbon of danger and delight. Sometimes the Mississippi floods, but other times it dwindles to a point where barges and boats can't navigate. It can teem with dangerous microbes and snakes, but it can also nourish beautiful birds, and fish that can be delicious. Its banks can be an ugly resting place for old tires and industrial trash, but they also are home to colorful lilies and spry white egrets. Despite its many good qualities, the Mississippi is ultimately inconsistent and sometimes deadly, just like every other river in the world.

The Redeemed River of Revelation is nothing like the Big Muddy — or like any river in the Bible since Eden. First of all, it's not muddy; it's "bright as crystal," which is a reference to its multifaceted purity. It isn't subject to floods or shortages; it flows steadily. Its water, the "water of life," never kills; it always revives. Its banks are never lined with refuse, but always with beauty and vitality. There we find the tree of life, which always yields perfect, life-giving fruit. This Redeemed River is consistently vital.

The reason heaven's river is so pure and life-giving is because it originates from the "throne of God and of the Lamb." This phrase signals the Bible's final description of God as our Fountain, which we first explored in Chapter 9. Here we again see that all life comes from Him. We see Him as the Source of Sources. In the closing chapter of God's Bible narrative, we find ourselves in proximity to this God and His River, basking and splashing for our ultimate hydration. Revelation 22 goes on to describe the abundant presence of this blessed reality in verses 3 through 5.

> No longer will there be anything accursed, but the throne of God and of the Lamb will be in it, and His servants will worship Him. They will see His face, and His name will be on their foreheads. And night will be no more. They will need no light of lamp or sun, for the Lord God will be their light, and they will reign forever and ever.

Yes, greater appreciation of heavenly delights elicits a greater gush-out trifecta from those certain to receive them.

"I Never Want to Leave This Place"

One of my favorite movies is the Australian-made film *Danny Deckchair*. In this whimsical romantic comedy, a concrete-pouring bloke named Danny plans an experiment. After a tiff with his girlfriend, he decides to tie a bunch of helium-filled balloons to his deckchair to see if he can fly.

A scene or two later, in the middle of a backyard "barbie" (barbecue), Danny and his balloon-enabled deckchair lift off — to the shock and bewilderment of his girlfriend, friends, and neighbors.

As the story unfolds, Danny drifts all the way to Clarence, a charming and idyllic little town well outside the noise and bustle of Sydney. He lands in the backyard of the local parking cop, Glenda, who just so happens to be a gorgeous, single sweetie. Somehow, Danny is able to hide away in this heavenly place, and he begins to blossom as a person. He's quickly surrounded by happy friendships, and he falls in love with Glenda (surprise, surprise).

At one point later in the movie, during a tender moment between Danny and Glenda, Danny softly says, "I never want to leave this place."[4] As the audience, we can understand why. All the noise and chaos of his life in the big city seem absolutely absent. There's no traffic, no deceptive associates, and no manipulative girlfriend. At the same time, beauty and joy are abundantly present. Danny's in love with a sweet woman, and she's in love with him. He's respected. He has friends. He has meaningful work to do. The sun is shining, and the birds are chirping. For these reasons, we might be apt to join Danny in his confession of desire to stay in this heavenly place called Clarence.

Now that we've gazed at our heavenly future, we should first confess, "I want to *go* to that place." Because of Christ, we as Christians have the assurance that someday God will take us there. (If you still have doubts about whether you're a Christian, please stop and turn to Appendix A to settle the matter.) We can imagine confessing upon arrival, "I never want to *leave* this place." And then the greatest desire our hearts will ever have known will be satisfied: We'll never have to leave. We'll be caught up in the unfathomably beautiful nearness of God and be satiated by Him *forevermore*. So, with the apostle John at the very end of the Bible, let us say, "Amen. Come, Lord Jesus!"

Gushaholic's Prayer

Lord, thank You for Your promise of heaven! I'm looking forward to being with You in that blissful state. Please encourage me with Your promise when I face trials in this life. Come, Lord Jesus. Amen.

Gushercises

1. Describe heaven.
2. Like my practice of looking forward to vacations, how can looking forward to heaven give you strength and joy in your present struggles?
3. In one sense, heaven is perfected intimacy with God. One way to thrill at this promise is to thrill at God. To help you do this, spend some time pondering Appendix C, which is like a mini-résumé of God, based on the Bible. Write out your thoughts and feelings as you reflect on God as He's described in Appendix C.
4. Over the coming weeks and months, think about how you can apply some of the truths revealed in this chapter to whet your appetite for God's eternal gush in heaven. In so doing, perhaps your daily prayers will begin to include "Amen. Come, Lord Jesus!"

28

Our Voyage Continues

*May He be like rain that falls on the mown grass,
like showers that water the earth!* Psalm 72:6

It takes more than one rainfall to grow a tall, green, strong oak. It takes more than one sip of water to stave off thirst. It takes more than dipping one's toe in the pool to cool off. It takes more than one shower your whole life to stay clean. In the same way, the Christian life in the gush isn't a once-and-done event. We can't sip God once and expect to stay hydrated. Our life in relationship with God is a voyage — an *ongoing* adventure of ever-deepening thirst and satisfaction in the God who calls us His beloved ones. This book was written to help us gulp down and gush out those truths.

In the previous twenty-seven chapters, we navigated the ocean of the gushalicious life *one time*. Now that we've navigated that trip *once*, we must revisit the buoys and chapters of this book over and over as guides for our *ongoing* journey. They describe the general ebb and flow of our continuing life in the gush, and can help us pilot through that life. Here's what return visits to these familiar water-markers might look like.

Buoy I: Our Thirst

Contrary to popular belief, as Christians mature, our thirst becomes keener. As our hearts become more attuned to God, we begin to notice new kinds of thirst, and we also broaden our understanding of familiar thirsts. In addition, our perception of our thirst sharpens as we develop an increased awareness of the spiritual deadliness of the world, the dehydrating campaigns of the devil, and the dastardly attacks of our own flesh enticing us to eat desiccants.

Unfortunately, it can be difficult for us to remain sensitive to the pain of our parched condition. What may start as helpful alarm may give way to a resigned familiarity and spiritual complacency. There'll be ample opportunities to medicate, ignore, or deny this pain through addictions that are perceived as either wholesome (intense religious fervor or ministry) or sinful (drugs, promiscuity, and the like). Experiencing our thirst will require us to deal with the ways that we try to ignore, minimize, surrender to, or avoid our thirst.

As a trained eye detects disease that a novice's eye can't see, maturing voyagers will be able to spot more of our parching enemies' tactics. We'll have to fight off our enemies, who claw at us and say, "The truth you think you see is really just a mirage. Besides, a little sip of my worldly wares won't hurt you. You're taking this gushalicious life too seriously. Lighten up!" These chants are a siren song designed to lure us away from the open ocean of intimacy with God and dash us on the rocks of sin and misery.

The chapters around Buoy I will help us to stay honest about our need for God while guarding us from self-loathing. With God's help, we'll be able to regularly and increasingly say to ourselves and to God, "Yup, I'm thirsty again. And it's worse than before. The world is hitting me with a whole new parching wind that I never knew existed. Let me tell you about it, Lord." Remember: It's normal to feel our thirst throughout the Christian life. Admitting our thirst is healthy and tunes our hearts to hear God's invitation at deeper and more satisfying levels.

Buoy II: God's Invitation

The ever-expanding awareness of our thirst, which comes from constantly revisiting Buoy I, should heighten our delight at rehearing God's invitation to find satisfaction in Him. We'll be like spiritual triathletes who become increasingly aware of the forces of dehydration and who therefore rejoice at the sight of the next hydration station. God is our hydration — and He's *everywhere*.

It may take some time to actually embrace the fact that God doesn't grow tired of us and our thirst. The world, the devil, and our flesh will work hard to convince us that He does. They'll try to steal precious water from us, saying, "You've got to be joking! God can't be inviting you to Himself *again*! Not for the same thirst you had last week! Heck, you've been struggling with this for *years*. He's sick of you and your neediness!" A great way to fight that lie is to soak in this hydrating passage (Isaiah 40:28–31).

> Have you not known? Have you not heard?
> The LORD is the everlasting God,
>> the Creator of the ends of the earth.
> He does not faint or grow weary;
>> His understanding is unsearchable.
> He gives power to the faint,
>> and to him who has no might He increases strength.
> Even youths shall faint and be weary,
>> and young men shall fall exhausted;
> but they who wait for the LORD shall renew their strength;
>> they shall mount up with wings like eagles;
> they shall run and not be weary;
>> they shall walk and not faint.

Revisiting the concepts around Buoy II is another great way to continually hear God's invitation and respond with an enthusiastic "Yes, God!" Healthy Christians are those who say "Yes" to God over and over — not to be re-saved, but to be rehydrated in their salvation. If we're properly hydrated, we'll run to God more freely and more quickly when we *do* sin and thirst. We'll do this out of an increasing conviction that God's invitation is indelible and inexhaustible — and that He provides the satisfaction He promises.

Buoy III: Water-Pictures

I'd like to meet the person who invented the soaker hose — that blessed garden implement that constantly trickles water so that plants stay hydrated. That person obviously understood that long-term, consistent hydration is essential to plant health, especially during dry seasons. Buoy III presents a type of spiritual soaker hose as a series of water-pictures that gush into our hearts for our ongoing hydration. Receiving the gush embodied in these amazing pictures of God is especially important to the soul that's realized its thirst for God and has begun to turn from sin back to Him.

This kind of soaking is what we did when we visited Buoy III. It's what we'll need to do over and over again. We need to let God flow into us for long periods so that we can fully recover from our bouts of dehydration. One violent cloudburst of God won't do. We need the soaking rains described in Hosea 6:3, which we discussed in Chapter 11.

> Let us know; let us press on to know the LORD;
>   His going out is sure as the dawn;
> He will come to us as the showers,
>   as the spring rains that water the earth.

Our enemies don't want us to soak (i.e., immerse ourselves over time) in God. They'll try to convince us that soaking is a waste and that God isn't really that interested in being with us for such long periods. They'll stand there, fire hose in hand, promising a quick fix through some mountaintop seminar or some how-to formula. As "dusty" human beings (Psalm 103:14), we can grow weary of the sustained effort that's required to receive, enjoy, and serve God. All too often, our frailties make us like visitors to a world-class art museum who glance for only two seconds at each of its wondrous artworks. Buoy III beckons us to become people who linger for hours at a time in awe at the wonders of God reflected in the Bible's water-pictures.

As we mature, we'll spend *more* time with God — not less. We'll realize that time spent soaking in Him will give us *real* water. We'll learn that distractions from this joy are nothing more than shiny baubles luring us into the desert. As with any relationship, the more we share time and experiences with God, the more familiar with Him we'll become and the more intimate our relationship will be. We'll taste more sweet flavors in Him as our spiritual palates relax and get tuned to His delectability. Our relationship with God, the Person, will become more personal and more engaging as we soak in Him throughout our years voyaging in His gush.

Buoy IV: The God of Gush

Buoy IV continues the hydrating trend started around Buoy III. It offers more ways we can soak in God by marveling at who He is and at what He does for us as His beloved. If there's any part of this book that I wish could have been longer, it would be Buoy IV. That's because God is so magnificent! He's incredibly opulent and amazing. In addition to Buoy IV, Appendix C — chock-full of Scripture references — is a tiny, yet valuable, attempt to encourage further study and to encourage us to marvel at the God who continues to gush toward His beloved ones in Christ.

The important thing about Buoys III and IV and Appendix C isn't that they're the last word on God (because they certainly aren't!). As hydrating appetizers, they're designed to heighten our yearning for the Full Meal. Revisiting them is good, and using them to deepen our understanding of God by delving more deeply into His Word is even better. So it's important that we spend lots and lots and lots of time with God. He's like an endless sea of wonders and delights to our souls. Getting to know Him is the most important endeavor of our lives. Our ongoing life in the gush depends upon our ongoing intimacy with God.

Buoy V: Life in the Gush

As we return frequently to sail around Buoys I through IV, our life in the gush will become richer and more multidimensional. Buoy V helps us understand, appreciate, and embrace the truths God reveals to us as we go about our everyday living. For example, we'll grow in our ability to actually walk with God in honest relationship through the changing circumstances of our lives. We'll become more sensitive to His movement within us, and we'll learn to trust Him by going with His "flow." We should get better at seeing the law of the gush in our lives and at gushing out a trifecta of praise back to God, love for ourselves, and love for others.

As we continue to revisit Buoy V, we'll become increasingly aware of how mutinous we remain. We'll become more sensitive to our constant leakiness, and we'll feel sad as the world, the devil, and our own flesh incessantly strive to pull us away from God. The pain of our temporary spiritual insanity will at times be so intense that we'll wonder if we're growing at all in the gushalicious life. So we'll groan.

Coming back again and again to Buoy V will remind us that we're not abnormal for feeling the sorts of things we read about in its pages. Such reminders won't give us license to sin or to abandon the Christian life. Instead, they'll release us from trying to attain the impossible, unrealistic standard that we, and our skewed Christian subculture, often think should characterize the Christian life. These reminders are both liberating and sobering, and we need to embrace them again and again. So revisit Buoy V to get realigned with some of the key themes of our voyage on this side of heaven.

Buoy VI: Gush Everlasting

During our ongoing voyage, our minds will return with increasing frequency to the themes presented in Buoy VI. As we "grow up" in the Christian life, the reality of what we've been saved from (hell) and what we've been saved to (heaven) should gain prominence in our hearts. While we remain faithful to each day's challenges, visiting Buoy VI should rightly heighten our excitement about leaving the groaning of this present life for the bliss of the next. We should be like children who get more and more rambunctious as the family drives to their vacation destination. Excitement builds as each road sign shows fewer miles to their goal — finally becoming almost unbearable.

The sometimes sweet, sometimes excruciating, monotony of continually revisiting Buoys I through V will heighten our longing for our final harbor. "Are we there yet?" is a healthy cry for those with a proper longing for heaven. Like so many squirming kids packed in a beach-bound family minivan, we join the chorus of gushaholics of old who became increasingly fascinated with their heavenly destination. In 2 Corinthians 5:1–5, Paul puts words to our desire. As we hear Paul say "Are we there yet?" let's remember that he'd been an apostle (i.e., a mature believer) for about twenty years when he wrote these words:

> For we know that if the tent [our physical body], which is our earthly home, is destroyed, we have a building from God, a house not made with hands, eternal in the heavens. For in

this tent we groan, longing to put on our heavenly dwelling, if indeed by putting it on we may not be found naked. For while we are still in this tent, we groan, being burdened — not that we would be unclothed, but that we would be further clothed, so that what is mortal may be swallowed up by life. He who has prepared us for this very thing is God, who has given us the Spirit as a guarantee.

As we continue navigating Buoys I through V, we must remember the stupendous news that one Day all Christians will reside in the heavenly eternal gush of God. Revisiting Buoy VI will help us remember.

Voyagers, Ahoy!

Maybe it's a little surprising — even annoying — that life in the gush is like an ongoing voyage. Perhaps you expected to pick up this book and find a shortcut to total soul-hydration. After all, that's the way our culture works. Even our Christian subculture can work that way, promising instant virtue and joy without acknowledging the ache and work involved in the journey of faith. In either context, the temptation is to believe that everything can be fixed quickly and easily. One Day God *will* fix everything for all eternity for His beloved ones in Christ! But for now, we must embrace the ongoing nature of our voyage and gain our sea legs for it.

First, let's expect what author Brennan Manning aptly describes as "magnificent monotony."[1] That's an interesting label, because it pairs two words that, like oil and water, don't seem to mix. *Magnificent* makes us think of words like *beauty*, *pleasure*, and *excitement*. *Monotony* stirs up ideas like *tedium*, *boredom*, and *dreariness*. The radical nature of life in the gush encompasses both of these ideas: Its basic themes never change (monotony), yet those themes happen to be wonderful and exciting (magnificent).

The Christian's magnificently monotonous life is a bit like eating a steady diet of your favorite food every single day until you die. On one hand, you could say that it's monotonous. But on the other hand, it's *your favorite food!* Sure, it's the same basic thing over and over again. But what a thing it is!

In our ongoing voyage, we get to know *God*. Not our favorite food. Not sports cars. Not religion, success, material wealth, a spouse, sex, or a better body — but *God*. What could be better than that? Nothing! So what if it seems a bit routine at times? Consider the point of it all, which is getting to know the most amazing, beautiful, holy, powerful, gracious, good Person in the entire universe. We can revisit Appendix C to refresh ourselves on who this Person is, and to encourage us to explore His Word, where He's robustly revealed.

Second, let's scrape off our rigid expectations. Like barnacles encrusting our hearts, they'll hamper our spiritual mobility, hindering our freedom to respond to God. Let's scrap strict ideas about how long we should linger at any particular buoy or where we should be in our journey. Let's keep looking to God, and resist the catcalls from below deck. These chiding voices will try to rattle us with threats like "You should be over that by now. What's taking you so long? You don't have time to linger."

We can also abandon any preconceived notions about how frequently we should round the buoys. We'll go through the process as many times as we need to, so forget about keeping count. Counting isn't important. And forget about always moving in a linear direction. We may backtrack, get blown off course, or get disoriented along the way and make a wrong turn. Subjective or rigid expectations will just make matters worse. So let's toss those overboard, too, and look to God — no matter where we find ourselves in the voyage. Being with Him is always the best place to be, even if our circumstances don't meet our expectations.

Third, let's force our fleshly compulsion to evaluate ourselves against others to walk the plank. God will help us banish this mutinous enemy — at sword-point if necessary! If we don't quell the mutiny, our constant comparing will cause our souls to get seasick. This is a phenomenon that our enemies — the world, the devil, and our flesh — love to exploit. They'll flash neon signs pointing to other ships (i.e., Christians) that appear faster, prettier, and more nimble in living the gushalicious life — all the while whispering, "Wow, look at *that*! You should be more like that by now, don't you think?"

Remember that we're *persons* — completely unique and wonderfully created individuals made by God in His image (Psalm 139:14). God is also a Person. Among other things, this means that we're in a *personal* relationship with God through Christ. It means that each individual Christian's voyage with God will be special. In many ways, it will be unlike the journey of anyone else who has ever lived or *will* ever live. So enjoy it! Rejoice in your exquisite distinctiveness and thrill at the journey God is walking with *you*. Never mind what He's doing with others.

Fourth, let's drop anchor in God. Well, maybe a *sea* anchor — one that keeps us stable *while we're sailing*. Remember that *knowing God* is the point of this voyage. Our trip isn't primarily about rounding the buoys faster or more efficiently. We're after intimacy with God, the Lover of our souls in Christ. Revisiting Chapters 17 and 18 will help to remind us of this preeminent ideal. Knowing God in intimate relationship should be our North Star, that immovable point from which all other points derive meaning and perspective.

Gushaholic's Benediction

Instead of a prayer, we conclude with a benediction. That's a blessing from God to gushaholics. This particular benediction gushes with the themes we've explored in this book — namely, that God is a gushing God and that to live in relationship with Him is a gushalicious life. To receive this hydrating blessing, first hear God's invitation from Psalm 81:10b (NIV) — "Open wide your mouth, and I will fill it." Now drink in God's opulent blessing from Ephesians 3:20–21.

> Now to Him who is able to do far more abundantly than all that we ask or think, according to the power at work within us, to Him be glory in the church and in Christ Jesus throughout all generations, forever and ever. Amen.

Gushercises

1. List and briefly describe the six buoys of your ongoing life in the gush.

2. Based on what you know of Him, what encouragements is God giving you as you continue on your ongoing voyage?
3. How does God's gushing benediction in Ephesians 3:20–21 inspire you as you move forward?

Appendix A

Am I a Christian?

If you've turned here, you're probably wondering what it means to become a Christian. It's quite simple, really. Know first of all that God wants you to become a Christian, as He says in 2 Peter 3:9 — "The Lord is ... patient toward you, not wishing that any should perish, but that all should reach repentance." He puts it this way in Isaiah 55:6–7:

> Seek the LORD while He may be found;
>   call upon Him while He is near;
> let the wicked forsake his way,
>   and the unrighteous man his thoughts;
> let him return to the LORD, that He may have compassion
>   on him,
>   and to our God, for He will abundantly pardon.

To be a Christian is to believe (i.e., trust, or count as credible and reliable) what God says about you and Him, regarding your moral position and your eternal destiny. Here are the basics you need to believe in order to become a Christian. The strange-looking words and numbers in parentheses in the latter part of each paragraph are books, chapters, and verses in the Bible that prove the statements they follow. If you want explanation and support for what is said in the first part of each paragraph, check out the references provided.

1. I believe that I'm a sinner. I offend God by breaking His law by doing what He tells me not to do and by not doing what He tells me to do. Because I'm a sinner, I believe that I deserve God's judgment and wrath. (Genesis

6:5; Psalm 59:5; Proverbs 6:16–19; Ecclesiastes 9:3; Isaiah 13:9; Jeremiah 23:14; Ezekiel 22:30–31; Daniel 9:11; Mark 7:20–23; John 3:36; Romans 1:18, 3:9–20, 7:14–25)

2. I believe that Jesus Christ, the Son of God, lived the perfectly obedient life that I cannot live. I believe that when He was crucified on the cross, Jesus Christ bore all of God's judgment and wrath that I deserve for my sins. I believe that three days later Jesus rose from the dead to secure eternal life for me. (Jesus is the "Passover Lamb" foreshadowed in Exodus 12:21–23 and specifically named in 1 Corinthians 5:7; Isaiah 53 [this text predicts Christ's work, which would be fulfilled 700 years later, in paying the penalty for your sins]; Matthew 5:17, 14:33, 26:27–28; John 1:29; Romans 3:21–26, 5:9–11, 8:3–4; Ephesians 1:7–10; Hebrews 2:17, 9:22–28; 1 John 2:2, 4:10; Revelation 1:4–6)

3. I believe that I cannot make up for my sins and earn my way into heaven by my own effort. Instead, I turn from trusting in my own efforts, and I trust in and rely solely upon Jesus Christ and His perfectly obedient life, His payment of the penalty for my sins through His death on the cross, and His resurrection from the dead to give me eternal life. I receive His forgiveness, the free gift of eternal life, and ongoing, intimate, and sweet relationship with Him. I trust Him to be the loving Lord of my life. (Matthew 10:37–40; Mark 8:34–38; John 6:29, 20:30–31; Acts 16:31, 19:4; Romans 3:21–25, 10:8–9; Galatians 3:22; 1 Timothy 1:16–17; James 2:17–26; 1 John 3:23)

That's it! Of course, there's nothing magical about the words you've just read. Merely reading them doesn't save you. Believing them, actually acknowledging their reliability and truth, is what you do to experience the forgiveness and relationship with God that He offers you. If you've sincerely confessed in your heart the biblical truths above, God heard you. He has forgiven all your sins, and He has brought you into a peaceful relationship with Himself through Jesus Christ. This is what He promises in Bible passages like Romans 10:8–10.

> But what does it say? "The word is near you, in your mouth and in your heart" (that is, the word of faith that we proclaim); because, if you confess with your mouth that Jesus is Lord and believe in your heart that God raised Him from the dead, you will be saved. For with the heart one believes and is justified, and with the mouth one confesses and is saved.

If you've just read and believed these truths, you've taken your first real gulp of God. You've also uttered your first prayer, which is simply conversation with God. That's wonderful! It's important now that you tell someone you think is already a Christian — someone who seems to be living in sincere relationship with the God of the Bible — about what you've done. If you don't know someone like that, look for a pastor in a church that affirms the Bible's truth, and tell him.

When you talk to this person about trusting God for the first time, ask him or her for help learning how to walk with Him consistently and share every aspect of your life with Him. There are many reliable resources to help you with this. This book is one of those resources! Your Christian friend, a reliable pastor who acknowledges the Bible's truthfulness and authority, biblically-sound websites, and a local Christian bookstore will have suggestions for other resources. Just make sure that the resources you choose are, like this book, rooted in the Bible.

Welcome to the family of God!

Appendix B

Gushcabulary

Think of gushcabulary as word-buckets into which we can collect some of the water themes of the Bible. From those buckets, we can "handle" and more readily benefit from some of God's richest communication to us. The following gushcabulary, or word-buckets, form the basic glossary for our voyage. The meanings of most of these words are intuitive, and are therefore easy to figure out, even without the glossary below. Each entry word is followed by its part of speech (noun, verb, or adjective), its definition, and a sentence that uses the word in context.

anti-gush *n.* that which is contrary to and opposes the God of gush and/or the gush of God: *Beware the anti-gush of the devil, who came to kill, steal, and destroy our connection with the God of gush.* *adj.* of that which actively opposes the God of gush and/or the gush of God: *David lived in an anti-gush world, and so do we.*

dehydrate *v.* to deprive of spiritual nourishment from the gush of God: *The devil's goal is to dehydrate our souls.* **dehydration** *n.* the lack of soul-satisfaction due to the lack of an intimate relationship with God: *The world, the devil, and our own sinful nature can lead to our dehydration.*

desiccant *n.* anything that deprives people of God's hydration; i.e., anything that causes them to sin: *We Christians retain an annoying internal affection for desiccants.*

God or **God of gush** *n.* the triune God of the Bible described as Father, Son, and Holy Spirit; the God who describes Himself as Israel's Fountain in Psalm 68:26. *God is a gushing God.*

golden hoses *n.* Christians who are connected to God the Faucet, thereby allowing Him to gush into and out of them: *Our life and fruit-*

fulness as golden hoses depend completely on the Faucet and our connection to Him.

gush *n.* an opulent, abundant, excessive flow: *The gush of God toward His people in Christ is full of grace and truth.* *v.* 1. to break forth in opulence, abundance, or excess: *God gushed Himself radically into my heart in early 1999.* 2. to be amazed by the God of gush and to be swept away in the gush of God: *We get gushed by God only through Jesus Christ.* *adj.* having to do with the God of gush, the gush of God, and anything related to these: *He told about his amazing gush experience.*

gush of God *n.* that which naturally flows from the God of gush; the outward radiance of God's inherent nature: *Only those who trust Christ can experience the particular, joyful gush of God.*

gushability *n.* the propensity, or capacity, to gush: *When it comes to gushability, God is infinite.*

gushaholic *n.* a person who's happily addicted to the God of gush and the gush of God: *The aim of this book is to create joyful gushaholics.* *adj.* characterizing a gushaholic: *Soaking in God is the center of the gushaholic Christian life.*

gushalicious *adj.* of a person or experience, deliciously opulent or abundant: *God is completely gushalicious.* **gushaliciousness** *n.* the quality of delicious opulence or abundance: *God's gushaliciousness is unfathomable.*

gushcabulary *n.* the vocabulary of gushspeak; words and phrases that are "word-buckets" by which we can grab hold and make sense of the water images God uses in the Bible: *It's important to learn gushcabulary for our voyage into the God of gush.*

gushensity *n.* one's propensity or ability to gush; a measure of one's gushability: *God's gushensity is infinite.*

gushercise *n.* an exercise that helps a person connect with the God of gush, enjoy the gush of God, grow as a gushaholic, increase in gushabililty and gushensity, and become more gushalicious: *The gushercises at the end of each chapter will help you grow closer to God.*

gushfest *n.* a state marked by abundant gush resources: *Within the Trinity, God experiences an infinite gushfest.*

gushflush *n.* the effect of God's gush in one's heart, especially to oust sinful desire and practice: *Christians increasingly desire God's gushflush in* *their own hearts. v.* to oust sinful desire and practice: *God gushflushes our hearts in Christ, much as a flood flushes a pile of old tires out of your backyard.*

gushiness *n.* passionate expression: *We are now ready to enjoy the sopping gushiness of verses 9 through 13.*

gushocity *n.* the velocity, speed, rapidity, or volume of a gush: *It's impossible to measure the gushocity of God that comes to us in Christ.*

gushology *n.* the study of the God of gush, the gush of God, and everything related to these: *This is a book about gushology.* **gushological** *adj.* pertaining to, or involved with, gushology: *In gushological terms, "other suitors" are the other "fountains" from which we've been trying to satisfy our supreme thirst.*

gushphrase *n.* an expression particularly and positively related to life in the gush or gushology: *God's invitation to "come to the waters" in Isaiah 55:1 is a beautiful gushphrase.*

gushsong *n.* a song, the lyrics of which brim with gushology and are therefore useful for nourishing the soul of a gushaholic: *William Cowper's hymn "There Is a Fountain Filled with Blood," written in 1771, became a famous gushsong.*

gushspeak *n.* the language of gushology: *Gushspeak reflects the water images of the Bible.* **gushspeaker** *n.* one who knows and uses gushspeak: *A natural byproduct of being caught up in the God of gush is that one becomes a gushspeaker.*

gushstory *n.* an account of a gush experience: *This verse is part of an amazing gushstory from Exodus 17:1–7.*

hydrate *v.* to spiritually moisten or saturate with the gush of God: *We can't sip God once and expect to stay hydrated.* **hydration** *n.* soul-satisfaction achieved by relationship with God: *God loves parched people and invites them to Him for hydration.*

law of the gush *n.* the principle that whatever comes into our hearts will work its way into and through our lives: *The law of the gush is one reason why we need to guard our hearts.*

leaky *adj.* of Christians, unable to maintain perfect intimacy with God; unable to perfectly gush Him in and out: *God is compassionate toward His beloved, yet leaky, jars of clay.*

soak *v.* to spend extended, unhurried time with God (i.e., in His gush), leading to a closer relationship with Him and deepened faith: *To soak* *in God's truths is to revisit them, ponder them, marvel at them, and above all, believe them.*

thirst *n.* spiritual and relational separation from God, accurately manifested in a yearning for Him, but often manifested in a misguided yearning for things that, unlike God, lack the capability to satisfy: *Only God can satisfy our soul's thirst.* *v.* to experience thirst: *Our souls thirst for God.*

Appendix C

The Attributes of God

If God were a diamond, this list would describe some of His brightest and most apparent facets. As you read, remember that God is infinite, so this list is merely a starting point to describing Him. Remember, too, that life in God's gush consists of growing more intimate with this amazing God, who sent his Son to live, die, and rise again for *you*, and who longs for you to know Him and adore Him.

1. Faithful: consistently trustworthy and reliable (Deuteronomy 7:9–10; Psalms 33:4, 36:5; Lamentations 3:22–23; 2 Timothy 2:13)
2. Glorious: unfathomably awesome in splendor; exceptional in loveliness, weightiness (literally "heaviness"), significance, wealth, and abundance (Exodus 15:11, 24:15–17; 1 Chronicles 16:28–29; 2 Chronicles 5:13–14; Psalms 3:3, 24:8–10, 138:5; Isaiah 4:2, 60:1–2; Luke 2:9; John 1:14; 2 Corinthians 3:9; 2 Thessalonians 2:14; Revelation 5:11–14)
3. Good: perfectly whole and suited to His role as God; lacking nothing; upright, agreeable, beautiful, and pleasant in His essential being and actions (Exodus 33:19; Psalms 27:13, 31:19, 69:16, 73:1, 142:7, 145:7; Mark 10:18; 2 Corinthians 9:8; Galatians 5:22; 3 John, v. 11)
4. Gracious: lavishly willing to gush, through Christ — on undeserving people — favor and blessing that is unmerited and unearned (Exodus 33:19; Deuteronomy 7:7–8; Romans 5:8–21, 11:5–6; 1 Corinthians 15:9–10; Ephesians 2:8–9)
5. Holy: morally pure and perfect; separated, or "set apart," from all other beings by His essential attributes, and especially by His moral

perfection (Leviticus 11:45, 20:7; Isaiah 6:2–3; Ezekiel 22:26; Mark 1:24; John 14:26, 17:11; Hebrews 13:12)

6. Immutable (Unchangeable): devoid of all alteration, not only in His being, but also in His perfections, and in His purposes and promises (Exodus 3:14; Numbers 23:19; 1 Samuel 15:29; Psalm 102:26–27; Hebrews 13:8; James 1:17)
7. Infinite: free from all limitations outside those He puts upon Himself by His own uncoerced pleasure and wisdom; with reference to time, eternality; with reference to space, immensity (Exodus 3:14; Deuteronomy 3:24; Job 9:4–12; Psalm 145:3; Ecclesiastes 7:13; Matthew 19:26; Mark 14:36)
8. Just: morally correct. God is the Originator of pure moral standards for good and evil, the Evaluator of all beings by those standards, and the Distributor of rewards and punishments according to one's adherence to those standards. (Deuteronomy 32:4; Job 8:3–6, 34:12; Psalms 7:6, 33:5, 45:6–7, 89:14, 103:6; Isaiah 5:16; Matthew 12:18; Luke 18:7–8a; 2 Thessalonians 1:6)
9. Loving: sincerely, sovereignly, and sacrificially committed to work divine good for/in/through/to *His people, specifically*. Not only does God do this as an *action*, but this is the *essence of His being*. (Deuteronomy 7:6–8; Jeremiah 31; Romans 8:38–39; Ephesians 3:18–19, 5:1–2; 1 John 4:19)
10. Omnipotent (All-Powerful): able to bring to pass whatever He pleases at any time, at any place, in any way without any hindrance whatsoever. He cannot be checked, restrained, or frustrated by anything. God is absolutely and completely unstoppable. (Genesis 1 and 2; Exodus 1–15; Job 37:9–18, 40:15–24; Psalms 104, 107:23–32; Matthew 8:13, 9:22, 12:15 and 22, 14:14, 15:28, 17:18; 1 Corinthians 15:55–58; Colossians 2:13–15; Hebrews 1:3, 8:1, 10:12, 12:2; Revelation 20:10)
11. Omnipresent (Present everywhere): free from all spatial limitations; everywhere present all the time (1 Kings 8:27; Psalms 33:13–15, 65:9–13, 139:7–10; Jeremiah 23:23–24; Matthew 1:23; Revelation 14:10, 22:1–5)

12. Omniscient (All-Knowing): knowing all things across all time (Psalms 90:7–8, 139:1–4 and 23–24, 147:4–5; Job 23:10; Ezekiel 11:5; Daniel 2:22; John 21:17–19; Hebrews 4:13)
13. Patient: forbearing, especially in His willing and free restraint of His wrath and anger toward those who rebel against Him (Exodus 34:6; Nehemiah 9:17; Psalms 86:15, 103:8, 145:8; Joel 2:13; Jonah 4:2; Nahum 1:3; Romans 9:22, 15:5; Galatians 5:22–23)
14. Solitary: singularly unique and exclusive as God. There are no other Gods but God. (Exodus 20:1–7; Deuteronomy 4:39; 1 Kings 8:59–60; Isaiah 44:7–11, 45:21–22, 46:9; Matthew 6:24; Mark 12:32)
15. Sovereign: being the absolute and highest cause of all things, either directly or indirectly by means (1 Kings 8:16; Psalm 135:6; Isaiah 46:9-11; Daniel 4:35; Acts 17:26; Revelation 19:6b)
16. Unified: free from division into parts, therefore from compositeness (Exodus 3:14; John 10:30; Galatians 3:20)
17. Wrathful: having justly furious feelings and actions against Satan, demons, and unrepentant sinners (Ezra 7:23, 8:22; Isaiah 51:20–23; Jeremiah 10:10; Nahum 1:2; John 3:36; Romans 1:18; Revelation 14–19)

Appendix D

Postscript: Life in the Desert

All this talk about the world as a dehydrating desert is sure to raise questions. Perhaps the most obvious is this: Is there *any* legitimate nourishment to be had in or from the world? Let's address this excellent question by affirming the Bible's most obvious teachings on the subject.

If by "world" we mean "the system embraced by non-Christians and opposed to all that is godly," then the answer is a clear no. Doing things God forbids, or not doing things God commands, may bring a temporary thrill, but in the end those actions will dry up our hearts and cause our lives to blow away like the dust (see Proverbs 5:3–4).

On the other hand, if by "world" we mean "legitimate physical pleasures and sensations," then the answer is a qualified yes. God says, as in Psalm 104:14–15, that the proper enjoyment of physical things, such as food, includes genuine and appropriate pleasure. Proper enjoyment basically means not making such things the ultimate source of your personal security or significance.

In other places, God affirms the proper joy associated with one's work (Ecclesiastes 2:24, 3:12–13, 3:22; Isaiah 65:22), sex between a man and a woman who are married (Genesis 2:23–25; Song of Solomon), good news of others' welfare (Philippians 2:18), and other activities. It's important, however, to remember that the joy and nourishment we get from God's good gifts are themselves gifts from God. In the end, then, we must affirm that God alone gives legitimate pleasure from temporal things. Here's an example of that principle regarding our work, eating, and drinking, from Ecclesiastes 2:24–25.

> There is nothing better for a person than that he should eat and drink and find enjoyment in his toil. This also, I saw, is from the hand of God, for apart from Him who can eat or who can have enjoyment?

The obvious answer to God's rhetorical question in Ecclesiastes is "Nobody." Real enjoyment — through eating, drinking, work, relationships, sex, material stuff, or anything else in the created world — is a gift from God.

Finally, we must guard against setting our deepest affections on anyone or anything but God. When we fail to reserve our deepest affection for God, we become guilty of idolatry, which is, quite simply, substituting anything — even legitimately good things — for God as our Ultimate Satisfaction. The problem isn't finding *joy* in temporal, physical things; it's in finding *ultimate soul-satisfaction* in them. If we rely on anything other than God to satisfy our supreme thirst (Chapter 4), we'll be like the tormented person described in Isaiah 29:8.

> As when a hungry man dreams he is eating
>   and awakes with his hunger not satisfied,
> or as when a thirsty man dreams he is drinking
>   and awakes faint, with his thirst not quenched,
> so shall the multitude of all the nations be
>   that fight against Mount Zion.

Notes

Giving Thanks

    1. Robert Louis Stevenson, "My First Book — Treasure Island," *The Courier* 21.2 (1986): 77–88 / http://surface.syr.edu/libassoc/206/. 10 Mar 2012.

BUOY I: OUR THIRST

Chapter 1: Life in the Desert

    1. Bibleworks Version 5.0, Bibleworks LLC, Norfolk, Virginia.

Chapter 2: The Devil, Our Dehydrator

    1. Bibleworks.
    2. Ibid.
    3. Ibid.
    4. Ibid.
    5. This phrase is widely used in addiction recovery programs and literature. It was originally coined in *The Big Book*, now published by Alcoholics Anonymous World Services, Inc.
    6. Bibleworks.
    7. You may have looked up this note because of James 1:13, which says, "Let no one say when he is *tempted*, 'I am being *tempted* by God,' for God cannot be *tempted* with evil, and he himself *tempts* no one" (emphasis added). The Greek word commonly used for *tempt* (*peirazo/peirasmos*) is used four times in this verse. The easy resolution is to acknowledge that *peirazo/peirasmos* are general words meaning "to experiment, try, or test to learn one's character." Such a test can be administered with either evil intent or holy intent. The proper interpretation of this word comes from its context. In the case of James 1:13, all four occurrences of the verb are negative — temptation with *evil* intent to do *evil*. Therefore, the best interpretation of the last "tempts" is this: God Himself tempts no one with evil intent for evil purposes.

God *does* tempt us (yes, the same word that is used for the devil's temptations), but for the purpose of strengthening our character and our relationship with Him (Exodus 16:4, 20:20; Judges 2:21–22, 3:1; 1 Chronicles 29:17; James 1:1–4, 1:12; 1 Peter 1:6–9). His tests have *holy* motives, using *holy* means for *holy* ends. Because of these tests' value in strengthening faith, mature Christians have been known to ask God to test them (Psalm 26:2)!

Sometimes it's hard to tell whether a test is from God or from the devil. Trying to determine the source of the test is often not the best use of our spiritual energy. Instead, our focus must be on trusting God and obeying His Word in the midst of the trial. Often, the road to mistrust or to sin seems easier. But that's the path to dehydration. It's the path the devil will be working hard to entice us to follow. We must realize that the external factors that entice us to sin and beckon us to do evil are from our parching enemy.

An interesting example of this kind of situation is when the devil tempted Jesus at the beginning of His public ministry (Matthew 4:1–11). Jesus was led by the Spirit of God, not by the devil, into this time of tempting (v. 1). The devil, who actually *did* the tempting, meant the test for evil. He misquoted Scripture, trying to get Jesus to sin. God, however, was involved in the test for holy purposes. Jesus' test was part of His fulfilling His priestly role for us (Hebrews 2:18, 4:15).

Chapter 3: An Appetite for Desiccants
  1. *Pirates of the Caribbean: The Curse of the Black Pearl*, directed by Gore Verbinski (Walt Disney Pictures, 2003), DVD (Walt Disney Home Entertainment, 2003).
  2. Rich Mullins, "Hold Me, Jesus," *Songs*, Reunion Records, 1996.

Chapter 4: Our Supreme Thirst
  1. Bibleworks.

BUOY II: GOD'S INVITATION

Chapter 8: Saying "Yes" to God
  1. Hebrew *qal* imperative followed by the *qal* infinitive absolute of the verb *shama*.

Buoy III: Water-Pictures

Chapter 9: God, the Fountain

1. The phrase *"everything* He promises" is extremely important. It focuses us on the things God has explicitly said in His Word that He'll do or be so that we can accurately set our expectations for fulfillment/hydration. Some of those things include the fact that He will never leave us nor forsake us (Hebrews 13:5), and that He will surely carry true believers to our heavenly home (John 14:1–14). We must not expect things from God that He has not promised us — like marriage, children, or a trouble-free life! Doing so sets us up for heartache and dysfunction in our relationship with God. Let's avoid that trap, fellow gushaholics, by enjoying the "everything" of this phrase within the blessed confines of His promises!

2. William Cowper, "There Is a Fountain Filled with Blood," 1771, from *Trinity Hymnal* (Norcross, Georgia: Great Commission Publications, 1990), 253.

Chapter 10: Like the Dew

1. *Amazing Grace*, directed by Michael Apted (FourBoys Films, 2006), DVD (Twentieth Century Fox Home Entertainment, 2007).

Chapter 11: Like the Rain

1. *Forrest Gump*, directed by Robert Zemeckis (Paramount Pictures, 1994), DVD (Paramount Home Entertainment, 2006).

2. Dan Vergano, "Parched U.S. Overheated into Fall," *USA Today*, August 17–19, 2012, 1.

Chapter 12: Like a Flood

1. *Lord of the Rings: The Two Towers*, directed by Peter Jackson (New Line Cinema, 2002), Special Extended DVD Edition (New Line Home Entertainment, 2002).

2. Ibid.

3. God will execute the final "flood" of judgment with fire, not water. Though the element used is different, the sense of action is the same. It involves complete, inescapable, and righteous condemnation by the holy God. For more detail, see Matthew 3:11–12, 2 Peter 3:10–12, and Revelation 21:8.

Chapter 13: Like a River

1. These amazing Amazonian facts were compiled from several websites, 28 Nov 2012: http://en.wikipedia.org/wiki/Amazon_River, http://library.thinkquest.org /04oct/02004/pages/mammals.htm, http://rainforests.mongabay.com/amazon/insects.html, http://www.mbarron.net/Amazon/wildlife.htm, http://www.unique-southamerica-travel-experience.com/amazon-river-fish.html.

Buoy IV: The God of Gush

Chapter 14: The God Who Gushes

1. As we move into the hydrating frenzy of verses 9–13, let's keep in mind that in the Bible, the physical often points to the spiritual. While there's no doubt that this psalm celebrates a lavish physical harvest, it's perfectly reasonable to rejoice at what its images say about an abundant spiritual harvest as well. Trusted Old Testament commentator Derek Kidner celebrates Psalm 65 this way: "Here we almost feel the splash of showers, and the sense of the springing growth about us.... It would be hard to surpass this evocative description of the fertile earth, observed with loving exactness at one moment and poetic freedom at the next, culminating in the fantasy of hills and fields putting on their finest clothes and making merry together." [Derek Kidner, *Psalms 1–72: An Introduction & Commentary* (Downers Grove, Illinois: InterVarsity Press, 1973), 229 and 232.]

2. John Foxe, *Foxe's Book of Martyrs* (New Kensington, Pennsylvania: Whitaker House, 1981), 235.

3. I have rendered these definitions in the singular to emphasize to the reader God's concern for individuals. This meaning is faithful to the original text. However, there is a strong corporate element in the text, too. The corporate element emphasizes God's care for all His people. So, while it is appropriate to apply God's actions here to individuals, it is equally — if not more — appropriate to apply them to God's people as a corporate body.

4. As explained elsewhere in this book, our continual repenting and trusting is not meritorious. We don't turn regularly from our sin back to God to get Him to love us. He loves us because of Christ alone. There's no merit in our actions. Our regular repenting and trusting opens us to receive — not earn — God's gush.

Chapter 15: Our Superlative God

1. "Box Office History for Super Hero Movies," *The Numbers.* http://www.the-numbers.com/movies/series/Super-Hero.php. 2 Sept 2014.

2. "superlative," Encarta World English Dictionary, Microsoft Corporation, 1998–2005.

3. Bibleworks.

4. "superlative," Encarta World English Dictionary.

5. "Niagara Falls Facts," *Niagara Falls, Canada.* http://www.niagarafalls.ca/about_niagara_falls/for_students.asp. 9 Jul 2010.

Chapter 17: Being God's Beloved, Part I

1. Art Garfunkel, "I Only Have Eyes for You," 1975, iTunes.

2. Bibleworks.

3. Ibid.

Chapter 18: Being God's Beloved, Part II

1. The phrase "big sins" is in quotes because we Christians often categorize our moral errors as "big" or "small" vis-à-vis God's judicial response. "Big sins" are those we figure have the unique power to merit, hasten, or exponentially increase God's displeasure, chastisement, or wrath. The Christian subculture in the late twentieth and early twenty-first centuries has often listed the following as "big sins": homosexuality, abortion, and adultery.

In its answer to Larger Catechism question number 152, the Westminster Confession of Faith very helpfully clarifies our thinking about categorizing sins in this way: "What doth every sin deserve at the hands of God?" The answer rightly reveals that "Every sin, even the least, being against the sovereignty, goodness, and holiness of God, and against His righteous law, deserveth His wrath and curse, both in this life, and that which is to come; and cannot be expiated but by the blood of Christ."

2. Texts that describe Jesus as The Beloved of God include Matthew 3:17, 12:18, 17:5; Mark 1:11, 9:7; Luke 3:22; Ephesians 1:6; Colossians 1:13; and 2 Peter 1:17.

Buoy V: Life in the Gush

Chapter 19: Relationship and Radiance
   1. Bibleworks.
   2. Remember — we can approach God without a veil only because Jesus is our S-O-N-screen. His righteousness, which is a gift we receive by faith, assures us direct, safe access to God's consuming holiness. God dramatically introduced a new veilless era when Jesus paid the penalty on the cross for our sin. Matthew 27:51 tells us that at the time of Jesus' death "the veil of the temple was torn in two from top to bottom" (NASB). This veil was not worn on one's face; it was a big curtain that separated the Most Holy Place (a unique symbol of, and special location of, God's presence) from human beings. The tearing of this veil from top to bottom indicates that it was the work of God, not man. This tearing of the veil meant that the barrier between God and man (sin) had been destroyed by Christ's sacrificial, atoning death on the cross for those who trust in Him. These truths should elicit peals of praise from gushaholics as we thank God for doing all the veil-removing work that allows us to have unfettered access to Him.

Chapter 20: Going with the Flow
   1. *Kingdom of Heaven*, directed by Ridley Scott (Twentieth Century Fox Film Corporation, 2005).
   2. Bibleworks.
   3. The term "golden hoses" was inspired by the Puritans, who were fond of calling Christians "golden pipes" for the same reasons I have coined the term "golden hoses."
   4. Bob Dylan, "Make You Feel My Love," *Time Out of Mind*, Columbia Records, 1997.

Chapter 21: The Law of the Gush
   1. The context of John 7 helps us know that believing in Jesus is the key to understanding His instruction in verses 37 and 38. Earlier verses in the chapter show lack of belief that led to a negative application of the law of the gush. Verse 1 indicates that the Jews wanted to kill Jesus, their ultimate gush-out of evil coming from the gush-in of disbelief and hardness of heart. Verse 5 says "Not even His brothers believed in Him." Jesus acknowledges in verse 7 that the world doesn't believe in Him, but instead hates Him. "The people" in verse 12 are "muttering" about him, debating

whether He was a good man or a false teacher. They cry out in exasperation in verse 26, "The rulers do not really know that this is the Christ, do they?" (NASB).

2. Don't be fooled by my use of the word *consume*. It doesn't mean that we can completely exhaust God the way we might consume a candy bar so that it's gone. God is infinite! So He's beyond total consumption. *Consume* is used here to imply robust imbibing. It signals that we're to let God flow into our hearts in large quantities.

3. Creed, "Beautiful," *Human Clay*, Wind-up Records, 1999.

Chapter 23: Gush-Out Trifecta, Part II: To Others

1. "John" is my friend John O. Dozier, Jr. His first book, published in January 2010, is titled *The Weeping, the Window, the Way — Will Suffering Make You Bitter or Better?* It is available at www.amazon.com.

Chapter 25: The Reality Sandwich

1. Chris Rice, "Untitled Hymn (Come to Jesus)," *Run the Earth, Watch the Sky*, Rocketown Records, 2003.

BUOY VI: GUSH EVERLASTING

Chapter 26: The Wrathful Gush of Hell

1. The Bible clearly teaches that all human beings, including those who are now Christians, begin life under God's wrath. This is true because Adam and Eve's sin is imputed to us by God (Genesis 2:16–19, Psalm 51:5, Romans 5:12–21, and 1 Corinthians 15:21–22). Some theological traditions call this "original sin." In addition, all human beings are also condemned because they themselves commit sins in keeping with this inherited nature (Psalm 14:1–3, Romans 1–3, and 1 Corinthians 6:9–11). The sixth chapter of the *Westminster Confession of Faith* is very helpful in probing the depths of this important doctrine.

2. Jesus is frequently referred to as the "Lamb" of God in the Bible: John 1:29, 36; Acts 8:32; 1 Corinthians 5:7; Revelation 5:6, 7:17, 15:3, 19:9, 21:23, 22:1, 3.

3. "gush," *The Free Dictionary*. http://www.thefreedictionary.com/gush. 7 Sept 2010.

4. This term is explained in Chapter 17, based on texts like these: Exodus 19:5, Deuteronomy 7:6, 14:2, 26:18.

Chapter 27: The Sweet Gush of Heaven

1. This sense of absolute departure is part of the lexical range for the word *aperchomai*, which is rendered "passed away" in the ESV. Examining its use in Revelation 18:14 indicates that "absolute departure" is a good definition of this word. "The fruit for which your soul longed / has gone from you [*aperchomai*], / and all your delicacies and your splendors / are lost to you, / never to be found again!" In this text, *aperchomai* is explicitly clarified and emphasized as meaning "never to be found again." In heaven, everything that causes thirst will be *aperchomai* — never to be found again!

2. Bibleworks.

3. There can be some confusion over the idea that the tree of life has leaves of healing. The question centers on whether or not anybody needs healing in heaven. The plain answer to that question is an emphatic *no*. Other texts (especially Revelation 21 and 22) make it abundantly clear that heaven is eternally and irrevocably pure, and that God will never allow any "dis-ease" to infect it. That being the case, we may find the New Living Translation's rendering of Revelation 22:2b helpful: "The leaves were used for medicine to heal the nations." Like the ESV and the NASB, the NLT supplies a past tense verb for the sentence (there is no verb in the original Greek). This helps us understand that the tree's healing leaves are not needed now (in heaven) as they were then (on earth). It also assures us that this is indeed a tree of *vitality and blessing*, not death or cursing. In this sense, the tree is the embodiment of heaven's blissful reality and should give us great joy and strength in our present hardships.

4. *Danny Deckchair*, directed by Jeff Balsmeyer, film (Crusader Entertainment, 2003).

Chapter 28: Our Voyage Continues

1. Brennan Manning, *Ragamuffin Gospel* (Sisters, Oregon: Multnomah Publishers, Inc., 2000), 34–50.

About the Author

Rev. Merkey is founder and president of Churches for Life, a Christian nonprofit whose mission is to nourish churches as gospel-driven champions of life. By God's grace, Churches for Life accomplishes this mission by helping individual churches start and sustain a Life Team that equips their church to live as gospel-driven "rescued rescuers." This work reflects "the law of the gush," a spiritual principle explained in Chapter 21 of this book. Using this principle, Life Teams equip Christian communities (e.g., churches) to enjoy God's rescue in the gospel and to naturally gush out that joy by rescuing those in imminent physical peril — the unborn, embryos, the elderly, the infirm, and others. For more information about Life Teams and how Churches for Life can serve your church or organization, visit www.getintolife.org.